The Art of Survival

Born and raised between the Pennines and the Yorkshire Dales and with a great love for this part of Britain, Steven Marshall is no stranger to rugged and often hostile conditions. Skills learnt as a boy scout have been finely tuned by military service in the jungles of South America and the arctic cold of Scandinavia.

He now passes on his ever-increasing knowledge to young and old alike, through active youthwork, scouting and talks.

His outgoing manner and enthusiasm for the outdoor life, coupled with his humorous style of teaching, make him a regular guest at many schools, groups and camp fires.

The Art of Survival

STEVEN MARSHALL

ROBERT HALE · LONDON

© *Steven Marshall 1997*
First published in Great Britain 1997

ISBN 0 7090 5807 1

Robert Hale Limited
Clerkenwell House
Clerkenwell Green
London EC1R 0HT

The right of Steven Marshall to be identified as
author of this work has been asserted by him
in accordance with the Copyright, Designs and
Patents Act 1988.

2 4 6 8 10 9 7 5 3 1

Photoset in North Wales by
Derek Doyle & Associates, Mold, Flintshire.
Printed in Great Britain by
St Edmundsbury Press Limited, Bury St Edmunds
and bound by
WBC Book Manufacturers Limited,
Bridgend, Mid-Glamorgan.

This book is dedicated to the memory of my mother
Dorothy Marshall
for she taught me to become a survivor.
Also to my father
Norman Marshall
for smoothing my rough edges and teaching me to focus.

Contents

Acknowledgements

Special thanks must go to Christine Hession for the many months of hard and committed work in not only typing this book but also for her patience with me and my scribbled notes. Someone up there must have liked me, to have introduced us.

Thanks also to Dan Nelson for carrying on the teaching when my father stopped. More than a friend, a brother.

Not to forget Ian Melvin who stepped in at the last minute to do the illustrations for Fig. 17, 18, 20–31, 101 & 106. Somebody please give this talented artist a well paid job.

The equipment shown in the front and back cover illustrations was supplied by Boyce's Army Surplus Store, Nelson, Lancs. and Dan Nelson, Settle, North Yorks. respectively.

Last but not least John Hale for his patience, honesty and help in making my dream come true.

Illustrations

Foreword

When I started this book, it was with the intention of producing a booklet which a rambler could keep in the pocket of his anorak or backpack to consult in an emergency. However, as I thought more about the subject, I considered the various reasons why people find themselves in a survival situation:

Involuntary
1 Out walking, bad weather causes delays
2 Member of party injured

Voluntary
3 Want to get away from it all or get back to nature
4 Need to lose yourself, keep low, etc.

Then there are the survival situations brought about by natural disasters – conventional war, civil unrest or the ultimate disaster, a nuclear war – what I term 'The Event'.

Because of this, I have divided the book into sections. Section One deals with walking, equipment, etc. Section Two deals with how to cope with minor setbacks to plans, enforced stops, etc. Section Three deals with deliberate isolation and survival and Section Four deals with coping with natural disasters.

By its nature, I hope the book will appeal to a wide variety of outdoor people with different levels of expertise, from the novice to the expert survivalist. My apologies now to the experts – I hope you will find something of interest to you in this book and will not feel patronized. Actions which are commonplace and common sense to you need to be explained to the beginner. For the beginners – who knows, what started out as a terrifying ordeal that you survived, may make you interested in being a survivalist and learning more.

I have purposely limited the book to the British Isles and similar temperate climates found throughout Europe and North America and to problems you might find in these places. Much of the information included you may have already seen in other books or magazines. This is not surprising as all survivalism follows standard guidelines and common sense plays a large part. I hope I have managed to state these guidelines with a different outlook and from a different angle but, above all, in a way which keeps the reader's interest and stays in the memory for future use. The value of the information lies in how you perceive it and how you use it.

Introduction

To survive in times of need is one of man's natural instincts, but to know how to survive is not. One must learn this. This book is a basic start to that learning and will give you a better chance of surviving most hardships, although it is actually directed towards ramblers, hill walkers or anyone who wishes to spend time on the moors, mountains and the few remaining wild areas of Great Britain.

One often hears stories of people dying on the bleak and barren landscapes of the North Yorkshire Moors, the Lake District, the Brecon Beacons, Dartmoor and anywhere where the weather can be unpredictable, because they were not prepared for the unexpected to happen. Town and city folk seem to be the ones who fall into this category because of their lack of experience and their ignorance. My biggest tip to any would-be rambler is 'If you have no common sense – stay at home'. Not many people however are prepared to admit to this, because common sense is seen as an important ingredient of life.

People tend to class outdoor pursuits as a hobby. They are not. In fact they are a very serious topic to the likes of the men who form the nation's rescue services. They do not risk their lives for fun, yet people seem to think that the men of the Air/Sea Rescue, RNLI Mountain Rescue, Cave Rescue Organization and the Moorland Rescue do all their practice for fun. They do not. They do it out of respect for life, for the sea, the mountains, moors and earth we inhabit. These men have grown to understand the areas they patrol and in doing so, have learnt much on the subject of survival.

We all know the dangers of rock climbing – well, I hope we all do – and of potholing, but few people seem to realize the dangers lurking on the heather-covered moors of this country or in the hills and dales of, for example, Yorkshire. The weather can end a man's life in hours if he is not careful. Sunday strollers can be clumsy and careless, and this can be fatal. This book will help you to understand the dangers, help you to avoid them and, hopefully, show how to survive until you get back to civilization, or the rescue services get to you if you do get into trouble.

You could find yourselves trapped for a few hours or even days.

There have been stories of men trapped on the moors for weeks and even that is believable. Their will to survive gave them the break they needed to get home. One story is told of a man who had a broken leg after falling down a hole. He lived off roots and leaves as he crawled back to civilization. Another man had somehow severed his foot. It is claimed that he used his foot to sustain himself until he found it easier to move. He also chewed roots into pulp and used this as a poultice on his wound. Both men, although they did so well, made one big mistake which could have solved their problems a lot sooner. They failed to tell anyone where they were going. I cannot guarantee the authenticity of these two stories, but then again, they could be as true as life itself.

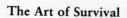

The Art of Survival

Part One

1 The Will to Survive

The experience of thousands of servicemen since 1939 has proved that survival is largely a matter of mental outlook. The 'will to survive' is the deciding factor.

Whether you are alone or with a small group, you will feel some form of emotional trauma, resulting from fear, despair, loneliness and boredom, in addition to the mental hazards of injury, pain, fatigue, hunger and thirst, which will tax your will to live. If you are not mentally prepared to overcome all obstacles and accept the worst, your chances of coming out alive are greatly reduced.

If you are on your own, the shock of finding yourself isolated and alone in a desolate area can be reduced or even avoided if you remember the key word – SURVIVAL.

    S   Size up the situation
    U   Undue haste makes waste
    R   Remember where you are
    V   Vanquish fear and panic
    I   Improvise
    V   Value living
    A   Act calm and laid back
    L   Learn basic skills

Size Up the Situation

Consider yourself, the country and the obstacles which could obscure or hinder your progress.

1   *Yourself*: Hope for the best but be prepared for the worst. Recall all you have read, learnt or heard about survival training. Get to a safe, comfortable place as soon as possible. Once there, look things over – form a plan. Once you have decided how to proceed your fears

will lessen and your confidence will increase. Stay calm.

2 *The country*: Part of your fear may come from being in a strange environment. Therefore, try to determine where you are by landmarks, compass directions, etc.

3 *Obstacles*: Type of landscape – hills, valleys, etc. No use walking over hills if you can go round them, this will only increase your fatigue.

Undue Haste Makes Waste

Do not be too eager to move, it will make you careless and impatient. You may begin to take unnecessary risks. Do not lose your temper, it may cause you to stop thinking. When something happens to irritate you, stop, take several deep breaths, calm down and start again. Face the fact that danger does exist – trying to convince yourself otherwise can be just as dangerous.

Remember Where You Are

Try to remember your route or where you have been. Take note of any landmarks you may have passed. Leave small markers along your route, even though you are not lost, because you may need to retrace your route later.

Vanquish Fear and Panic

To feel fear is normal and necessary, and it is nature's way of providing that extra shot of adrenalin just when you need it. Learn to recognize fear, what it is and how to control it. Look carefully at the situation and determine if your fear is justified. You will usually find that many of your fears are imaginary. When you are injured and in pain, it is difficult to control fear. Pain can sometimes turn into panic and cause a person to act without thinking. Panic can also be caused by loneliness. It can lead to hopelessness, carelessness and even thoughts of suicide.

Improvise

You can always do something to improve the situation. Figure out what you need, take stock of what you have and then improvise. Learn to put up with new and unpleasant conditions. Keeping your mind on survival will help. Do not be afraid to try strange foods.

Value Living

Hope and a real plan for rescue will reduce your fear and make your chances of survival better. Conserve your health and strength. Illness and injury will greatly reduce your chances of survival. Remember that hunger, cold and fatigue lower your efficiency and stamina and force yourself to be especially careful by realizing that your low spirits are due to your physical condition and not the danger. Remember your goal – *getting home alive*.

Act Calm and Laid Back

Panic is often caused by stress. Relax and stress will fade away. Believe in yourself and the problem will become clearer and once your problems are clear they can be sorted out more easily.

Learn Basic Skills

The best insurance is to make sure that you learn the techniques and procedures for survival so thoroughly that they become automatic. Then the chances are that you will do the right thing – even in panic. Be inquisitive and search for additional survival knowledge. You are never too old or experienced to learn.

2   Setting Out

Basic Rules

Before setting out on a journey, you must always plan your route. If you are camping, plan your sites and stick to them. That way you will always know:

1   Where you are
2   How many miles you have covered
3   Where the nearest town lies

Work everything out in advance. That way you don't have to worry about being lost, and it also leaves you time to think out the important aspects of any emergency you may encounter.

Always tell someone where you are going, your proposed route, how long you will be away and when you expect to be back. If possible, try to phone home every two days or so, this will help to stop the family from worrying. Let them know any change of plans or routes, how you are and if there is any illness among your team. (I call it a team because that's how you must act, as a team.) If at all possible, advise the local police or rescue service of your plans. They will give advice and help freely and it is most valuable. Expect the unexpected, it inevitably happens just when you least expect it, so be prepared.

Always pack enough clothing to last for your journey and if you are walking or rambling, dress as if for bad weather, even if there is a heatwave at the time. If you have foul weather clothing with you, you can't go wrong, and you can always take clothes off if you are too warm; you can't put them on if you haven't brought them. Before setting off, make sure your equipment is serviceable, damaged kit can be a death trap. What good is a tent that won't give you shelter or waterproof clothing that won't keep you dry?

Always take a first aid kit with you and all the relevant dressings you may need. If you are rambling, take enough food to last you a few hours, just in case you happen to get lost in that fog that seems to appear from nowhere. Never walk so far that it is impossible to return the same day. Never go out alone. Take an up-to-date map. If you can't read one, take the time to find someone to teach you. Get hold of a good compass: they may be expensive but they are well worth it.

Even if you are just rambling, make up a survival kit. This won't cause a hindrance whilst walking, but it is an invaluable aid to your survival. It may seem unnecessary, but out in the wilds it can be turned into numerous different tools that could prolong your life and increase your chances of surviving until you are rescued. Just having the necessary equipment to keep you warm and fed can make sure you will get home. If you are lost or hurt on the moors, you will find a survival kit is essential to you.

A Simple Survival Kit

1 *The container*. A tobacco tin will suffice to hold most of the small kit. The lid can be used as a heliograph and the tin can be used for cooking if the need arises.

2 *Matches and striker*. These must be made waterproof by the simple process of dipping them in melted wax. This will not only keep them waterproof but will help to keep them alight. The wax does not hinder the match from striking as it will just fall away.

3 *Candles*. These are excellent for starting fires. They do not have to be table size either, birthday cake size will do.

4 *Razor blade or knife*. These must be sharp, just in case you find yourself having to skin or gut game. It might be better to carry a few razor blades as well as a knife as they don't take up much room.

5 *Safety pins*. These simple items have a thousand uses, from fastening bandages to securing your tent. They can also be used as fishing hooks and even for holding up your trousers.

6 *Condy crystals (Potassium Permanganate)*. This can be bought in any chemist shop, and in my view it is a wonder crystal. It can be used as an antiseptic, a water purifier, a fire lighter and, if sprinkled in snow, it will stain the snow red and become a ground-to-air signalling device. (There are differing schools of thought as to whether potassium permanganate is toxic. Too much can cause problems for some people, so use in moderation. See end of chapter for more information about potassium permanganate.)

7 *Fishing line and hooks*. It is always handy to carry this kind of kit around. Stick the hook in a cork and wind the line around the cork.

8 *Notepaper and pencil*. If you find yourself lost, what better way of letting people know which way you are heading if the need to move arises. It also burns well.

These are the basics of my survival kit, but every person has his own special needs and so every survival kit differs slightly.

Sample Survival Kit

Kit held in army bag:

1   Gas stove and fuel
2   Hexemin burner and fuel
3   Waxed matches
4   Flint and saw blade
5   Billy can
6   Razor blades
7   Sewing kit
8   Compass
9   Packet rice
10 Dried meat
11 Biscuits
12 Plastic sheet 6 x 6ft (2 metres square)
13 Medical kit
14 Emergency flares
15 Emergency flood survival blanket
16 Para cord
17 Tea/sugar/dried milk
18 Spoon (for use when eating)
19 Spare pair of socks
20 Plastic bag or balloon
21 Needle and cotton
22 Snare wire

In addition the water bottle on the belt contains sterilizing tablets and a hook on the back of my belt can fit an entrenching spade or small fold-away shovel.

My Survival Kit

I never go out on the moors without my kit, because if I get lost or something goes wrong – and believe me that can happen to the expert as well as the novice – my kit has everything I need and everything has a purpose.

If I do get lost, the first thing I do is light up the gas stove and make myself a cup of tea, this helps to boost the confidence and gives me time to assess the situation. If I run out of gas, there is my solid fuel burner and the flint and striker are there in case anything should happen to the matches or I run out of matches. Using the striker is much easier than rubbing two sticks together. The razor blades have a million uses. The machete is for chopping trees to make a shelter or for decapitating game. When the plastic sheet is stretched out overnight, it will collect morning dew, which is drinkable, or you can wrap it around your space blanket or sleeping bag and it will keep the rain off you. It can also be made into a tent and, if wrapped round two poles, it easily becomes a stretcher.

As you become more experienced and the areas you visit change, so will your survival kit. I know mine did – it became smaller and more compact.

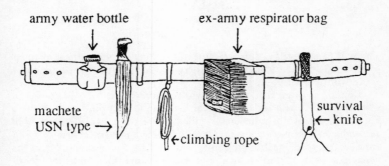

army water bottle

ex-army respirator bag

machete
USN type →

←climbing rope

survival
← knife

Fig. 1 My survival belt

Potassium Permanganate

Potassium permanganate is normally sold as small, purple crystals and is one of the most versatile items you can have in your survival kit. It can be used for purifying water, disinfecting wounds, firelighting or as a dye stuff for distress signals.

To purify water: add three or four crystals to every litre and leave for thirty minutes. It will stain the water slightly but it is safe to cook with and drink.

As a disinfectant: to clean cuts and abrasions or treat fungal disease, dissolve crystals in a glass of water, one by one. When the water turns purple, you have added enough. Use to bathe a wound.

To start a fire: take one part sugar and two parts potassium permanganate, mix and grind between two pieces of dry kindling. If the kindling is sufficiently dry it will burst into flames.

3   The Psychological Aspects of Survival

The will to survive is of paramount importance in the natural instincts of all animals. Man is an animal, therefore his instinct to survive takes precedent over all other thoughts.

Mention is often made of 'the will to survive' but no explanation of what the will to survive really is can be found. Dr John Leach wrote a fascinating article for a magazine called *SWAT* (*Survival, Weaponry and Techniques*; now *Survival and Outdoor Techniques*) in February 1988 entitled 'Survival Psychology', in which he wrote about a study on the behaviour of people in survival and disaster situations. Statistics identified three phases of psychological reaction: period of impact, period of recoil and period of post trauma. Although the statistics were split into three, they do in fact highlight different stages of the same syndrome.

The Period of Impact

This lasts from the moment the disaster becomes obvious until the immediate danger is removed. It rarely lasts more than one hour. During this period between 12 and 25% of people will remain calm, assessing the situation, making plans, retaining their awareness. 75% will be stunned and bewildered with impaired ability to reason. They may feel sick, weak and trembly; they may also find themselves perspiring profusely. This is a normal reaction and will pass. The remainder will be panic-stricken, screaming and weeping, and, in some cases, paralysis will occur.

The Period of Recoil

This occurs when the danger is passed. During this phase there is a gradual return to awareness. In effect, the shock wears off. Survivors will often show an infantile dependency and an overwhelming need to be close to other people. Many will become withdrawn with a strong need to vent their feelings. This may often be directed at any would-be rescuer. Apathy often sets in at this phase as does an undue concern for silly little things – a person may fret constantly over a torn shirt or a broken shoe lace.

Period of Post-trauma

This is the phase that comes into being after the survivor has been rescued. They often show signs of guilt, anxiety and depression, often with recurrent nightmares and psychosomatic disorders. There may be feelings of guilt over the loss of loved ones. It is during this phase that the survivor will come to realize the full extent of what has happened to them.

Panic

This is a common reaction to a disaster. It stems from the fear of what may happen as opposed to what is actually happening. Panic is contagious and every effort must be made to calm down panic victims.

Depression

A large percentage of survivors will find themselves numb and will often just sit and stare blankly at what is going on about them, not talking to anyone and shrugging off help. Less affected victims can easily be snapped out of this phase by gentleness or by giving them very simple jobs to do.

Anger

Hostility, aggression and anger are very common amongst victims and survivors. These reactions can often be aimed at the rescuer or at other victims who are made into scapegoats. This must be prevented at all costs – the last thing needed after a plane crash is a lynch mob hanging the pilot after having held a kangaroo court which found him guilty of pilot error.

Hyperactivity

Some victims will become hyperactive. Although they may dash around helping, they are easily distracted or become bored. Invariably tasks will be left half finished. It is common for victims who were depressed to become hyperactive.

Guilt

A very common symptom. Guilt for not having helped enough or even guilt for surviving when others have died.

Irrational behaviour

Some victims will become blatantly irrational. In some cases victims might collect pebbles or flowers instead of helping injured victims.

Apathy

The most common symptom of the onset of psychological breakdown in survivors is apathy. This can often lead to despair or even suicide and can often be triggered by rescue aircraft or ships failing to spot the victims. Some victims have been known to commit suicide after they have been rescued.

Knowing what to expect is half the battle – all the reactions mentioned here are common and victims cannot be blamed for suffering from them, in the same way that a man with a broken leg is not blamed for slowing down the rest of the group. Dr Leach actually states that the more he studies survival psychology, the more he comes to believe that the phrase 'the will to survive' is meaningless. Although I agree with him on all the aspects mentioned above, I believe there is a will to survive in all people which operates almost instinctively.

1972 Air Crash

A classic example of the will to survive is clearly shown if you refer to the events involving a group of men in 1972. In that year a plane flying over the Andes mountains crashed and only twenty-eight people out of forty-five survived the crash, which was caused by navigational errors on the part of the crew. The rescue services could not find them and after three weeks the search was called off because everyone believed they were dead.

How did they survive? Simple – they had no choice. The will to live was the greatest gift God had given them or so they believed. Their will to survive and their faith in God helped them to overcome the fact that under normal circumstances they were doomed. They had crashed high in the mountains and the plane had scattered to the four winds. In freezing blizzards and with hardly any food, the men from that plane crash survived for seventy-two days. They managed this by eating the flesh of their dead comrades. Having agreed not to eat the flesh of dead relatives, they sustained themselves by eating the flesh of the crew and strangers. They stripped the dead of all clothing and used it themselves to keep warm. They were unable to eat untreated snow because of the shock it would cause to their system and so they had to melt the snow, first by body heat and later using reflective aluminium trays. The meat stayed fresh because it was frozen. They used foam from the aircraft seats to make snowshoes. Finally two men reached civilization and seventeen of the twenty-eight people who survived the crash were rescued.

How does man now look upon cannibalism? Barbaric? Yes, but let's face it, we are meat, we are still part of the food chain. How many times have bodies been pulled out of rivers and lakes partly consumed by fresh-water fish? How many dead bodies have been found with rat bites and even cat bites? When does a dog stop smelling the scent of his dead master and start smelling the scent of food if a body is left to rot? Do we not eventually get consumed by insects and maggots ourselves? If man was pre-packed and put on a supermarket shelf, labelled as pork, would we really know the difference?

There are many reasons for cannibalism. The old belief that cannibals eat anyone and anything is ludicrous. The fact is that cannibals ate the bodies of their enemies in the belief that they would also consume his strength in battle. Some eat only loved ones in the belief that, being consumed, the dead person will live forever in the bodies of future generations. For whichever reasons cannibals eat human flesh, being hungry is not one of them. However in a survival situation, where man has no choice, religion does not come into it. You must eat to survive and, once the initial worries about eating human flesh have been overcome, it is no different to eating any other kind of meat.

Part Two

4   Travelling

Different Types of Terrain

Moorland

If moving on moorland areas is not practical because of the weather, find shelter where animals shelter – behind walls, woods, copses, bankings, caves, etc.

If visibility is restricted and you are on your own, take cover until visibility improves. Poor vision can be caused by fog, heavy rain, snow or nightfall.

If there is a group, take a compass bearing from any visible landmark, e.g. hill, pylon, lights of a town in the distance, then tie a white or fluorescent cloth or object to the backpack of one of your group and send him off, shouting instructions to him to keep on the bearing (left, right, go on, etc). When it becomes difficult to see him, shout to him to stop and the rest of the group can then move to join him; the first man will warn the group of any obstacles they may have to cross. When you reach him, re-check your bearings and send him on again. Keep this up until you reach the landmark you were making for, or a road, then head for the nearest town.

If you arrive at a road and there is no indication of which way to go, send a member of the group off in each direction with instructions to walk for fifteen minutes before returning. Each man then gives the group any information he has found from road signs, houses, villages, etc., and the group then decides which way to go after assessing the information.

Remember if in doubt, in moorland areas, civilization is usually downhill. This also applies in mountain areas.

Mountain

When walking in mountain areas try to stick to tracks made by previous walkers. If the track starts to rise up the side of a fell, then it is possible that it is a sheep track rather than a path. Do not attempt to climb down loose shale or scree. Follow streams downhill; they will sooner or later meet rivers which will lead to towns.

In mountain areas, what looks like a single ridge line from a distance can be, in reality, a series of ridges and valleys which are difficult to climb. Follow the directions of ridges and valleys and don't try to cross them.

To save time and energy during hill and mountain walking, keep the weight of your body directly over your feet, by placing the soles of your shoes flat on the ground. Do not try tiptoeing up a mountain. Doing this will make your calves ache. When you climb, lock your knees briefly at the end of each step in order to rest your leg muscles. Traverse steep slopes in a zig-zag direction, not straight up. Turn at the end of each section by stepping off in the new direction with the uphill foot. This prevents crossing your feet and possibly losing your balance. Take plenty of rests.

Forest

If you come across a forest while travelling, attempt to go round it unless there is a very obvious path with signs of motor transport using it, e.g. LandRovers or tractor tracks. Tracks peter out very quickly and you can't see to get a bearing once in the forest. If you have no option but to travel through a forest, spread out in single file with a few yards distance between each man. This will help stop you walking in circles. The last man should attempt to mark the route they have followed, just in case it becomes necessary to backtrack.

In plantation forest, there will invariably be wide breaks between each group of trees which makes travelling easier.

Coast

When walking on shores, it is easier to walk on compacted wet sand than on dry sand, but be aware of the possibility of quicksand and test the ground ahead regularly. Always keep an eye on the tides and beware of getting cut off.

Marsh

When walking in marshy areas, travel from tree to tree, since the ground will be more solid round the roots of trees because the trees soak up the water.

Keep your eyes open for any areas that do not look solid. These are often shown by flat, black areas without any vegetation. Beware also of bright green areas of sphagnum moss.

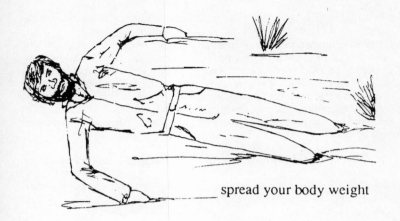

spread your body weight

Fig. 2 Getting out of quicksand/marsh/bog

Use a stick to test the ground – infantry officers in the First World War were issued with willow walking sticks so that they could test the depth of mud in the trenches. The modern swagger sticks are just for tradition. If the map shows that there is a marshy area ahead of you, cut yourself a stick about three to four foot long. Do not use dead wood, it will break too easily. Tossing rocks on to the ground ahead will also show any boggy areas.

When travelling in a group, walk in single file and always follow the first man's path exactly unless he is obviously in trouble. The second man should carry the rope in case of any problems.

Getting out of a bog

If you do get into trouble, spread your body weight over as much area as possible and move very slowly and deliberately. Do not throw your arms about as this will draw you under more quickly.

If you are alone, use your arms and legs as paddles with a very slow breaststroke movement to get yourself to the edge. Use any roots or grass clumps you see to pull yourself along.

If you are with someone, wait quietly while they throw you a rope or a pole or something to grab hold of and let them haul you out.

Walking in Winter

Do not venture on mountains in snow and ice conditions unless you are experienced or are with someone experienced. You need to know how to use an ice axe expertly, from how to carry it to how to use it to stop yourself from falling. You also need to be expert at compass work in case 'white out' conditions come down.

Remember that fresh drinking water will be difficult to find and be prepared by carrying extra water with you. Shops, cafes and hotels may well be closed.

1   Wear the right clothing and carry extra with you as well as water-proof kit
2   Don't go alone – companions will keep you going if the weather breaks
3   Plot your route – allowing for shorter daylight hours
4   Avoid steep grassed areas near potential hazards. Waterproof nylon clothing will slide too easily over icy grass

If you get caught in a blizzard:

1   Get yourself on the leeside of some natural protection, such as a wall
2   Make a small crater to sit in
3   Put on all the clothing you have with you (except for your anorak, until you have completed the next two steps)
4   Undo bootlaces, belts, cuffs and collars to ease the circulation of warm air
5   Make something to sit on, a book, a map, folded towel, camera case, food box – anything to get you off the ground
6   If you have a bivi bag, climb into it, sit on your improvised seat, slip your feet into your rucksack and wear your anorak over all. Do not put arms in sleeves but tuck your hands under armpits
7   Do not eat anything – you may need to ration the food you have so that it lasts longer and also you tend to feel drowsy after eating and going to sleep when caught in a blizzard is potentially dangerous
8   All of the group should huddle together
9   Keep wriggling fingers and toes and keep awake – sing if necessary
10 Wait until conditions improve before moving

Walking at Night

Travelling at night over unknown territory can be very dangerous. The night is never completely dark and night vision is not totally lost but because it is difficult to see things clearly, it is easy to become disorientated and lost. If a compass is used, you can maintain a set heading and therefore dispel the fear of getting lost.

Mountain Safety Code

1   Carry warm, water and wind proof clothing and spare woollens. Wet, wind and cold are the enemies at high altitudes even in summer

2   Wear strong footwear, i.e. boots with a good grip. If the soles have worn thin, get them re-soled. A sole can be cut out of an old tyre in a survival situation

3   Carry extra food. A pocket full of sweets will give energy in a concentrated form

4   Always carry a whistle

5   Learn sound rope management, abseiling, rock climbing, etc., under expert tuition

6   Obtain knowledge of local conditions and take heed of them and learn to understand the signs of changing weather conditions

7   Make sure you know where the mountain rescue post and huts are on the high fells. Learn the recognized emergency signals

8   Inform someone of your route before setting out. Inform them when you return so they don't call out the rescue services for nothing

9   Accidents are most likely to happen when you are tired – conserve energy, stay alert

10   Be prepared for the unexpected

Additional safety rules

1   Check the weather forecasts before leaving

2   Keep to the planned route if possible, but

3   Let your route suffer rather than yourself and turn back if conditions get worse

4   Phone those expecting you or the police if you end up at some point away from your original destination to avoid search parties being sent out

5   Follow the Country Code

6   Don't ignore the risks of crossing swollen streams, detour instead, even if it adds several miles to your trip

7   Try not to travel alone in hills and moorland

8   Don't split your group up

9   Don't walk in groups of less than four or more than six on moun-
    tains and moors. Too many is risky in case of accident and difficult
    to keep together in bad weather

5   Finding Your Way

At this moment, you probably know where you are. Perhaps you are sitting at home thinking about a trip – but the main thing is that you are secure and comfortable. The purpose of this section is to help you carry that security with you when out in the country.

In the past, knowing how to find your way without any maps, just by an in-built sense of direction, or hearsay, was a way of life. Nowadays we use this skill very little, and most people can get through life without needing to do more than find their way round a new town or a diversion caused by roadworks; but as the wild areas in the countryside get smaller, they become more interesting, and anyone venturing out into areas with few inhabitants needs to know how to find their way.

Maps

We now have maps of virtually the whole world easily available to us. Drawn maps date back to 600 BC in Greece and there were probably others in Egypt and China before then. Compasses appeared in China around 2500 BC and were amongst the items Marco Polo brought back to Europe in the thirteenth century. If you can master the use of both map and compass the chances are slim that you will ever be totally lost, provided of course you are carrying these items.

You can use an accurate map as if it was an aerial view of your surroundings. Many of the Ordnance Survey maps are actually taken from aerial photographs. They indicate mountains, valleys, water, roads, buildings, steepness of the land, marshes, etc. Having a good map can save a lot of unnecessary climbing and struggling through bogs.

The symbols used on an Ordnance Survey map are generally standard. North is generally at the top of any map and the scale of the map will be printed somewhere on the front cover or the bottom, i.e.

1:24,000 which means 1 cm on the map equals 24,000 cm or 240 metres. The two most commonly used maps are 1:50,000 and 1:25,000. The large scale maps show a small area in great detail, whilst the small scale map will show a larger area in less detail, although all the important information will still be shown. The scale of the map (usually at the bottom) will give you an idea of the area each square covers.

Ordnance Survey (OS) maps have super-imposed on them a series of horizontal and vertical lines. This is called the National Grid. This grid system provides a standardized method whereby any point can be defined accurately on any map by a reference to these lines: this is called a Grid Reference. Maps have a series of numbers running up the sides and along the top and bottom of these grid lines. These numbers indicate the reference number of each line.

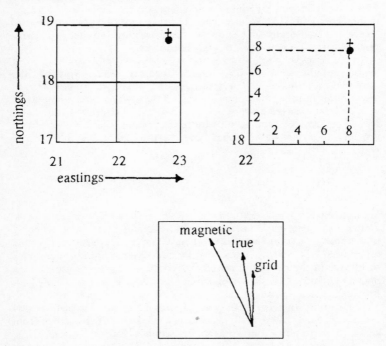

Fig. 3 Grid references

The numbers running vertically up the map are called Northings and the numbers running from east to west are called Eastings. To give a Grid Reference, firstly run your finger along the Eastings; these numbers although running horizontally refer to the vertical lines. The vertical rising numbers refer to the horizontal lines. This can often cause confusion. Run along the Eastings until you reach the grid square you require, then run your finger along the Northings until you come to the grid square you want. The Grid Reference is taken from the bottom left-hand corner of the square where the two lines cross.

Most maps give a wealth of information about the topography or contours of the land. Land areas are shown in green, water in blue. Marshy areas are represented by blue tufts of grass on a green background. The brown lines are counter lines indicating elevation: the elevation or height of all points on a given contour will be the same. The thicker contour lines normally give the height of that elevation somewhere along the line; therefore if you find two thick lines and read their heights, you will be able to work out the elevation of the thinner lines in between. The number on the darker lines indicates the height above sea level. The steepness of the slope is indicated by the relative density of the line – lines close together show a steep slope whilst lines at wide intervals indicate more gentle slopes. The height of a summit is usually shown in the centre of the highest contour.

The first requirement for a map reader is to 'set' the map. This can be done in two ways.

1   By use of compass
2   By visual means

Setting the map visually is a very simple procedure, but like everything else it requires practice.

When using a map, keep the majority of the writing the correct way up. The top of the map is north, the bottom south, the left west and the right east. You then need to find a prominent feature, such as a church or a road junction. Hold the map out in front of you and move it around until the symbol on the map lines up with the feature. A map does not have to be read like a book or a paper, you can read it from any angle.

Making your own route map

At some point you will need to make a map yourself, either to keep track of your whereabouts or to show a friend how to find somewhere. You don't need any sophisticated materials, just paper and pencil. Begin by indicating north, then indicate a scale, such as 2 cms equals 100, 500 or 1000 paces.

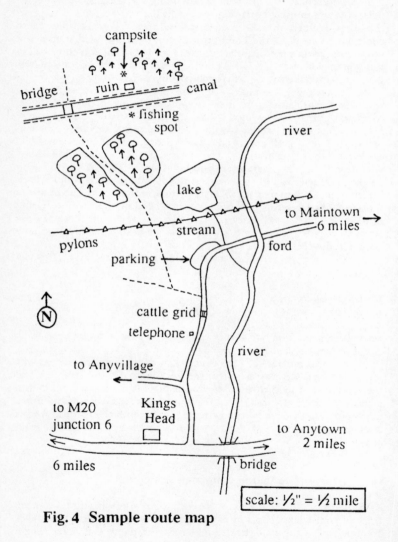

Fig. 4 Sample route map

Indicate the access to the area of the map, i.e. a motorway, major road, river or some other familiar landmark. Include the approximate locations of any features, natural or man made, that will reassure the user that he is on the right road (see Fig. 4).

It will be helpful to remember that on flat and open terrain an average walker covers about 100 paces a minute. Knowing how fast you walk will save you counting each step.

A rough rule of thumb calculation is that you will walk at 2½ mph (4 kph) plus an extra half hour for every 700 feet (210 m) climbed. This calculation does not allow for rests, extra weights carried, companions who prove unfit or delays caused by the weather.

Making an Emergency Compass

A compass is a balanced strip of magnetized metal which is free to swing in any direction. You can make one yourself by stroking a needle in one direction (preferably from eye to point for safety) with a piece of silk and then floating it in a still liquid such as a puddle or a cup of water. To keep it from sinking, oil it lightly first, by running it through your hair if no other oil is available, then lower it very gently, using looped strands of thread or grass blades. Once it is afloat, remove the supports. The needle will turn until it comes to rest in a north-south direction. The part of the needle you stroked from will point north.

This is a simple home-made emergency compass, but one which is inconvenient for normal use because it has to be re-magnetized frequently and needs gentle handling. Compasses which you buy are much easier to use, because north is clearly marked and the arrow is suspended on a point and protected by a case. Some compasses have a fluorescent needle which glows in the dark, clips for fastening the compass to clothing, a mirror and sighting apparatus to project a bearing on to a vertical landmark. It is best to carry two compasses because it is possible for one to jam or de-magnetize. These should be kept away from each other and checked against each other. If there is a difference between the two, favour the compass on which the needle moves more freely.

Using a Compass

To use a compass, hold it still and level until the needle comes to rest. Then double check by moving the compass to ensure the readings are the same. If the compass does not show the other cardinal points on the housing you will have to fill these in mentally.

Most compasses have three basic parts: a magnetic needle, a rotating compass housing marked with the cardinal points – north, south, east and west – and markings from 0–360° and a clear base marked with an arrow (DOT – Direction Of Travel arrow).

Place the compass on the map with the base plate along a line which connects where you are now and where you are going, with the DOT arrow pointing towards your destination. Turn the compass housing until the orienting arrow points due north on the map itself, i.e. to the top of the map, parallel with top to bottom grid lines on the map.

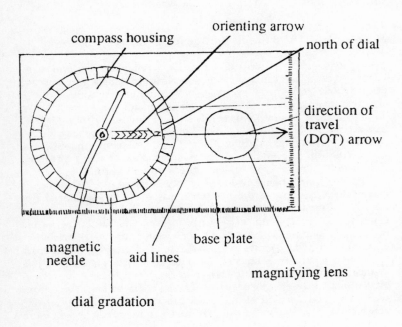

Fig. 5 Standard compass

Find the degree mark on the housing which touches the DOT arrow: this gives you your bearing. Allow for magnetic variations which will be printed on the map; for example, if your bearing was 45° and the local variation is 15° east from True North, turn the compass housing until

60° nudges the DOT arrow. Hold the base plate of the compass with the DOT arrow pointing away and turn yourself until the red magnetic needle points north. Keep the red needle pointing north and walk following the DOT arrow.

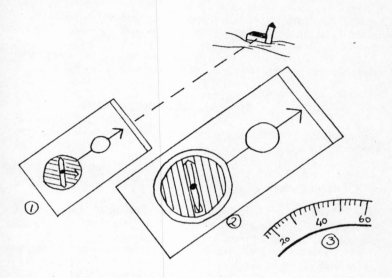

Fig. 6 Taking a bearing

Using a Compass to Find Your Position

Look round for a clear landmark such as a church spire or a known mountain. Find the landmark on the map. Lay the straight edge of the compass or other straight edge on the map so it touches the symbol for the landmark. Sight along the base plate and turn the plate, without moving the map, until it points at the landmark. Draw a line along the straight edge. Repeat the procedure with a second and third landmark. Where the lines cross is your position.

It is often useful to determine the direction of visible landmarks when you come to high ground or a clearing because at a later stage, even if the landmark is obscured, you can use your compass to walk towards it. However you must allow for the fact that magnetic north and north as shown on the map are not identical.

Taking a Magnetic Bearing with a Compass

Hold the compass horizontal at about waist height so that the direction of the compass needle points to the feature you are travelling towards. Keep the base of the compass steady in this position and turn the housing until the north on the rim is opposite the red end of the compass needle. Read off the number of degrees at the index pointer; this gives the magnetic bearing.

Compass needles are susceptible to metal objects, so always take compass bearings away from vehicles or large metal objects.

Magnetic Variation

When working out your bearings, a simple way to remember the magnetic calculation is:

Mag to Grid   Get rid
Grid to Mag   Add

When transferring a compass bearing to a grid reference, deduct the difference shown on the map; when transferring a grid reference to a compass bearing, add the difference.

Remember that magnetic bearings are taken by pointing the compass needle at an object such as a church and that a grid bearing is taken by using the map and then in effect travelling towards an object.

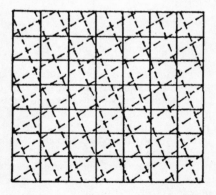

Fig. 7 Adjusting a map for field use

Compass work and map work are not the easiest subjects to learn by reading and it is much simpler to get an experienced person to show you how to map read. To adjust a map for field use, re-draw the lines of longitude and latitude to reflect the fact that Magnetic North and Geographic North differ.

There are three types of north:

True North	The actual direction of the North Pole
Magnetic North	The direction towards which a compass needle points
Grid North	The direction of the vertical gridlines from the bottom to the top of the map

Only two of these concern the map reader, these are Grid North and Magnetic North. The difference between True North and Grid North is given at the corner of the map. The variation is caused by the difficulty of representing the curved surface of the earth on a flat sheet of paper.

When travelling with a map and compass, a distinction must be made between the Geographic North Pole (on which maps are based) and the Magnetic North Pole which controls the compass. In 1985 the Magnetic North Pole was a point in the Upper Hudson Bay area of Canada about 217 m (350 km) from the Geographic North Pole but it is moving north at about 6 m (10 km) per year. In the British Isles, the greatest variation is on the Isle of Lewis in the Outer Hebrides where Magnetic North is 11½° west of True North.

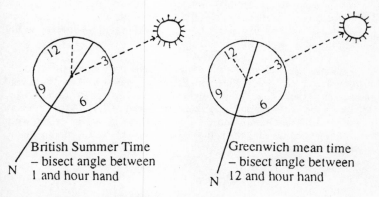

British Summer Time
– bisect angle between
1 and hour hand

Greenwich mean time
– bisect angle between
12 and hour hand

Fig. 8 Using a watch as a compass

A watch is useful when you are away from civilization because it is easier to measure the distance you have travelled in time rather than miles or kilometres. You do not need to know how far you have walked but if you return over similar ground at the same pace, then you should take a similar time for the return trip. You must bear in mind though whether you were climbing or going downhill on the outward journey.

A watch can also be used as a compass if the sun is casting a shadow and you have the watch set to local standard time. Hold the watch face horizontally, with the hour hand pointing to the sun. This can best be done by holding a twig vertically at the edge of the dial so it casts a shadow directly along the hour hand. North will lie midway between the hour hand and the number 12. If you were to do this at 9 a.m. a line from the centre of the watch to a point midway between 9 and 12 would point to the north (see Fig. 8).

If You Get Lost

If you get lost and have no map you should still be able to reach safety:

1 Consider returning to the last main road you crossed
2 Look round for any buildings or telegraph wires, which are usually near roads and head for them
3 If there is a landmark, such as a road or a river ahead of you that you know crosses your path, head for that
4 If no landmarks are visible, use the sun to give you an idea of which direction is which. The sun rises in the east and sets in the west and will be due south at midday in Great Britain
5 If the sun is obscured by clouds, hold a knife blade or something similar upright on to a shiny surface. The sun will be directly opposite the shadow cast by the blade

If you are lost and you reach a road, follow it to the nearest village or town. If you are looking lost and distressed, people will not mind you knocking on their door late at night. Try to keep your morale up by singing – there is always a chance that a farmer may shout 'What the hell are you making that bloody noise for at two in the morning?', then, with a pleasant smile, ask him for help or directions. He will probably moan at you but at least you won't stay lost.

Natural Guides

If you find yourself in the wilds without a map and/or compass, there are other guides that you can use, such as the sun, vegetation, winds and rivers. Remember that these are general indications of directions and not always reliable.

The sun

The sun is the most widely used indicator because we know the sun rises in the east and sets in the west. If we take this literally however we could get in trouble because there are only two days of the year, 21 March and 23 September (the spring and autumn equinoxes), when the sun rises and sets exactly true. It can vary by as much as 23° from these directions at the equator. At other points on the globe the variation is even greater. The table given below is correct to within a few degrees of 50°N, i.e. northern Europe. The error increases sharply nearer the North Pole.

Date	Variation from true east at sunrise and true west at sunset at the equator
1 January	23 degrees south
1 February	18 degrees south
1 March	8 degrees south
1 April	4 degrees north
1 May	14 degrees north
1 June	22 degrees north
1 July	23 degrees north
1 August	18 degrees north
1 September	9 degrees north
1 October	3 degrees south
1 November	14 degrees south
1 December	22 degrees south

Fig. 9 Variations on compass points

The direction of the sun at sunrise and sunset is further complicated by the fact that it is rare to find an ideal horizon. Even a low range of hills will obscure the sea level horizon and cause an error of as much as 10–15°.

It is therefore simpler to note the position of the sun at true noon, i.e. after taking into account putting clocks forward in summer.

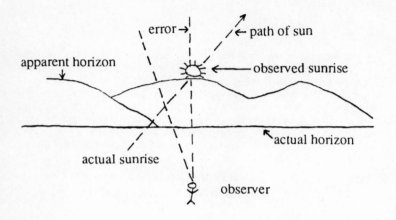

Fig. 10 Horizon distortion

The stars

Navigating by the stars is simple and reliable, although it can only be used when the night sky is clear. It is wise to use the stars to double check your daytime readings.

The North Star or Polaris, which is the absolute and invariable indication of True North in the Northern Hemisphere, is easy to find. A bearing taken on the North Star is never more than one degree away from True North. While the other stars move across the heavens nightly and change positions with the seasons, the North Star always seems to stand still while the other stars pivot round it.

To find the North Star

1 Find the Plough (see Fig. 12)
2 Extend an imaginary line through the two pointer stars which form the side of the cup farthest away from the handle, approximately five times. A line drawn straight from these two stars and one drawn from the centre star of Cassiopeia, will converge at the North Star

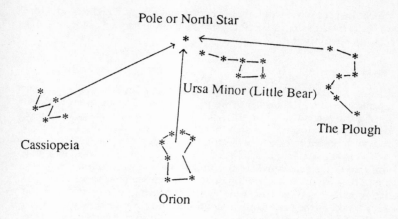

Fig. 11 Finding the North Star

Vegetation

The old adage that moss grows thickest on the side of the tree which is in the shade, i.e. the north, can be helpful. It will only work in the Northern Hemisphere and when the tree stands in the open and gets sunshine full on to it. In addition, some growths which resemble moss grow on the sunniest side of the tree. Unless you can tell which is which, this method does not always work.

The relationship of growth to light does help however. Trees and other vegetation grow more profusely on a south-facing slope. Tree rings which are visible on tree stumps, tend to be wider on the sunnier side of the tree.

Winds

The wind does not blow in random patterns. Each area has its own prevailing wind pattern. If the pattern is known for the region you are in, it can serve as an approximate guide. As prevailing winds are usually averages, this method is inexact in most places.

The prevailing wind patterns can help in more indirect ways. Trees generally fall in the direction of strong prevailing winds and sand banks and sand dunes tend to be narrower and lower in the direction from which the prevailing wind usually comes and they are higher and wider on the leeward side. Indications such as these are usually more reliable than the wind itself.

Water

Streams of water always flow downhill and, as even the smallest stream usually joins a bigger stretch of water, it is generally true to say that following the current will lead to civilization. 'Sod's Law' being what it is, however, there is always a possibility that the stream could flow into a lake with no outlet or go underground.

To cross a stream, always look for the widest part, because as a general rule this is usually where the stream is shallowest. Rather than trying to balance on a slippery log or stones, remove your shoes and cross barefooted. If you have to wade, remove clothing to keep it dry. Avoid steep banks as they are likely to continue being steep below the water.

Game tracks usually lead to water and tend to bypass swampy areas. They don't bear any relation to compass directions but are a help in finding a gradual descent from high ground and in avoiding natural obstacles.

The return journey

When travelling through unfamiliar territory, look behind you occasionally to see what the route looks like from behind. This trick, which is often overlooked, will help on the return trip.

Landmarks

To walk a straight line out in the wilds is not as easy as it sounds because the tendency is to walk in circles. To help you, pick out three landmarks all in a line. When you reach the first, select a fourth beyond the third and proceed to the second. Continue in this manner. With practice you will be able to walk a straight line with only two landmarks.

6   Frostbite and Exposure

Frostbite

When the surrounding temperature falls, it causes the surface blood vessels to contract. When they have fully contracted the body temperature begins to fall. A further lowering of temperature, or an increase in the time of exposure to that temperature, will lead to an increase in the severity of the effect of cold. The body's protective mechanism of shivering will cease to be effective and give way to muscular rigidity and finally, as the body temperature continues to fall, unconsciousness will occur.

Paradoxically, severe cooling of the hands and feet usually causes the blood vessels to relax and dilate or to alternate between relaxing and constricting, which aggravates the loss of body heat in cold conditions. This mechanism is not fully understood, but may be due to paralysis of the constrictor muscles in the small blood vessels in low temperatures. The effect of wind chill can create a serious additional hazard by lowering the effective temperature and increasing the possibility of frostbite.

Frostbite can occur in any part of the body exposed to very low temperatures. In such a situation, the natural closing down of the surface blood vessels is so complete that the circulation stops completely. The onset of frostbite may be gradual and painless but in some cases a feeling of numbness or a tingling sensation is felt, and this may be used as a warning sign. In the early stages, the affected parts are white and waxy and surrounded by a red zone. Later, they become purple or blue and eventually the area becomes gangrenous. The most commonly affected areas are the extremities, such as fingers, toes and nose, but in severe conditions any exposed areas of skin may be affected. Even without the cold conditions, the wind chill factor can cause frostbite, similar to Bells Palsy where the facial muscles become paralysed.

Treatment

Rapid re-warming of the frozen tissues should be carried out as soon as possible. The way to do this is to immerse the affected area in hot water or urine in the groin area. Massage the area to stimulate the circulation, but on no account should it be rubbed vigorously with snow or ice.

Preventive measures

There are few preventive measures apart from the usual 'dress properly and keep as dry as possible'. The extremities should be kept moving. Pull faces in order to keep the facial muscles working.

Exposure

This is not a strict medical term, but in general it describes the serious effects which result from exposure to climatic extremes. It is generally limited to the effects of cold environments and is similar to frostbite. The only difference being that instead of causing actual frostbite, the body temperature becomes so low that it causes hypothermia. Once the temperature of the body falls this far, it is very hard to make it rise again.

This ailment is not uncommon amongst climbers, ramblers and other people who engage in outdoor activities. It seems to be caused by a mixture of fatigue, cold, anxiety or mental stress and can be extremely dangerous. It also hits the physically exhausted, so the rule is not to carry on regardless, but to conserve as much energy as possible.

Signs and symptoms

1 Unexpected and unreasonable behaviour, often accompanied by a feeling of cold and tiredness
2 Failure to respond to or understand questions or directions
3 Failure of or abnormality in vision. This is a usual occurrence and, when noted, should be treated with extreme seriousness
4 Some slurring of the speech and the victim may speak quite strongly before collapsing
5 Sudden shivering fits
6 Violent bursts of energy, possible physical resistance to anyone wishing to help – violent language
7 Constant falling down

It should be noted that not all these symptoms may be noticeable, especially if the person has a strong personality. It is vital that the deep-core body temperature of 98.4° is maintained at all costs. If not, it can lead directly to mental deterioration and loss of muscular co-ordination which will eventually lead to unconsciousness, heart and respiratory failure and in the most extreme cases – death.

Unlike cases of frostbite, sudden surface warming is dangerous. Using hot water bottles, vigorous rubbing and the administration of alcohol must be avoided, as all these cause sudden heat surges on the body surface and therefore actually cause the problem to worsen.

Treatment

1   Get the victim into a sleeping bag, or wrap round with a sleeping bag to insulate above and below. Strip the victim completely naked
2   Get a fit companion, also stripped, into the sleeping bag alongside the victim so that body heat can be passed more easily
3   Build a wind and waterproof shelter round both the victim and the companion, a tent or polythene bivouac
4   If the victim is able to take food, give sugar or condensed milk

There are many factors to consider before getting the victim back to 'civilization'. I would suggest that waiting for the rescue team is the safest method if at all possible. If you decide you must send men to fetch help, organize the remainder of the party into setting up camp and making hot drinks for everyone. Get food down all your members and when everyone is satisfied and the camp set, send off your chosen party.

Non-suffering members must keep warm at all costs. When the rescue party arrives, they will take over and organize the 'casevac' (casualty evacuation). Never class the return of the victim's temperature to normal as the end of the problem. Keep building up a reserve of energy and temperature until help arrives.

7   Reading the Weather Signs

Clouds

There are three main cloud types – cirrus which is wispy, cumulus which is heaped up and stratus which is in layers. These forms are combined to give the various cloud types.

High clouds – cirrus, cirrocumulus and cirrostratus – extend from about 20,000 ft (6 km) – 50,000 ft above ground. They are composed of ice crystals and develop and disappear rapidly. Cirrus clouds are the wispy 'mares tails', cirrocumulus look like ripples in wet sand (mackerel sky) and cirrostratus is a sheet of thin cloud. These clouds indicate a warm front moving in from the west when they appear after a clear sky.

Medium altitude clouds – altostratus and altocumulus – are made of water droplets and are usually about 4 km (7,000–20,000 ft) above ground. They change in shape and colour as they move between layers. Altostratus clouds, which appear to be striped and have the appearance of frosted glass, often turn into low level nimbostratus clouds. Altocumulus forms puffy parallel patches and foretells possible rainfall.

Cumulo-nimbus – the thunder cloud – is a towering mass of cloud which can stretch from about 3,000 ft (1 km) above ground to 19,000 ft (6 km). It has the classic anvil top and ragged base. It foretells squally winds, heavy rain, thunder and possibly hail.

Cumulus and stratus are basic low cloud forms which lie at about 7,000 ft (1 km) above ground. Cumulus are mounded clouds, like cotton wool, with flat bases and fluffy, rounded tops. They foretell fair weather coming, unless they begin to pile up on top of each other which could then grow into the thunder cloud. Stratus are the wet layer-like clouds that gather on hill tops like a fog, although they don't usually touch the ground. They usually produce drizzle rather than rain. Nimbostratus lies between the cumulus and the stratus as dark sheet-like layers which bring steady rain or snow.

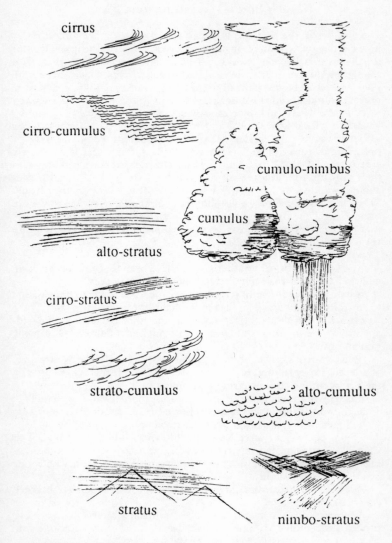

Fig. 12 Clouds

Weather Lore – Forecasting from Nature

The weather in the first few hours of the day gives a fair indication of how the day will continue. In summer a dew will soak the grass, in winter the frost will cover grass. If dew or frost are missing, there is a change in the weather coming. Hard-edged clouds, clean, hard blue skies and vivid dawns generally mean bad weather. Dusky, heavy skies precede thunder, whilst soft mists, skies and colours mean fine weather.

Animals, birds and insects can sense what weather is coming. Pheasants 'clock' at distant thunder and bees rush home, whilst rooks gather in the trees to shelter. Many insects hatch in the humid weather preceding a storm, including the warble fly – this insect is practically eradicated in Great Britain but if you see cattle or horses running with their tails up, for no apparent reason, there are probably warble flies about. Swallows fly low at this time to catch the insects as they hatch. When there is rain about, owls hoot more at night and cocks crow more often. Seagulls make for land if heavy winds are coming and ducks fly low. Pigs get very upset if heavy rain is coming and animals generally are very restless before bad weather.

Many of the traditional weather sayings have been based on observation and do have valid reasoning behind them. For example:

A halo round the moon usually means rain and strong winds within about thirty-six hours. The bigger the halo, the nearer the rain. These haloes are produced by the refraction of light through ice crystal clouds and are frequently followed by a warm front and a depression bringing rain and gales.

'Red sky at night, shepherd's (or sailor's) delight'. The western sky where the sun is setting, reflects the sunlight and if the sky is very dry, the red portion of the spectrum predominates.

'Red sky in the morning, shepherd's (or sailor's) warning'. The light from the sun rising in the east is reflected from the underside of very high clouds, which are often the forerunners of rain.

'When rise begins after low, squalls expect and clear blow'. This rhyme, referring to barometric pressure, accurately describes the passage of a cold front. The clear blow is the north west wind with lifting cloud and good visibility.

'Clear moon, frost soon'. The cooling of the earth's surface is greatest on clear nights.

'Mackerel sky and mares' tails make tall ships carry low sails'. The broken altocumulus of a mackerel sky (small clouds like scales of a fish) may be a forerunner of fronts with wind and rain.

'When clouds appear like rocks and towers, the earth's refreshed by frequent showers' is an accurate rhyme describing shower clouds.

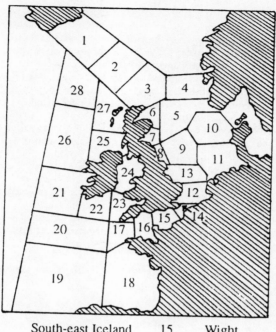

1	South-east Iceland	15	Wight
2	Faeroes	16	Portland
3	Fair Isle	17	Plymouth
4	Viking	18	Biscay
5	Forties	19	Finisterre
6	Cromarty	20	Sole
7	Forth	21	Shannon
8	Tyne	22	Fastnet
9	Dogger	23	Lundy
10	Fisher	24	Irish Sea
11	German Bight	25	Malin
12	Thames	26	Rockall
13	Humber	27	Hebrides
14	Dover	28	Bailey

Fig. 13 Coastal shipping areas

'A northern haar brings fine weather from afar'. A 'haar' is a sea mist in the north of England and east of Scotland and is caused by anticyclone conditions which often bring fine weather when the mist clears.

'Mackerel sky, not long dry'. The mackerel sky is often caused by ripples in high level cloud associated with an advancing front.

'If Candlemas Day (2 February) be fair and bright, winter will have another fight. If Candlemas Day be clouds and rain, winter is gone and will not come again'. A mild break early in February often develops into a cold spell later in the month.

The weather around St Swithin's Day (15 July) can often indicate what lies ahead, although rain on the day does not mean it will rain for forty days and nights.

'For every fog in March, there'll be a frost in May' has been investigated by the Met Office and found to be accurate.

'Oak before ash, we shall have a splash. Ash before oak, we shall have a soak'. Refers to the oak and ash coming into leaf.

A copper-coloured sunset is a warning of a gale or storm while a yellow sunset indicates wind and rain. A green sunset foretells a thaw.

Seagulls flying inland indicates bad weather at sea making its way to land.

'Rain before seven, fine before eleven' is usually more accurate in flat areas than hilly ones.

Shipping areas

If you have a radio with you or have access to a radio, listen out for the shipping forecasts. If you know the areas the broadcaster is talking about, you will have an idea of what weather may be coming your way.

8 Clothing

Choice of Clothing

Clothing is always going to be one of the items which is hardest on the survivalist's pocket. Some survivalists believe in the self-sufficiency ideal, doing the impossible with nothing at all. However, many survivalists are mountain climbers, moorland ramblers – outdoor people who will already have some equipment.

I don't think anyone can say for sure what is the best type of clothing to take with you when hiking or camping, but one can give guidelines. For example, it needs to be:

Light
Waterproof
Easy to pack away
Warm

Nylon seems to have most of these properties, so I would suggest nylon water-proof kit as well as the conventional 'woolly pully'. Corduroy trousers seem warmer than denim jeans, but, from my personal experience, army issue lightweight trousers are the best. They dry quicker than most others, but even when wet they seem to keep the legs very warm.

The best bet is that clothing should be bought to suit oneself. There are hundreds and thousands of outdoor centres, scattered all round Britain where you can go and buy the kit you need. These are the kinds of shops where you go in to look for one thing and come out after buying something else or something besides your original intention.

There are many types of outdoor clothing on the market with as many different ranges of prices as there are styles. With many you are paying 'over the odds' for a name. I can tell you what I prefer – Rohan clothing. I've struggled to afford it, but it's good, it's hard-wearing, it's practical and it's comfortable. I go out on the fells quite a lot and I wear

Rohan for all the reasons I've mentioned. All good quality outdoor clothes are tested in one way or another to make sure that they will live up to expectations but you must beware of cheap imitations. In other words whilst making sure you don't get 'ripped off' for a name, don't buy rubbish either!

Always remember that walking shoes or boots are the best to wear. It makes sense – you don't go swimming in boots, so don't go rambling in flip-flops. Ladies should remember that heels and hills don't mix.

Clothing lists differ depending on where you are going and what you are doing. It is as pointless climbing a mountain in an army trench coat as it is trying to remain camouflaged in a bright yellow cagoule. Your clothing must be chosen bearing in mind the outdoor pursuits you follow. If you are living off the land, camping and hunting, you need clothes that will hide you from your prey; if you are mountain climbing and fell walking, you need bright clothing in case you get lost, so that you can be found easily.

Don't just buy a pair of boots the day before you set off, get them a couple of weeks before so as to stretch them in over a short distance, otherwise they will end up breaking you.

Clothing

Wear thin layers to trap air in between – a string vest, wool shirt, one or two light jerseys. A proofed nylon anorak or cagoule will keep off most rain, although even good ones leak to some extent. A zip right down the front helps ventilate you and prevents too much condensation building up.

Packing a Rucksack

Other items which may be needed include a wool hat to prevent the 25% heat lost through the top of the head, a pair of mitts, climbers-type breeches or long warm woollen pants (not jeans), long woollen socks, rain-proof over-trousers, long zip-up snow gaiters.

Supplies to take with you include Kendal mint cake or dried dates to be chewed to stave off hunger and provide a steady source of energy. A flashlight with a spare bulb and battery, a whistle for emergencies, a bivi bag, high energy food, maps, a compass and a first aid and survival kit.

You gradually will build up a packing list that will incorporate minimum weight with maximum protection and give more room in your rucksack. The space that is left can be put to good use with the many other things one needs to take. Always pack the least important items at the bottom of the rucksack.

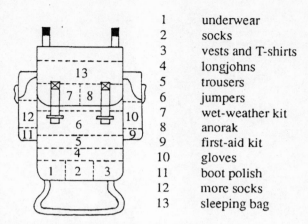

1	underwear
2	socks
3	vests and T-shirts
4	longjohns
5	trousers
6	jumpers
7	wet-weather kit
8	anorak
9	first-aid kit
10	gloves
11	boot polish
12	more socks
13	sleeping bag

Fig. 14 Packing a rucksack

A Comfortable Rucksack

When carrying a rucksack it is important that the weight of your pack is in alignment with your centre of gravity and that you keep the load high and forward.

Fig. 15 Sideways view of a rucksack

65

Fig. 16 Samples of clothing and equipment

9 First Aid

Introduction

Learning first aid is simple. First aid means treatment given on the spot before the doctor arrives to see the patient. To be able to give adequate treatment, you need:

A little knowledge of the body and how it works
To keep calm
To use common sense
To act quickly
NOTHING MORE, NOTHING LESS

Do not be afraid of asking for help or getting other people to help. Tell them what to do if necessary. Send someone off for the doctor or ambulance. Do not stand about talking, the patient needs your help. Always try to improvise with what you have, use whatever is hanging about. Above all, do not forget the injured man – talk to him, try to cheer him up. Ask him what happened because this will help both you and the medical team when it arrives.

There are three things that kill:

1 Breathing stopping
2 Bleeding
3 Shock

Bleeding

A man suffering from severe bleeding always suffers from shock. Sometimes a man can be bleeding internally, and this will only show if he coughs up, or vomits blood or even passes blood from his back passage.

It is difficult to stop internal bleeding, so the important thing is to treat the patient for shock (see below) and get medical help.

Shock

Any injury to the body will cause shock to a greater or lesser degree. This can be a serious condition, which by itself can kill the patient. Bad news or an unpleasant sight may also cause a milder, but rarely fatal, form of shock.

How to recognize a patient in shock

He will look pale and clammy.
His pulse at first may be slow, later it will be fast and faint.
He will look frightened and may be shivering.

Treatment
Remove him from danger.
Rest him down comfortably, putting something under his head.
Reassure him.
REMEMBER – the three Rs.

Keep the patient comfortable by putting a blanket or coat above and below him to protect him from the weather. Do not use a hot-water bottle or give him spirits. Do not give fluids in cases of burns or crush injury, because of a possible delay in evacuation. Take the greatest possible care in handling him. Treat the injuries and get him to a hospital as soon as possible.

General Treatment of Broken Bones

Broken bones generally

A broken bone is a painful injury causing shock. The man usually cannot move the injured part and the site of the break will be painful to touch. It could also be crooked and swollen. Sometimes the skin over the break may be torn and a jagged piece of bone may be protruding.

The first thing to do is relieve the pain and so relieve the shock. You can relieve the pain by good treatment. When you treat a broken bone, you must support it and stop the broken ends moving about. Never try to set it yourself and move the limb as little as possible. If you see a bit of bone protruding, never try to push it back, just put on a dressing. Be very gentle when handling broken bones, because movement of the bone ends increases pain and shock.

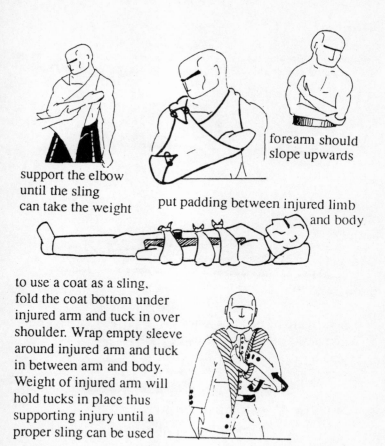

support the elbow
until the sling
can take the weight

forearm should
slope upwards

put padding between injured limb
and body

to use a coat as a sling,
fold the coat bottom under
injured arm and tuck in over
shoulder. Wrap empty sleeve
around injured arm and tuck
in between arm and body.
Weight of injured arm will
hold tucks in place thus
supporting injury until a
proper sling can be used

Fig. 17 Supporting an arm injury

Broken collar bone, upper and lower arm, hands or fingers

All these bones can be broken by a direct blow or by falling on out-
stretched hands. The simplest treatment is to immobilize the arm and
get medical help. Move the arm as little as possible. If it is lying straight,
splint it to the side of the body. If it is lying bent, put it into a sling, supporting the injured limb until the sling is in place.

69

Broken ribs

Place the arm on the injured side in a sling. If the patient coughs up blood, sit him up and do not let him lie down. Attempt to get proper medical help because this could mean he has also damaged his lungs.

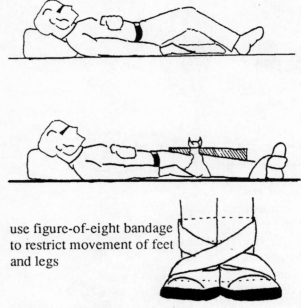

use figure-of-eight bandage to restrict movement of feet and legs

Fig. 18 Treating a leg injury

Broken back or neck

The backbone is broken by a fall from a height or a heavy blow on the back or neck. Sometimes the arms and legs will be paralysed below the level of the injury. The patient may be unable to move his head or there may be tingling, numbness or pain in shoulders or neck.

If you think the backbone is broken, do not move the patient unless it is absolutely essential. Loosen clothing, reassure him and get medical help to him as soon as possible, but above all, try not to move him unless there is no alternative. If you do have to move him, do so as follows:

70

Remove all hard articles from his pockets. If you have to strap his arm to his side, place some padding between the arm and his side (see Fig. 17). Place some padding between the knees and ankles then strap the legs together. Do not bend or twist his back. If he is lying on his face, place him on the stretcher on his face but always try to keep his body completely static whilst moving him.

Broken thigh bone

First place the limbs together by gently pulling the ankles downwards. Move the uninjured leg to the injured one and place padding between the knees and ankles and tie the ankles together. Put a long piece of wood on the outside of the broken leg then tie the piece of wood by bandages to the ankles, knees and thighs.

Broken foot or ankle

Remove footwear by cutting if necessary and immobilize with thick cushioned padding.

Fig. 19 Broken foot or ankle

Moving an Injured Person

Assess the injury before moving the victim because you can cause severe damage whilst moving the victim. Cover him with a coat or blanket whilst waiting for medical help.

If he must be moved, move him lengthways, not sideways (see Fig. 20). Try to slip a coat or blanket under him so he can ride on that or improvise a stretcher from a door or wide board or use jackets fastened together with poles running through the sleeves (see Fig. 21). To get an injured person downstairs use a chair carried by two people.

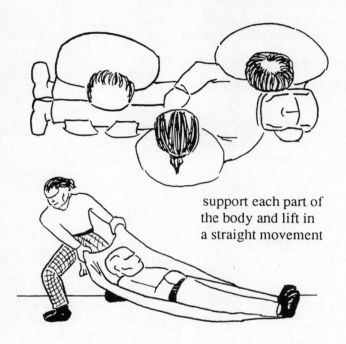

support each part of
the body and lift in
a straight movement

Fig. 20 Moving an injured person

Unconsciousness

Lay the victim down in the recovery position (Fig. 22). This is the best position for all unconscious victims because it stops the tongue from falling into the back of the throat and lessens the possibility of the victim choking on blood, saliva or vomit, as well as keeping the airway clear for them to breathe easily.

Remove any false teeth, wrap them up and put them in his pocket, loosen clothing round his neck and waist to make him comfortable. Do not give fluids.

Watch the victim carefully to ensure he does not stop breathing. If he does give mouth to mouth respiration.

take two jackets and turn the sleeves inside out. Pass two poles through the sleeves of the jackets, as diagram.
Button or zip up the jackets to form a stretcher. Test the strength of the stretcher before using

Fig. 21 Improvising a stretcher

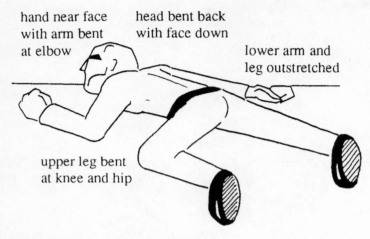

Fig. 22 The recovery position

Drowning

When a half-drowned man is taken out of the water he may seem to be dead. You may not be able to see him breathe or feel a pulse but do not give up unless he is quite stiff. You should try to revive him however hopeless it might appear.

Waste no time because every second counts. Lay him face down as for unconsciousness. Lift his hips off the ground to help drain the water from his windpipe and lungs. Start artificial respiration but remember that you may have to keep this up for a long time. Send for medical help in the mean time.

Breathing Stopped

If breathing has stopped, look into the mouth and remove any blockage. Watch patient's chest and hold fingers in front of the nose and mouth to test for breathing. Feel pulse to see if the heart is beating.

If the heart is beating and breathing has stopped due to drowning, electric shock, fumes, etc., apply mouth to mouth respiration. (Make sure the electric current is broken before touching victim in a case of electric shock.)

If you cannot feel a pulse, assume the heart has stopped and apply external heart compression (EHC), which entails intermittent mouth to mouth plus closed chest heart massage.

Artificial Respiration

Lay the victim on his back. Wipe any blockage away from the mouth with fingers. Place one hand under the neck to arch it up and tilt the head back with your other hand. Pull the chin up and open the mouth. Take a deep breath. Place your mouth over the victim's mouth, pinch his nostrils shut and blow hard enough to make his chest rise. (If victim is a small child, put your mouth over his mouth and nose.) Remove your mouth and listen for exhaled breath. Repeat process.

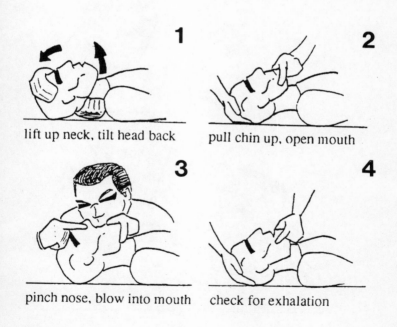

1 lift up neck, tilt head back

2 pull chin up, open mouth

3 pinch nose, blow into mouth

4 check for exhalation

Fig. 23 Artificial respiration

If there is still no exhalation, check the victim's head and jaw position and check whether something is blocking the air passage. Check his mouth again. If you still get no air exchange, turn the victim on his side and slap several times between the shoulder blades to dislodge any foreign body. Wipe his mouth clean again and repeat procedure.

For adults, deliver one vigorous breath every five seconds, for children blow shallow breaths every three seconds. Don't give up until the victim starts to breathe. When he does, get medical help and keep the victim warm.

If you prefer you can place a clean cloth over the victim's mouth before starting the procedure.

Fig. 24 External heart compression

External Heart Compression

Stretch the victim flat on the floor on his back. Kneel at his side and feel the victim's chest to locate lower tip of breastbone. Put your index and middle fingers of one hand on the cartilage. Put the heel of your other hand (never use the palm) on the breastbone and move down until it meets your index finger. Place first hand on top of the other, interlocking the fingers. Now push down with quick firm thrusts. Use sufficient force to press lower one third of breastbone down 1½ ins (4 cms), letting your back and body do the work. Now lift your weight. Repeat this compression once per second.

If you are alone, stop after each 15 compressions and give 2 deep mouth to mouth breaths and continue this 15/2 rhythm until help arrives. If someone is with you, get them to give mouth to mouth at a rate of 12 times a minute – 1 breath for each 5 compressions you perform.

Continue until the victim revives – i.e. pupils constrict, colour improves, breathing begins, pulse returns. A person can be kept alive this way for one hour.

Do not give EHC if victim has obviously broken his ribs, as this treatment could puncture lungs.

Poisons

Find out what has been taken by asking the patient, if conscious, or by looking to see what is lying around. Get medical help and tell them what has been taken. Follow their advice whilst waiting.

For swallowed poisons dilute the poison by giving liquid, preferably milk or water if the patient is conscious. Do not try to make the patient sick as this could cause further harm. If the patient has inhaled the poison take him away from the source of danger and into unpolluted air outside.

Keep any vomit and the suspected poison to show the doctor.

If the victim is unconscious put in the recovery position, do not attempt to make him sick or administer liquids. Keep a close check on the breathing and heartbeat and be ready to take necessary action if required.

Stopping External Bleeding

Grazes

Grazes or small cuts soon stop bleeding by themselves. Clean the wound by washing away from it with soap and water. Remove any debris from the wound with fingers or tweezers if possible. Tweezers should be sterilized in several match flames and the carbon wiped off with a clean cloth before using. Then apply a dry pressure dressing.

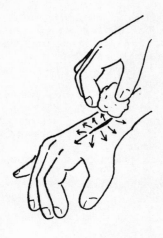

Fig. 25 Cleaning a wound

If something is in the wound which you cannot remove, put a pad round the wound to keep pressure off the foreign body and bandage over that (see Fig. 26).

Infected wounds

Even a small cut can become infected. The signs are:

1 Red, painful, swollen area around the wound
2 Red streaks radiating from the wound, up arm or leg
3 Tenderness in groin or armpit area

Cover the wound with clean dressing. To reduce swelling, elevate and support the injured area. The patient should visit the doctor but if the infection worsens he should be taken to hospital.

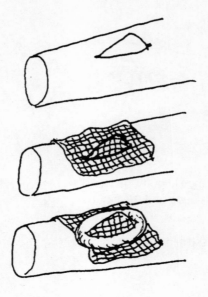

Fig. 26 Foreign body in wound

Deep cuts

Deep cuts continue to bleed. The first thing to do is to raise the damaged limb – provided it is not broken – so that it is higher than the heart, then cover the wound with a clean dressing and secure it tightly. In most cases this will stop the bleeding. If it is on too tightly, the patient will complain of pins and needles and the area below the wound will begin to go blue. Loosen the dressing if this should happen. If bleeding continues, press on the nearest pressure point above the wound. Release after ten minutes.

If all this does not work and you cannot stop the bleeding, you will have to apply a tourniquet, but remember:

A tourniquet is a last desperate effort

Use a tourniquet only if you have tried everything else and failed or if the man has lost a limb.

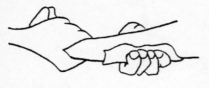

applying direct pressure

choose point between
wound and the heart

Fig. 27 Pressure points

To put on a tourniquet

Use a handkerchief, bandage or any piece of soft, strong material. Tie
the cloth with a half-knot just above the wound and over his clothing.
Avoid using anything which will cut into the flesh. Next put a stick in
position over the half-knot and complete the knot over the stick. Twist
the stick round and round until the bleeding stops but no more. Fix the
stick in position with a bandage and release it every ten minutes. If the
patient is evacuated out of the area, write on his forehead the letter 'T'
and the time (e.g. T0940 hours) so that whoever takes over will know
when to release the tourniquet again.

Wounds to Chest and Abdomen

If a man is injured in the chest, the wound will appear as a hole in the
chest area and air will be sucked into the wound via the hole. This is
very dangerous. Plug the wound with a dressing or anything you have
handy that is clean. Do not give the patient anything to drink. Put him
in a position where he is comfortable, even if it is lying on his injured
side. Lying on the injured side reduces the likelihood of blood flowing
into the good side. If breathing becomes laboured, prop him up into a

half-sitting position, tilted to the injured side to ease the actual mechanics of breathing.

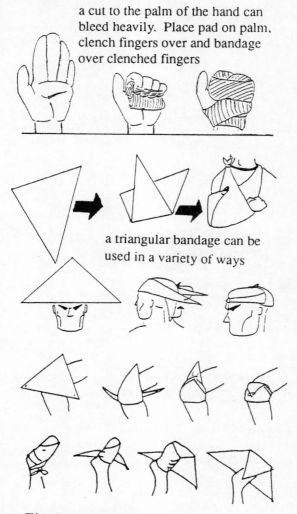

a cut to the palm of the hand can bleed heavily. Place pad on palm, clench fingers over and bandage over clenched fingers

a triangular bandage can be used in a variety of ways

Fig. 28 Types of bandages

81

Any wound to the abdomen should be classed as very dangerous and treated at once. Raise the patient's knees, cover the wound and any protruding gut with a dressing. Do not give him anything to drink. Just moisten his lips with a wetted handkerchief if he complains of thirst. Do not try to push the gut back into place. This injury, together with the internal bleeding which may occur, produces severe shock. Evacuate as quickly as possible.

Internal Bleeding

There are no external signs although blood may come from mouth, ears, etc. The victim will have a weak rapid pulse and be thirsty. Put into head down, legs up position and do not let him move. Do not give liquids.

lift thighs to reduce pull on wound

lie victim on his back on wound

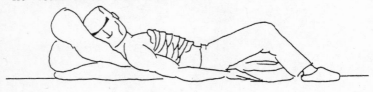

Fig. 29 Abdominal wounds

Head Injuries

If blood comes from the ears, this indicates a head injury. Do not plug ears or put in head-down position.

Various complications can develop as a result of a blow to the head which can be very serious. The treatment depends on the victim's situation:

Conscious and alert – keep under observation but make him rest
Dazed – put into recovery position and observe closely
Unconscious – treat as for unconsciousness

Bites

Wash the wound thoroughly as soon as possible with clean water. Cover with a dressing or clean cloth. Consult doctor if wound needs stitches, i.e. if it is large or deep. The patient may also need a tetanus injection (injections last five years).

Insect bites will often swell and itch. Apply calamine lotion or antihistamine cream. Ice in a cloth or a cold towel will help swelling.

Snake bites in Great Britain are usually only dangerous to the old or very young and panic or shock cause more problems than the poison. Keep the victim calm and still. Get them to lie down to slow the blood circulation. Do not suck the wound or apply a tourniquet to try and stop the poison going into the blood stream. Cover with a dry dressing and immobilize the limb. Again medical help should be sought and a tetanus jab may be needed.

Burns

If clothing is on fire, smother flames with coat, rug, blanket, etc. Keep the victim lying down and still, to lessen the shock. Cut clothes away from burns. If clothes stick, do not pull them off: cut round them leaving cloth stuck to burn. Cover burn with a dressing or clean cloth. If necessary use freshly laundered sheets or towels. Do not apply ointment, oil or antiseptic. Get medical help immediately. If burns are to a large area of the body, the patient will be in shock and should be treated accordingly.

Electrical burns should be treated as above, i.e. as major burns, because although they may only be small, they can be very deep. If the burn is caused by electric shock make sure that contact with the electric current has been broken before touching the victim.

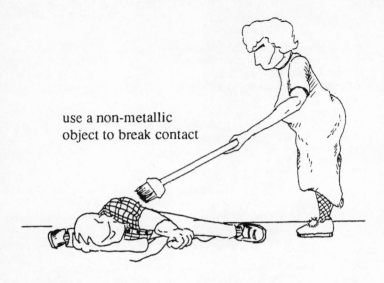

use a non-metallic
object to break contact

Fig. 30 Breaking an electrical current

To move victim away from source of shock, use dry, non-conductive
material (e.g. dead wood, stick, leather belt, chair) to pull the wire off
the victim, or the victim off the wire. Make sure you are standing on a
dry surface. Don't touch the victim until you are sure the current is broken. Check if the victim is breathing and if a pulse is present. If, however, electrocution is caused by high voltage overhead power lines it is
advisable to keep clear of the body. Electricity from such sources has
been known to jump large gaps and re-earth itself through the person
attempting to rescue the victim. In such cases it is best to contact the
emergency services.

Chemical burns should be bathed with lots of cold water to dilute the
chemicals.

Carbon monoxide poisoning

Symptoms are headache, dizziness, difficulty in breathing, vomiting, followed by collapse and loss of consciousness. Can be fatal. Finger nails,

lips and skin may be pink or red. Get victim into fresh air immediately or open all doors and windows. Turn off stove or car engine or other source to stop any more gas being emitted. Begin artificial respiration if he is not breathing or breathing is irregular. Use EHC if heart has stopped. Keep him quiet to minimize oxygen consumption. Cover the victim to keep warm. Get medical help and tell them the victim needs oxygen.

Choking

If a person is choking you need to clear the airway of the obstruction. If coughing does not clear the blockage, give the patient five slaps on the back between the shoulderblades. If there is no success, stand behind the patient and try an abdominal thrust. If this doesn't work after five times alternate with five slaps on the back. For a choking child, place over your knee and slap on back, but more gently than for an adult. Place a baby along the length of your forearm and carry out the same treatment, but even more gently this time. Do not use the abdominal thrust for either child or baby unless you have specific training.

If patient loses consciousness and is still unable to breathe, give five slaps between shoulderblades after turning him on his side. If this fails place patient on his back and give abdominal thrusts. If breathing begins, put in recovery position and call for medical help. If breathing still hasn't taken place call for medical help first and start resuscitation.

Convulsions and epileptic fits

The victim's body may jerk uncontrollably. His lips may turn blue and his eyes roll up. There is little you can do other than try and stop the victim hurting himself or others. If possible, place victim on floor with head on one side to prevent choking. Place the victim in the recovery position and stay with him. Try to calm him with supportive, soothing words. Gently stroke his head while reassuring him that all is OK. This will calm him. Move furniture out of the way if necessary or possible. Apply cool, wet cloths to forehead if he is feverish. Convulsions only last a short time. Make the victim as comfortable as possible when fit ends. The victim will either not remember anything or feel very embarrassed. Give the victim time to reorientate himself. Some will wander off, some will just feel tired and want to sleep. GIVE THE VICTIM TIME TO RECOVER. If he seems to recover but then slips back into another fit get him to a hospital as soon as possible.

choose the method most suitable for size of patient

applying abdominal
pressure to standing
or lying patient

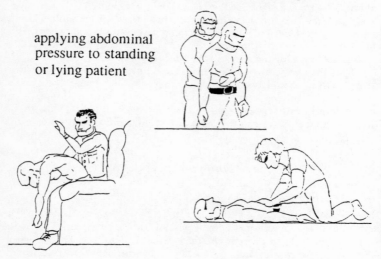

Fig. 31 Dealing with choking

Diabetic coma and insulin reaction

If the victim becomes confused, incoherent or unconscious for no
apparent reason he may be suffering from insulin reaction or diabetic

86

coma. Treatment is different for both so you must be able to tell which is which.

Insulin reaction

This is caused by a too rapid drop in blood sugar. Symptoms appear rapidly, such as nervousness, profuse sweating, rapid pulse, shallow breathing. He may be hesitant. If he is conscious, give him some form of sugar. The victim may resist, refuse help, even fight. If necessary, throw sugar into his mouth! If the victim is unconscious, summon a doctor and make no attempt to administer sugar or glucose. Keep air passages open while waiting.

Diabetic coma

Symptoms appear gradually. Skin becomes flushed and dry, the tongue is dry, the victim is drowsy, the breathing laboured and the breath smells of nail polish remover or pear drops. Diabetic coma can kill. Urgent medical help is needed. Do not give sugar as the blood is overloaded already.

Fainting

Caused by a variety of things – fatigue, hunger, sudden upset, stuffy room, etc. The victim's breathing is weak, the pulse feeble, the face pale and the forehead beaded with sweat. If the victim just feels faint, get him to lie down or sit down with the head below body level to restore blood supply to the brain. If the victim is already unconscious, place in recovery position with head low (see Fig. 22). Keep air passage clear and keep checking he is breathing. Loosen tight clothes, apply cold cloths to the face, administer smelling salts if available. When he comes round, give him a hot drink of tea or coffee.

Heart attack

Symptoms are shortness of breath, pain in centre of chest, sometimes radiating into neck and arms or occasionally pain in upper abdomen. The victim is pale or blue, with a fast feeble pulse, he may sweat and lose consciousness.

Call an ambulance. If victim is having trouble breathing, settle him into a position where he is most comfortable, not necessarily lying down. Loosen tight clothing, open window to provide fresh air but keep victim warmly covered. Don't give him anything to drink. Remain calm yourself and try to reassure victim. Be prepared to give EHC.

Heatstroke and sunstroke

If victim has heatstroke, he will be weak, irritable, dazed and/or nauseous. He stops sweating. His skin will be dry and hot. His temperature will rise dramatically. He may pass out. Cool him as quickly as possible by placing him in a cool shaded place and pouring cool water over him by the bucketful or wrap his head in a cold wet towel and his body in a cold wet sheet. Massage his legs upwards towards heart. If conscious give cool drink but no stimulants. Get medical help.

The symptoms of sunstroke are mild headache, extreme fatigue, dizziness, cold clammy skin and fainting. Treatment is rest in a shaded area with cold compress to head. Three or four glasses of cold water, each containing half a teaspoon of salt can be given, one every fifteen minutes. Make him drink slowly to avoid vomiting and further fluid loss.

Hyperventilating

This happens to highly strung, anxious people when they become emotionally upset. They begin to breathe too rapidly but complain that they cannot breathe. They may get tingling sensations in fingers and toes and a numbness around the mouth which makes them more anxious. The victim's colour is good and pulse remains strong.

The victim mainly needs reassurance. Treatment is simple. Hold a paper bag tightly over mouth and nose for several minutes and get them to breathe into this.

Puncture wounds

Wounds caused by nails, protruding wire, etc., tend to send contamination deep into the wound. Squeeze the wound gently to encourage bleeding to clean the wound before washing the area. Then deal with puncture as for grazes.

Snow blindness

Snow blindness occurs due to the reflection of intense sunlight from snow crystals on land and in clouds, when the sun is mainly at its highest. The symptoms are sensitive eyes followed by constant blinking and squinting. Vision becomes pinkish turning to red as time passes. At this stage the eyes feel as if they have grit, sand or dust in them thus causing intense pain. Get the victim into darkness or subdued light and apply cool compress to the forehead (heat will aggravate the pain). The condition will correct itself given time and rest.

Cover the victim's eyes with pads and get medical help. Normal vision should return in two or three days.

Childbirth

Get the mother to lie down and relax as much as possible. Keep upper body covered and warm. Wash your hands thoroughly and find something clean to wrap the baby with when it arrives.

Cut three pieces of string, roughly 9 ins (23 cms) long. Sterilize string and scissors for ten minutes in boiling water then wrap in clean cloth. Do not touch the sterilized blades.

The waters surrounding the baby will break at some point. Contractions will start at about thirty minutes apart, often with pains in back and lower abdomen and will come at successively shorter intervals until, when the birth is imminent, they are every two to five minutes.

Get the mother to lie on her back with knees bent and legs apart.She will naturally want to bear down with contractions. When the baby's head appears, put your hands over it to stop it being expelled too quickly. Tell the mother to pant to slow things down.

If you find that the cord is round the baby's neck when the head is out, this must be removed as quickly as possible, by passing it over the baby's shoulders, otherwise it could stop the air getting to the baby.

The next contraction should release the shoulders, after which you should hold the baby firmly under the arms and gently lift it out. Hold the head low to allow fluid to drain from its mouth and nose. The baby will be wet, so don't drop it. Do not try to pull the cord out; this will be expelled with the next contraction.

Use the sterilized strings to tie the umbilical cord. Tie off as tight as you can about 6 ins (15 cms) and 8 ins (20 cms) from the baby's navel. Cut the cord between the two ties. Make a further tie about 4 ins (10 cms) from the baby's navel. Put a clean dressing over the end of the cord attached to the baby. Wrap the baby warmly, especially his head as he will lose heat rapidly.

Lie the baby at the mother's side and cover him up. Cover up the placenta when it is expelled for the doctor to see, if one is on his way, so he can check it has all been expelled. If no doctor has been called, it should be burned or buried. If there is a lot of bleeding, rub gently but firmly on the mother's stomach at about navel level.

If the baby does not cry within two minutes, first try flicking the soles of the baby's feet with your index finger. Do not slap the baby's bottom. If there is no response, give artificial respiration but very gently and with small breaths completely covering the baby's nose and mouth with your mouth.

Most babies appear head first with their face down. If they arrive head up it will usually be a slower delivery. If the bottom appears first (breech birth), support the baby and when the shoulders are out, ease the baby's body up so the mouth is clear.

Sponge the mother to freshen her and make her feel comfortable. Fix a sanitary pad or clean cloth in place. Give her fresh clothes if possible. Put the baby to the breast if she wishes to feed it. If the mother is asleep, put the baby on its side in an improvised cot, warmly wrapped with its head slightly lower than its body.

10   Tools

Survival Knives

There are many survival knives on the market ranging in price from £8 to £300. Even a reasonably priced knife can usually be made good with correct and careful sharpening. Most knives, even when new, are in need of sharpening. Before buying a knife it is always worthwhile reading any reviews available and asking any knife-owning friends about their experiences.

There are many schools of thought as to the best type of knife. Some people praise the Bowie knife with its solid tang, and then attach a survival knife to the scabbard. Others prefer the hollow-handled cylinder type survival knife with a short tang, while many now prefer the new Wilkinson Sword survival knife, which has a tang extending through the handle to give strength and an area in the middle cut out to attach survival equipment. Some like the 'Buckmaster' and 'Rambo', because of the detachable spikes on the hilt which can be used for many different purposes. Others prefer not to have these types because of the possibility of causing accidents.

Many people carry Swiss Army knives as well as a sheath knife. A Swiss Army knife is undoubtedly one of the most practical knives on the market, as well as being world-renowned.

Whichever knife you pick, in a survival situation it is your most important asset. A sharp knife can be used for chopping, cutting, skinning, gutting and slicing. A blunt knife just becomes extra weight and a fancy shaped cosh. Your knife must be kept sharp, therefore it is best to re-sharpen it every time it is used. Once you have reached the desired blade, it should only take a couple of minutes a day to bring the edge back up to standard. Always keep the blade oiled, never let it go rusty. If you use any of the survival equipment attached to the knife, replace it at the earliest possible opportunity.

Survivalism is becoming commercialized and, as with any other product, the amount you pay for a knife does not necessarily reflect the standard you obtain. Knives go in and out of fashion, therefore be careful you are not paying a high price for a 'fashionable' rather than a useful knife. Many knives are sold under macho names like 'Rambo', 'Buckmaster' and 'Urban Skinner'. It does not always follow that a macho name makes a good knife, and it is also worth remembering that a macho knife does not necessarily produce a macho man. A good knife is used well, and a well-used knife, to its owner, is often a good knife.

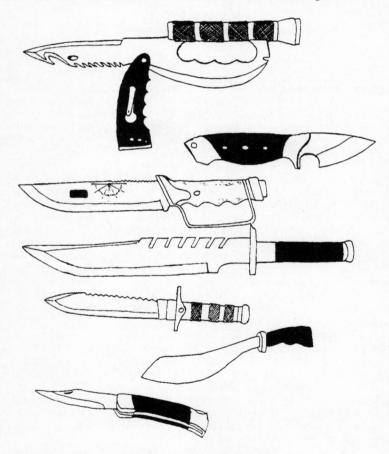

Fig. 32 Types of survival knives

It is worthwhile practising sharpening a knife on a cheap knife, as opposed to ruining the edge on your highly prized, and priced, survival knife. The knife is not just a tool or a weapon – when used correctly and to the fullest, it becomes an extension to your arm. Protect it, care for it – in the wilderness it can be your best and only friend. Mistreat it and it will become your worst enemy by not being sharp enough to do the jobs it was purchased for.

Axes

The hand axe is also a close friend of every survivalist. In a survival situation it is very important that you have a tool which can be used to chop. I feel that too much emphasis is placed on the survival knife and that, when you come down to it, a good sharp axe cannot be beaten.

A good stout steel-shafted axe can be bought for a few pounds at any ironmonger, and it is virtually indestructible. It is however worth remembering that an axe from a shop will need to be re-sharpened because the angle of the cutting edge will be too steep and will need to be ground back to make a more shallow angle. Always sharpen backwards from the edge; this will prevent any burrs on the blade.

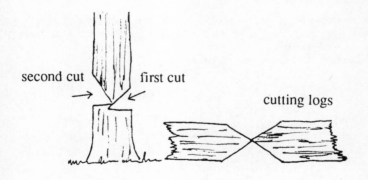

second cut → first cut

cutting logs

Fig. 33 Cutting standing wood

Your axe can be used to fell trees. Before felling it is important to examine the tree and surroundings to try and establish where it will fall or where you want it to fall. This is established by the weight of branches on each side, if it leans, which way the wind is blowing, etc.

Before felling, clear the area around where you hope it will fall. This should make it easier to swing your axe and lessen the chance of branches bouncing and hitting either you or anyone nearby. In the interests of conservation, which most responsible survivalists are involved with, I feel that you should plant at least one tree for every one you fell.

It must be remembered however that the axe is a lethal weapon in the hands of anyone who doesn't know how to use it.

The safety rules of axemanship

1 The person who has the axe is responsible for it
2 Mask the axe properly when not in use
3 Hold the axe properly when walking – head of axe in hand facing forward, with the haft running up the inside of your arm
4 Never throw an axe
5 Take off loose clothing or anything else which may get in the way when chopping
6 Never chop on to or into the ground
7 Always chop downwards and away from your body
8 Stop chopping if you become tired

Looking after your axe

Keep the head greased to prevent rust and keep the head masked either in leather or sacking. Always sharpen your axe after use – two minutes' work sharpening your axe could save time and energy later. Keep the haft oiled with linseed oil if possible.

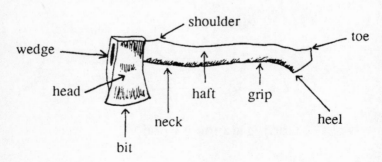

Fig. 34 Parts of an axe

There are many types of axe; all must be treated with respect. A machete is treated in the same way. When used for building shelters, fires, etc., the axe will show its real value. There is an old joiner's saying which goes 'look after your tools and they will look after you'.

Survival Tools

At the many outdoor shops which have already been mentioned, at youth hostel shops, sports shops and at some of the survival shops, which are now appearing as more people show interest in war games and paint ball, you will find a fascinating selection of survival tools. Most of these are small enough to slip into your pocket or attach to your belt or backpack, and they usually are designed to do several jobs. Here again, you can get 'ripped off' and pay a high price for something you will rarely use. On the other hand, of course, you might pick up a really useful tool.

Making Tools in the Field

A long bow

There are many good instruction books showing how to make a good long bow. Yew is the traditional material, but to make a yew long bow properly could take three years. Obviously this is not going to solve your immediate problem – hunger. If you are determined to have a bow, then it might be as well to actually buy a secondhand bow from a junk shop or an archery shop. There are many archery shops scattered round the country, and most of them sell by mail order as well as over the counter.

If you are determined to make a long bow, then a quiet word with the churchwarden or gardener might result in you getting a length of yew from the graveyard yew. Because yew is poisonous, there is not much to be found growing wild. If you get the opportunity to make your own yew long bow, it will give you an amazing feeling of satisfaction.

A hand arrow

A simpler item to make is a hand arrow. Take a length of bamboo approximately 30 ins (76 cms) long and fasten a piece of lead around the shaft near to one end. Sharpen this end and burn it in the fire to harden it. When you get more skilled, you could put a piece of sharp pointed flint into the arrow. Split the other end and attach flights to it. Then tie a length of string round the shaft. Wrap the other end of the string round your hand and throw the arrow like a sling shot. It can travel in excess of 100 yds (90 m) and with practice could be used to bring down small game.

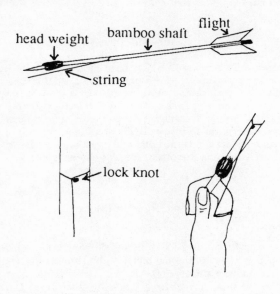

Fig. 35 A hand arrow

Catapult

Catapults are an under-estimated tool or weapon. They are only used now by small boys – and precious few of those since computers became popular – and fishermen, who use it to throw ground-bait. Catapults can be made fairly easily from a forked branch of strong wood and a strip of rubber band taken from a tyre inner tube. The rubber is fastened to either side of the fork.

Flint and stones

In the Stone Age, man used to make hunting tools from pieces of flint and from stones and points were made for spears and arrows with flint as well as hunting and cooking knives. Flint will break cleanly if hit, leaving a sharp edge. It is probably highly unlikely that we could produce tools such as were used by necessity in the Stone Age, but, in an emergency, I think you could produce a sharp enough edge if you tried. Stones were also used for throwing whilst hunting. They were used to make an item similar to the bolas still used by the South American gauchos, by finding three stones of similar size and chipping a channel into each stone into which a rope could be fixed which would fasten all three stones together. This is then twirled round the head before being hurled at the prey's legs.

If you are really desperate for some form of tool, a little thought and ingenuity should soon provide the ideas; failing that, desperation and hunger will!

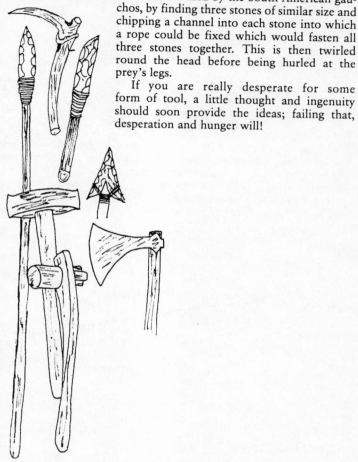

Fig. 36 Ancient Tools

11   Canoeing

Types of Canoe

The modern type of canoe made of glass-fibre reinforced plastic and aluminium has largely replaced canvas-covered wooden canoes, because they are lighter, maintenance free and cheaper. Rips to the canoe can be mended quite easily. If you are canoeing in a large open area of water, the canvas-covered type (or Canadian) is probably better because with its deeper keel and higher sides it has great stability, but for river and canal work a glass-fibre kayak is quite adequate.

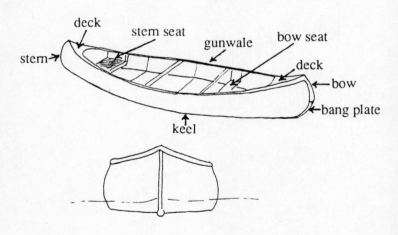

Fig. 37 A Canadian canoe

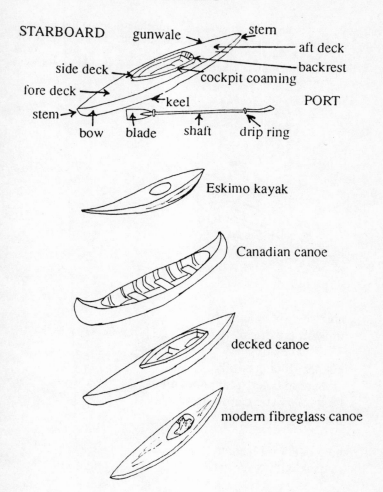

Fig. 38 Types of Canoe

If you have never been in a canoe before, spend some time in shallow calm water, getting used to moving about in the canoe (this is for a two-man canoe), changing places with your partner, by rising together and moving forward and aft in a low crouch, balancing against each other's weight and movement. Do not stand up tall, because it will over-balance the canoe.

Capsize situations are another manoeuvre which should be practised before moving out seriously.

getting in from
shore or banking

hold cockpit coaming
forward on far side

put near foot centrally
on bottom boards, far enough
forward so you can sit down
with moving foot

hold but don't lean on
to bank with other hand

put other foot behind first
and sit down, almost as one
movement

Fig. 39 Getting into a canoe

Getting Into a Canoe

Face forwards, grip the nearest rim with one hand. Place one foot in the centre of the canoe. Reach for the far side while shifting your weight on to the foot already in the canoe.

Position in Boat

When paddling, sit or kneel. If alone sit in the middle. With two oarsmen, one sits in the bow, the other at the stern.

correct sitting position

Fig. 40 Position in canoe

as with getting in from
banking except you place
hand to rear of coaming
and lean back

Fig. 41 Getting in from the water

Canoeing Alone in a Kayak

Always ensure that you have a splashdeck, as this will stop the water
from rushing into the canoe in the event of your capsizing. If you capsize when you are alone, whilst underwater, lean forward as low as possible and manoeuvre your paddle to face lengthwise, flat along the top
of the canoe. Holding the rear of the paddle in one hand and grasping
as far forward on the paddle with the other hand as possible, with one
sweeping motion, push the paddle vertically overhead, leaning back in
the process. This action will cause a sweeping current to right the canoe.
This is known as an Eskimo roll.

If, after trying an Eskimo roll, you find you still cannot right yourself or you constantly spin and capsize again, hold the paddle in one
hand, grab the front elastic or front of the splashdeck and pull hard. The
splashdeck should come away from the canoe and you should be able to
roll out of the canoe and submerge. Do not let go of the paddle. The
trapped air inside the canoe should be sufficient to allow it to float
upside down on the surface of the water. Use the canoe as a lifebuoy,

hold on to an end where it is narrower and swim to the bank. Once out of water, you can empty the canoe and resume your journey.

Fig. 42 Using the canoe as a float

Capsize with Two Kayaks

If while travelling in pairs, you were to capsize, lean forward in the canoe, place both hands round the hull and bang three times on the sides. Then in a sweeping motion, move hands backwards and forwards on the outside of the kayak. The sound should attract your partner, and the sweeping motion will allow you to feel your partner's canoe coming up alongside you. Do the banging and sweeping motion at least three times. If no one arrives, release the splashdeck and tumble out of the canoe. When you are free, swim towards your partner. When you reach his canoe, wrap yourself around the front of his canoe with your arms and bring your legs up either side. This will give your partner the chance to retrieve your canoe.

When the partner is alongside the retrieved canoe, he gives his paddle to the man holding on to the canoe, who holds the paddle for him whilst the next manoeuvre is carried out. The partner grabs the front of the submerged canoe, brings the point to his side, i.e. at right angles to him. He then lifts the point on to the top of his canoe and then begins to feed the canoe on to his own canoe, causing water to pour out of the canoe. When the canoe is half-way over, he tips the canoe backwards and forwards until all the water has been emptied out. When the canoe is empty, he lifts the canoe and turns it upright, pushes it into the water and manoeuvres it to the side of his canoe.

The man in the water then swims to the rear of the manned canoe.

103

The partner in the canoe stabilizes both canoes by putting his hands on both sides of the canoe alongside. The hand nearest the empty canoe holds the far side of the empty canoe, while the other hand holds the nearside of the empty canoe and his own canoe together.

The partner in the water climbs up the back of the canoe and then brings his legs up and slides into position. Refit the splashdeck and attempt to retrieve the second set of paddles, if they have not already been collected by the partner.

If the partner arrives before upturned man leaves his canoe, attempt the Eskimo roll again with the knowledge that the partner will steady you when you come up, or let the partner take hold of your hand and pull you and the canoe into an upright position.

Rescue Drill from the Shore

This rescue is where a canoe goes over, cannot right itself and is rescued by a swimmer from shore. As with standard rescue drill, use three bangs and a sweeping motion. The swimmer should then swim to the canoe. Once the man in the canoe has felt the body at the canoe, he should bring his arms into a folded position across his body or else hold on to the splashdeck. The swimmer, on reaching the canoe, swims up, leans over the canoe and puts his hand around the rim of the splashdeck on the far side from him. The other hand holds the nearside. Then the swimmer leans back, pulling on the splashdeck with the other hand. The canoe should come upright. The swimmer then tries to retrieve the paddle if necessary, before climbing piggyback on to the canoe to be taken back to the shore.

Turbulent Water

Lean away from the waves that are pushing you, using your paddle to balance. Reach out with the paddle to stop the water swamping the canoe. If you come to an obstacle, lean on to the rocks to steady yourself. Every movement is based from the hips.

Paddling a Two-Man Canoe

There are two positions for paddling: bow (front) and stern (back). The paddler in the stern controls the direction, speed and gives instructions to the bow paddler. This is where the more experienced paddler should sit. If both are experienced, the smaller man should sit in front.

Paddling on the right side, grasp the grip of the paddle loosely in the palm of the left hand and grasp the shaft with the right hand. Dip the paddle blade into the water ahead of you, pull back with the right hand and lift out of water. Repeat motion. Change hands to paddle on left side.

Sit comfortably and do not lunge at the strokes. Dip the paddle into the water, sit upright and pull back, keeping your paddle straight and close in to the canoe. A common problem with novices is that they throw their bodies around, which causes the canoe to ship water. You should sit relaxed and upright and let the arms and shoulders do the work.

For straight rowing, the oarsmen row on opposite sides in unison. To steer, keep the paddle slightly angled during the stroke and hold it a few seconds at the end of each stroke; this guides the boat left or right.

For an abrupt turn, the stern paddler digs the paddle in at the end of the stroke while the bow paddler makes the bows come round with the steering action described above.

Carrying a Canoe

This really depends on how much available help there is. If you are alone, tie the paddles securely to the seat to form a yoke centrally into which you can put your neck. Place one end of the canoe at an angle against a tree, step back into the yoke, position it comfortably and lift, moving back from the tree. The boat can be carried quite a distance like this.

Two men can carry a canoe holding bow and stern on either side, the front man on the right holds the bow, the back man holds the stern on left. A boat can be carried easily this way until the track becomes narrow or overgrown. The alternative way is for two men to lift the boat upside down on to their shoulders, again one man on either side of boat. This has the advantage of lifting the canoe over most undergrowth. Don't try to carry canoe and all the gear. Make two or even three trips instead.

Towing a Canoe

Tie a long rope to the bow and stern thwarts. Hold rope in centre from shore and steer boat round obstructions by pulling on the stern line. Pull the forward line to bring the boat closer.

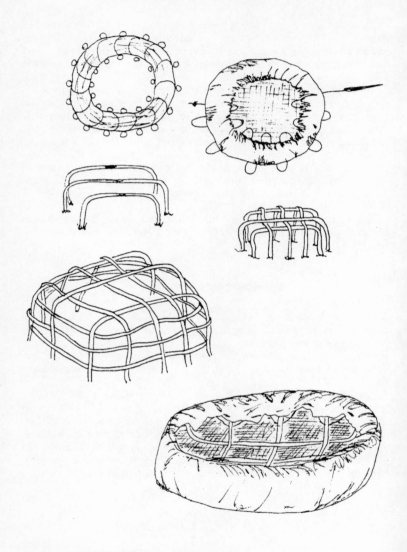

Fig. 43 Building a coracle

Building a Coracle

Knock two concentric circles of stakes into the ground with an inner radius of about 2 ft 6 ins (76 cms). This will give a finished circumference of about 20 ft (6 m; see Fig. 43). Pack in brushwood and twigs and bind tightly with string or thin rope.

Place on a canvas or tarpaulin and tie into position (or sew), binding through the tarpaulin as shown and pull tight. If you have any bitumen, cover liberally. Place board in bottom.

Collect lengths of willow, ash or chestnut and soak for twenty-four hours. Make sure lengths are ¾ in (2 cms) thick. Stick the end of the framework onto the ground, bend over the opposite pairs and lash together. Interweave the crossings, making sure the centre is flat. You can do this by putting stones on top.

Interweave lengths around the sides. These should be as long as possible but they do not have to go all the way round.

Temporarily lash the pieces near the ground so that the coracle won't spring apart when you pull the main stakes out of the ground. After you have pulled the stakes out, turn the coracle over on to a tarpaulin. Bend the stakes down and lash them to their neighbours. Stretch the tarpaulin over the framework and tie down tightly. Place a mat in the bottom of the coracle and form a paddle.

12   River Crossing

In the United Kingdom, most rivers can be crossed without too much effort because there are many bridges, and most rivers can be crossed at shallow points without the need to get wet at all. It is just a question of thinking logically. The same principles apply to canals, but if you wish to cross a stretch of water without the aid of a bridge, there are various ways. It is possible to pole vault across canals, and I believe this is actually done for fun in some parts of the country!

If you swim across a fast or deep river, swim with the current, don't try to fight it. In deep water rapids, swim head first with the current. In shallow rapids go feet first, using arms to keep you buoyant and steady.

Crossing on a Raft

The most obvious way to cross a stretch of water without getting wet is to build a raft and paddle across. This method is best used on a slow moving river or canal.

Depending on the prevailing weather conditions, if you swim across, remove your clothes and put them into a plastic bag or similar to keep them dry for when you get to the other side. If the weather is warm, this will not matter as much as if it is cold.

Pendulum Technique

On a fast flowing river, it is best to use the pendulum technique (see Fig. 44) if at all possible. This will save any of the party being swept away by the current and will also help if one of the party cannot swim.

Tie a rope to the first person, ideally the strongest swimmer, and the other end of the rope to a tree. The first person crosses the river, either by swimming or wading. He unties himself and ties the end of the rope securely on the far bank and the rest of the group uses the secured rope to get across.

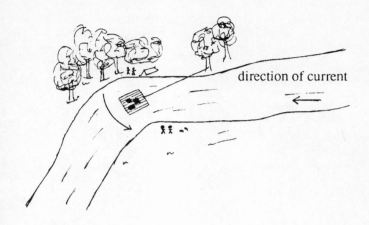

direction of current

Fig. 44 River crossing on a bend with a rope

If the rope is not long enough to go across the river, use it to rope members of the group together. Each member should carry a stick to feel the river bed in front of him and only one person should move at a time. The next person should brace himself against the current whilst playing the rope out. Keep the rope fairly taut, so that if the first man is swept away, you will be able to take the strain easily and not be pulled over yourself.

Floating Across

Use trousers to act as flotation bags by knotting the legs at the ankle, zipping the fly and swinging them above the head to fill the legs with air. Trap the air by grabbing the waistband whilst underwater and hold the trousers in front of you so that they can act as floats. Bin liners can be used in the same way.

You can hold on to a log held in front of you and use as a float, whilst kicking with the feet to get across a river.

Other Methods

Secure a loop around the chest of the strongest swimmer, then have the others play out the rope as the first man crosses the river, to stop him being washed away.

109

When he has crossed safely, he unties the rope and the second man ties himself on and proceeds across, controlled by the first man. When the second man has crossed, the third crosses in the same way as those before him, with the first man guiding him over and taking most of the strain whilst the second man is there in case of emergency. This method can be used with any number of people crossing.

Fig. 45 Crossing a river with a short rope

Crossing a Flooded River Alone

Firstly consider whether it is really necessary – is there a bridge which you could reach with a detour? If you decide it is the only way – remove your socks and then put your boots back on to give you a firm foothold on the riverbed. You can put your dry socks on after emptying the water out of your boots on the other side. Undo the waist-strap of your back-pack, so that in an emergency you can discard it, but leave it on your back to provide ballast. Use a stick to test the bed in front of you and to provide support. Walk either straight or diagonally across the river but face into the current so that you can brace yourself against the flow, i.e. walk sideways but be careful not to cross your legs.

You could also tie a rope to a tree on the bank and tie yourself to the other end of the rope and swim across, knowing you will not get swept away. Note that you will lose your rope this way unless you intend to return over the same route.

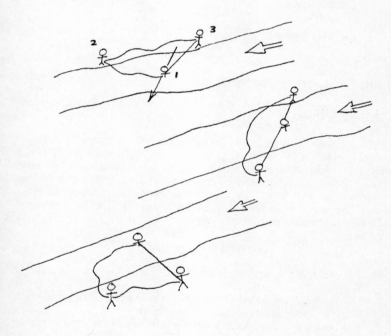

Fig. 46 River crossing technique

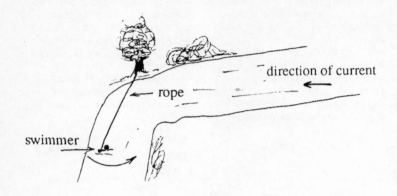

direction of current

rope

swimmer

Fig. 47 Crossing alone

Know the River

Before crossing a river, study how the water is flowing. Rocks under the surface usually cause waves that seem to stay in the same place. This is caused by the rock or boulder deflecting the water upwards. These rocks can cause considerable damage to canoes and often trip people wading.

Rocks close to the surface often cause eddies. Downstream from the rock, the water will appear to run backwards against the main flow. These underwater currents can pull swimmers under and are very dangerous.

Choosing a Crossing Point

1   Choose a broad stretch of the river, where the water should be slower and shallower
2   Do not wade across at a bend; the outside bend usually has much more powerful currents and a steeper bank
3   Use boulders and rocks as supports and handholds – not stepping stones – you may slip
4   Avoid submerged trees and high banks, as well as rapids and weirs
5   Avoid entrances to lakes or estuaries, because the flow is usually more powerful. Go upstream

13   Water Safety

If caught by the undertow it is pointless trying to swim against it, because you will just waste your strength. Let it carry you until the current eases and then swim parallel to the shore until well away from the undertow before turning to land. If in a river near to a bend, head for the inside curve where the current will be weakest.

Remember that water travels parallel to a beach as well as going in and out. Try to keep an eye open for landmarks so you have some idea how far you have drifted.

Floating

Practise this floating technique, which could help you stay afloat for a couple of hours, in the safety of a swimming pool beginning in shoulder-deep water. As you gain confidence, move into deeper water.

Take a deep breath and hold it. Put your face in the water, relax and float vertically with arms and legs dangling relaxed. Take another breath by raising your arms straight out in front and bring a foot forward in a scissors kick. Raise your head until your mouth is out of water. Press your hands down in a circular motion and close your legs. With your chin level with the surface, exhale through your nose and then inhale deeply through your mouth. Return to resting position. If you sink too deep, push down with your hands. Kicking will also help you rise.

Swimming Difficulties

If you get cramp

Stop swimming and float on your back. Stretch out the affected limb, using your hands if necessary. When the cramp goes, swim ashore.

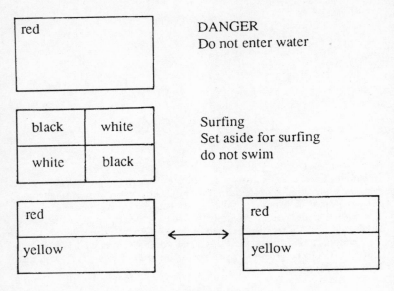

Fig. 48 Beach warning flags

If you get caught in weeds

Try to kick yourself free if you have no knife. If that fails, try and roll the weeds down your leg as you would do with a sock.

If you have to swim in very cold water

Get into the water gradually and allow your body to accustom itself to the cold. Consciously control your breathing.

114

Rules for Safe Swimming

1 Never swim immediately after a heavy meal or on an empty stomach
2 Test the water temperature before you go in. Don't swim in very cold water
3 Don't swim alone
4 Be aware of marker flags
5 Avoid water-filled quarries and sand pits; they are often deep and cold with steep sides and submerged obstacles
6 Never dive into water without knowing the depth
7 Do not go out of your depth
8 Look out for underwater hazards
9 Do not swim in the sea using inflatables – you may get carried out of your depth without realizing it.

Rescuing Someone from a River, Lake or Canal

Reach – Throw – Wade – Row.

If someone falls into the water near you, give him encouragement while you look for something to REACH out to him – a branch, rope, piece of cloth, your jumper, etc. Lying on the ground at the water's edge, anchor yourself, by hooking your ankles round a bush or get somebody to hold on to you, so you cannot be pulled in yourself.

If the person is out of reach, THROW something to him that will keep him afloat while you get help, such as a lifebuoy, a piece of wood, etc.

Before deciding to WADE out to a person in trouble, test the water temperature and look for signs of current. Test the bottom for depth and mud with a stick, before each step.

If a boat is available and you are able to use it, ROW out to the person, taking care that the boat does not hit and injure him or push him under. To lessen the risk of capsizing as you haul him aboard, bring him to the stern of the boat.

If no other method is possible and you are a good swimmer, swim out with something buoyant, a lifebuoy or a tyre, preferably with a rope attached so someone else can pull you both in.

Keep clothing on to combat cold, but discard shoes and anything heavy in your pockets.

Canal Locks

If somebody falls in a canal lock, never under any circumstances go in after him whilst the lock is filling or emptying, because the turbulence caused by open sluices or valves makes it impossible for even the strongest swimmers to stay afloat. If someone has fallen in under these circumstances, shut the sluices before going in after them.

If there is a boat in the lock, ask the skipper to stop his engines and pull the boat over to one side and tie up, so that the person in the lock is not crushed. There is invariably a ladder in a lock, so direct him to the ladder so he can climb up by himself or throw him a lifebuoy so he can be hauled over to the ladder.

Rivers with Strong Currents

If there are strong currents in rivers, it may be impossible to take a straight course to the bank. Move downstream and swim diagonally across the current. If there is a bend in the river, aim for the inside curve where the current will be less powerful and the water shallow. If the side is steep, as in a canal, lock or gravel pit, try to find something you can grasp hold of to stop yourself being swept away and then use the hand-hold to haul yourself out.

Lifting a person out of the water when the bank is steep is not easy. Keep him from submerging by tying a line under his armpits. Climb out yourself, keeping hold of the line, and use the line to help him climb out.

Thin Ice

If you fall in the water through thin ice, for example if it is snow-covered, tread water. Try to get your arms up out of the water so you can put pressure on the ice around you. Break and smash the ice all around until you come across some that is solid. Head towards the shore, where the ice is likely to be thicker. When you get to thick ice, keep your legs out behind you and keep your body as flat to the surface as possible and try to drive yourself out on to the ice. Stay flat and edge away from the weak area until you reach solid ground. Make for a warm place, do not stop or you will get cold.

Never venture on to ice without testing its strength. Throw large stones towards the middle to see if they will go through. Shallow water is usually safest because you will only get your legs wet if it does break. Where it is shallowest, vegetation will be sticking out through the ice. Ice is not thick in a uniform way. In some places it may be thinner than others. *Do not trust ice.*

If you are with somebody who falls through thin ice, throw them a rope and try to get them to follow the above advice. If it is a middle man in the group who falls in, throw a rope across the hole and let him use that to pull himself out, with somebody holding the rope at either end.

Safety in Boats

1   In sheltered waters, canals, tide-less reaches of rivers, small lakes and gravel pits, children must wear BSI standard buoyancy aids or life-jackets at all times whilst on the water

2   In tidal rivers, estuaries, inshore around the coast and on big lakes, adults as well as children should wear BSI buoyancy aids at all times when under way

3   Extra, warm clothing should be carried even on warm days. If any-one gets wet or the sun goes in, the wind chill can be dangerous

4   All boats must have an alternative means of propulsion, oars for a small motor boat or dinghy and an outboard engine for a larger boat

5   In coastal waters, there must be sufficient life-jackets of a size to fit all members of the crew and two lifebuoys available to throw over-board, one of which must have a water-activated light attached to it. Lifelines and safety harness must be available for crew working outside the cockpit in rough weather

6   Every boat must carry an adequate anchor

7   Boats going to sea must have adequate means of communicating with other vessels or the shore if in distress: basically flares and smoke signals. Any boat going offshore must carry at least a small inflatable boat as a lifeboat. If going out further than three miles (4.8 km), it should be life-raft equipped with a survival pack and a radio to receive weather and shipping forecasts

8   Small boats in any water should have sufficient built-in or installed buoyancy to keep them afloat when capsized or water-logged and no one should leave a capsized boat and try to swim to safety. A small boat, even upside down, is more visible than a person's head in the water, and remember that even the strongest swimmer can be defeated by an adverse tide

9   Boats with engines and galleys must carry adequate fire extin-guishers and all butane gas installations must be professionally installed and containers vented outside the boat

10 Good seamanship is good safety. A well-found and well-equipped boat, careful handling and attention to weather are better safe-guards than a lot of expensive safety equipment

If you see a boat in distress or if you get into difficulty yourself, con-tact the coastguard. If you have informed coastguards of your intended route before departure – a sensible precaution – do not forget to tell them when you arrive or else a search might be launched.

Part Three

14 Ovens and Fires

Fire is the only means of keeping warm out in the wilds, unless you class flapping your arms around to circulate blood as a way to keep warm.

It is surprising how many people cannot start a fire without the aid of a gallon of petrol. If you have ever sat cold and wet, trying to light damp matches, then you would wish for a gallon of petrol, but there are easier ways of starting fires.

Waterproofing Matches

Seal by dipping into hot wax. Cover half the stick and place them in a 35-mm film canister or similar sealable container.

Always carry candles. Remember the golden rule of fire lighting – one match, one fire. Before your candle is lit, build a small wind break, then light the candle and use it to start the fire. There are many other ways of starting fires. Burning grass with a magnifying glass is one way but for that you do need the sun.

One fancy trick I learned on an exercise in the mountains of Germany whilst in the Army, was using potassium permanganate and anti-freeze. Place about a teaspoon of potassium permanganate in the middle of a page taken from a newspaper, add a few drops of anti-freeze (taken from the radiator of your vehicle). Roll up the newspaper tightly and place in the middle of your kindling. Only use a small amount of anti-freeze because too much will only make combustion take longer. After a minute, the mixture will ignite and start a fire. This is an idea to bear in mind if you find yourself with a broken-down car out in the wilds.

In the wilds, always keep your fire alight, never let it go out. It is important to ensure that you have plenty of wood but that you use it sparingly.

Camp-fire Safety

1 Always allow enough room around your camp-fire to allow you to move safely
2 Never build a fire where trees with low hanging branches could ignite – or too near your shelter, for the same reason
3 Make sure the ventilation is good enough because carbon monoxide kills
4 Never use stones that have been in water for a long time to line the fire. Water may be trapped inside the stones, and when they are heated they could explode. Some boulders are also apt to explode because of their composition
5 Always keep your wood dry
6 Cracked stones may also explode. Try to keep the immediate area around the camp-fire clear, to lessen the danger of flying sparks

Starting a Camp-fire

Choose a spot in the open, away from trees and overhanging bushes. Carefully remove the turf and then dig a hole about 18 ins (46 cms) across and 6 ins (15 cms) deep. Keep the turf to replace when you move. Circle the hole with large stones. Build the fire in the centre using twigs and leaves as kindling and larger branches to keep the fire going. Keep a bucket of water handy in case it becomes windy and the fire looks like spreading. Never leave the fire untended. When putting out the fire, use lots of water, separate the burning pieces and soak each one. Throw water into the fire hole. Before leaving the site, replace the soil and turf over the ashes.

Ovens and Fires

Ditch oven

This is a simple oven to make. Dig well into a bank. As you can see from Fig. 50, it is fairly self explanatory. By moving the top slab backwards, this will reduce the heat inside, by moving it forwards, it will increase the heat.

Basic Oven

Light a fire inside the make-shift oven. When the stones are hot, remove the fire, place in the food and then block both ends in order to keep heat inside the oven.

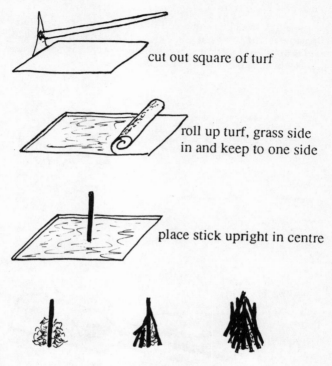

cut out square of turf

roll up turf, grass side
in and keep to one side

place stick upright in centre

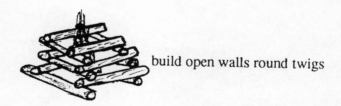

build tinder round stick   add kindling in teepee shape

build open walls round twigs

Fig. 49 Starting a fire

123

Trench and mud oven

Dig a shallow trench. At one end of the trench, use stones and mud to shape an oven. If you light a fire along the whole of the trench, this will serve as an all-purpose fire. You can add a roasting spit or a gypsy tripod on which to hang a large pot, etc.

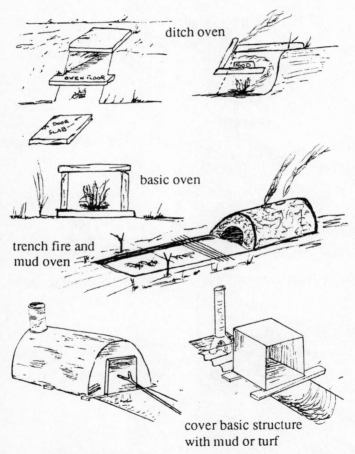

Fig. 50 Types of oven

Mud coating

Another way of cooking is to wrap your food in straw or grass, then in mud and bury it in the embers of your fire.

Star fire

This fire actually saves on wood. Start a small fire and add four logs in a star shape with the fire central (see Fig. 52). As the logs nearest to the fire burn, push them inwards. This is an ideal fire to sleep by.

Double log fire

A simple cooking fire, which is easy on wood and can be easily controlled.

All-purpose fire

This is so easy to start. It can be used for cooking and warmth and is one of the most effective fires.

Stone reflector fire

This rock-based fire gives off the maximum heat because the heat is reflected from the rocks.

Oil drum oven

Old oil drums can make a good oven by using a wire mesh to make a barbecue grill. See Fig. 51 for a sawdust stove using an oil drum. Remember to look around the area carefully, because what you need to improvise a good oven could be right under your nose.

There are many different types of fire, including gypsy fires, altar fires, wood reflector fires and many more. The reasons different fires are used is to help the person do the job in the quickest and easiest way. If you are going to stay in a location for a while, it makes sense to incorporate an oven into your fire. If it is just an overnight stop, any fire will do.

Night Fires

To keep a fire going through the night, bank round the fire, using stones or earth to reduce the amount of air draught to the fire and add slow burning hardwoods or green wood to the fire.

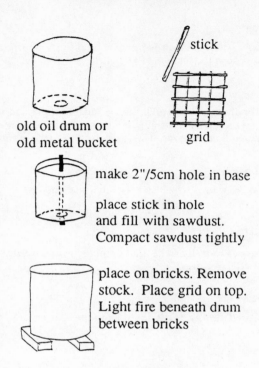

old oil drum or
old metal bucket

stick

grid

make 2"/5cm hole in base

place stick in hole
and fill with sawdust.
Compact sawdust tightly

place on bricks. Remove
stock. Place grid on top.
Light fire beneath drum
between bricks

this stove will burn for two
to three hours. Useful for
barbecues and cooking generally

Fig. 51 Sawdust stove

Firelighting

Always use dry wood whenever possible, unless the food is to be smoked when you do need damp wood. You also need damp wood to make a signal fire, so that it will give off lots of smoke.

Do not waste matches by trying to light a poorly prepared fire. Use embers, cigarettes, candles, etc., that can be lit with one match and will stay alight. Matches are one of the most valuable things you have with you in a survival situation and shouldn't be wasted.

wood reflector fire

all-purpose fire

stone reflector fire

old oil drum fires

double log fire

star fire

Fig. 52 Types of fires

Carry dry tinder in a waterproof container. A roll of toilet paper also makes good tinder; but don't use it all, you need it for the toilet.

Do not just think, I am going to camp here and start to collect wood and tinder. Whilst you are searching for a suitable site, also look for tinder. As you are going along, pick up any pieces that might be useful.

There are many ways to keep your fire overnight. If you don't actually need the fire overnight, cover the embers with ash and dry earth. When you uncover them next morning, they should still be smouldering, which will make re-building the fire easy.

You can build two or three fires in a ring round you, which will give off more heat than just one fire, but this obviously uses a lot of wood.

Build up a good supply of wood and tinder near you, so that you can keep the fire going. Nothing is more disheartening than spending time building a fire and then finding you have no more fuel to feed it. Good tinder is cedar bark, sawdust, fine wood shavings, dry straw, cloth, dry grass or leaves. In wet weather the bases of trees or under rock over-hangs and shrubs should produce some dry tinder. Birch bark will burn even if wet because of the oils in the wood. At a pinch, fluff from your pockets or shredded tissues will do. Kindling is larger pieces of fuel, which will bring the fire up to heat ready for bigger pieces. Use small twigs, split wood, heavy cardboard, etc., as kindling. Split branches will burn better than whole ones but add kindling sparingly. The large logs are only put on the fire at the final stage.

Hay Box Cooking

Meals which require cooking for a long time can often be cooked in a 'hay' box.

To make a hay box, get a wooden box – a small tea chest is ideal. Fill six cloth bags as big as the box panels with hay (or polystyrene beads or even polystyrene tiles if you have time to prepare). Fill the bags well with the hay or polystyrene and line the bottom and sides of the box. Make sure all joints are well sealed and padded. The sixth bag goes on top. The hole left in the middle should be big enough to take a casserole dish or stewpot snugly.

Start your stew, soup or porridge as usual in a pan. Bring to the boil and then simmer for at least twenty minutes before transferring it to finish cooking in the hay box. Cover the lidded stewpot with the final hay-filled bag and put on the wooden lid. A stew put in the hay box at breakfast will be ready for the evening meal.

Porridge can be cooked overnight using a hay box. For two people, boil half a pint (25 ml) of lightly salted water and sprinkle on 2 oz (60 g) of medium oatmeal and stir well to avoid lumps. Transfer to a hay box and leave overnight.

Open Pit Cooking

This style of cooking is best for large or tough cuts of meat, chickens or even sides of meat. It can also be used for cooking fish. It is very useful if you have made plans for the day but intend to return to your camp-site that night and is especially useful if the area is windy and keeping an open fire going without constant attention is difficult.

Dig a pit in damp ground about 2 ft square (60 cms square; but size will vary with whatever you are cooking). Collect large damp pebbles to line the sides and bottom of the pit and keep enough pebbles back to cover the bottom again in reserve. Collect wood and build a roaring fire in the pit and, once this is going, throw the spare pebbles in as well. Put your largest container, full of water, into the pit to boil and keep feeding the fire.

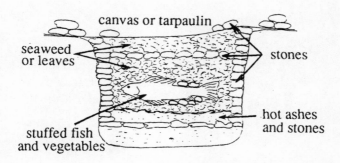

Fig. 53 Open pit cooking

Whilst the water is boiling, prepare the food ready for cooking and collect a quantity of damp seaweed (vine leaves, cabbage, sunflower or pumpkin leaves – or any other non-poisonous large leaf – can be used instead of seaweed.)

By the time the water has boiled there should be a good layer of ash and charcoal in the bottom of the pit. Rake out the spare pebbles and keep them to one side. Pour the boiling water into the pit, which will make the pebbles steam and sizzle. Quickly cover the pebbles with clean seaweed (or whatever else you are using) to a depth of about 3-4 ins (7-10 cms). Put the food to be cooked on to the seaweed, together with any vegetable which will take slow cooking, i.e. jacket potatoes, corn cobs in their husks, turnips, carrots, whole onions in their skins.

Cover this with another layer of seaweed 3-4 ins (7-10 cms) thick, then add the extra and still very hot pebbles and cover with another 3-inch (7 cms) layer of seaweed. Put a piece of canvas or tarpaulin over the top and weight it down so no steam can escape. This can then be left to cook slowly. A side of meat will take about six hours and a stuffed bird about four hours.

The most important thing to remember is that the steam must not be allowed to escape.

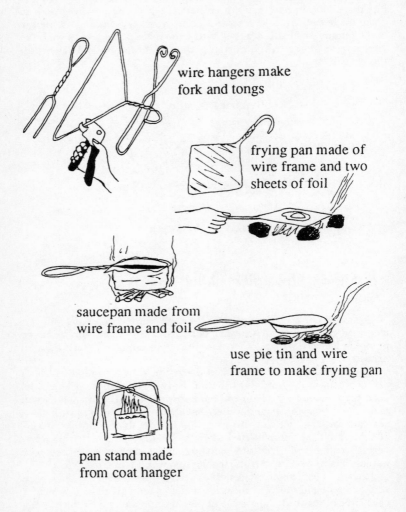

Fig. 54 Improvising cooking utensils

Cooking Utensils

These can be improvised from things you find around you or which you
take with you. For instance, wire coat hangers can be manipulated to
make a cook's fork and tongs, and a trivet for placing a pot on over a
fire. A frying-pan can be made with a wire coat hanger and tin pie plate.

15   Wood and its Uses

Alder. A soft wood which was once used to make the soles for clogs. It is an easy wood to use for wood-turning and can be used to make many household items.

Apple. Very suitable for hand carving, and wooden mallets can be made from crab apple trees. Aromatic when burned but wasted out of doors.

Ash. A light wood which is easy to cut and bend because it is strong and pliable. It has many uses but is not durable if in contact with the ground. Used for the shafts of carts, furniture, ladder poles, handles, shepherds' crooks, oars, tent pegs, hay rakes and toys. It is an easy wood to work with. The wood will burn green or seasoned and makes the best burning wood.

Beech. A strong wood which was once used to make wooden clogs or shoes and also to make chair legs. Clothes pegs and tent pegs used to be made from beech although it is not a good wood to use outdoors. Thin sheets of bark were used to write on in ancient times and beech leaves were used to stuff mattresses and pillows. A good burning wood.

Birch. The bark of the birch tree is hard-wearing and waterproof and can be peeled from the tree in wide pieces, but be careful not to ring the tree or it will die. The bark can be used for roofing, and the American Indians used it to make summer wigwams, sewing the sheets together with spruce roots. The bark was also used as a writing material. The twigs can be used to make the traditional besom broom and can also be used as a roofing thatch or as a bedding material. They can also be woven to make rough baskets after first soaking in boiling water. A good burning wood, but it burns quickly so is used to start the fire off.

Blackthorn. Good for burning green or seasoned, but be careful of sparks.

Brambles (commonly known also as Blackberry and Dewberry). Peel off the outer skin and you will have a strong material for weaving baskets or ropes. Wear sturdy gloves and pull the brambles through a strong fabric first to remove the thorns.

Broom. As its name suggests, it can be used to make brushes.

Cedar. Suitable for all stages of a fire.

Cherry. A beautiful wood to use for hand carving or wood turning and it turns a warm yellow colour when rubbed with almond or olive oil. Musical instruments and many other items are made from the wood.

Elder. The soft inner core of young branches can be pushed out to make flutes or pea shooters. The thicker wood can be dyed to resemble ebony, box or even ivory. Elder is useless for burning, and legend has it, that if you do burn it, then witches or the Devil will get you!

Elm. Once used for water pipes, pumps and water buckets because of its ability to withstand the effects of water. No use for burning when green but good for keeping the fire going once it has caught.

Hawthorn. The wood is used for door knobs, rakes teeth, mallet heads and tool handles. Good for burning.

Hazel. Hazel twigs make pea shooters and faggots. The fine branches can be used to make a rope. Hazel is the best wood to use to make a dowsing rod. Walking sticks, shepherds' crooks and baskets can all be made from hazel. Burns well.

Heather. The whole plant is used for brooms, packing materials, thatch, binding materials and heather beds.

Holly. Suitable for carving and can be dyed to imitate other wood. Holly burns well, green or seasoned.

Honeysuckle. The thin rods can be woven into baskets while the old wood makes an ornamental walking stick.

Hornbeam. Best for later stages of a fire as it is slow burning.

Horse Chestnut. This was used to make cotton reels before plastic was introduced. Good for chopping boards and hand carving. The nut contains saponin and will, in an emergency, act as a substitute for soap. Not much good for burning.

Laburnum. A hard wood used for flutes, ladles, cups and hand carving. Mallets and tool handles can be made from this wood.

Larch. Good tinder wood for starting off a fire.

Lime. Suitable for fine carving, boxes and cutting blocks as it does not blunt knives. The outer bark can be used as roofing tiles. The inner bark is fibrous and can be used to weave mats or as a tying material. Lime suckers can be woven into baskets. A poor burning wood.

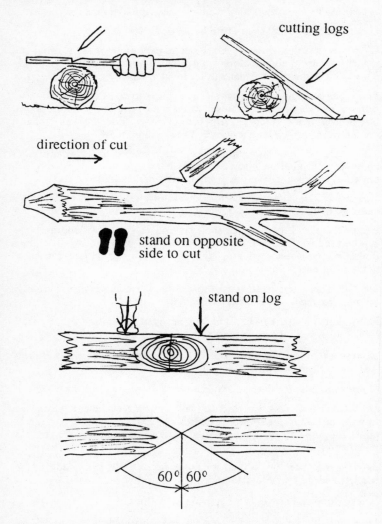

Fig. 55 Cutting wood

Maple. Burns steadily.

Oak. Tannin for tanning leather is obtained from oak bark. Oak wood has many uses including wooden pegs to use in place of nails, oak buckets, barrels and charcoal. Writing ink can be made from oak galls. Oak is very hard wood and when cut can be used for hurdles, fencing and roof tiles. Baskets were made by boiling the straight poles for some hours and then splitting them into thin bands while hot. The bands were then woven into baskets. Because of its strength, wheel spokes, barrels and ladder rungs were made of oak. Slow burning, useful for keeping a fire going in the later stages.

Pear. Used as apple and cherry.

Pine. This wood is often used to make furniture but pine wood baskets can also be made along the lines of a trug. Water pipes can also be made from trunks that have been bored hollow.

Rowan or Mountain Ash. Thin branches used to make rough baskets and tool handles.

Sweet Chestnut. Resistant to rotting and therefore suitable for outdoor use. Used for fencing, garden poles, sleepers, charcoal, chair legs and walking sticks.

Sycamore. Used for wood carving. Old kitchen table tops used to be made from sycamore because it would stand up to a lot of wear and scrubbing. Also used to make spoons, bread boards, boxes, meat skewers, rolling pins and butter prints. Not particularly good for burning.

Walnut. Used for wood carving and it is the cabinet maker's delight, although it is rare.

Willow. Used for basketry, for tool handles, toys, paddles, clog soles and cricket bats. Gypsies make split clothes pegs from goat willow. Willow catkins can be used to stuff cushions.

Yew. Fence posts made from yew are very strong and are said to outlast iron. Used by bow makers and useful for small carvings. Baskets can be made from the fine branches.

16   Shelters

Invariably shelters constructed in England would be better constructed for cold weather conditions. In summer, shelters can be built in the style of jungle shelter constructions, but that should not restrict the would-be survivalist from building any kind of shelter he wishes.

The construction of a shelter is not as important as the siting of the campsite. The building of a shelter is simple as long as it keeps you dry and warm and protected from the elements. But choosing a good site takes knowledge of the landscape. You will also need to know about fires, tools, basic construction, etc. This comes under the general heading of 'campcraft'.

Unsuitable Campsites

The best looking site may not always be the most practical:

- Hilltops could be exposed to high winds; always camp on the leeside of a hill
- Some hillside terraces may hold water; check for soggy ground
- Camp away from rock faces where there is a possibility of rock falls and avalanches
- Valleys and dells could flood or trap frost on clear nights and valley bottoms often contain pockets of cold air. When it comes down to motivation, a cold camp is more likely to keep you in your sleeping bag or pit when important work needs to be done
- Lush undergrowth invites insect attack
- Lone trees can be dangerous if there is the possibility of a thunderstorm

Suitable Campsites

Ideally you should have a plentiful supply of wood and water, although pitching camp too close to water can cause trouble with insects. Look for signs of high water marks, debris lines, etc. Heavy rain miles upstream could bring a flooded river right outside your camp. In mountainous areas small streams can become torrential floods in a very short time. Find flat ground with few rocks. Try to find space where ground to air signals can be laid out and seen if you are lost.

Types of Shelter

If the weather conditions are suitable you could sleep in the open. If light rain is a possibility, a tree could provide sufficient shelter. Equally, caves, over-hanging ledges, etc., could be used.

Your shelter will depend upon local conditions, what materials are available and how long you are likely to be there. For immediate protection, knock up a quick shelter. Once this is done, start building a bigger, more permanent shelter if it seems it will be needed, which can be added to when time and materials permit and will also improve morale.

If you are heading back to civilization, a small lightweight shelter that can be carried or simple bivouac shelters constructed at every stopping point is all that is needed. Alternatively you could use the simple modern back-packing tents if your isolation is from choice and you are on the move (Fig. 56).

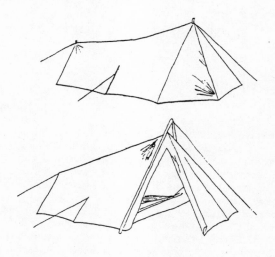

Fig. 56 Modern backpacking tents

If you have sick or injured members in your team, then a more permanent shelter would be worthwhile because it would give you the opportunity to recoup your strength and stockpile provisions.

In remote areas of Britain, the simplest shelters will have been constructed by nature in the form of caves and hollows. In winter, snow walls can be made by rolling snow. At very low temperatures snow will be solid and therefore, you will need a tool to cut your blocks out. Snow trenches make good simple shelters and you only have to look at an igloo to see that a substantial shelter can be built out of snow. To build a snow house, cut blocks of snow with a saw or a machete and build the igloo in a spiral. Once the walls are built, cut a hole for a doorway and fill any gaps between the blocks with loose snow.

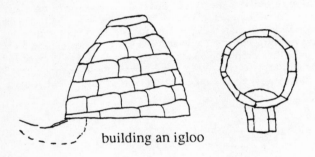

building an igloo

Fig. 57 An igloo

Long-term shelters are advisable if you hold out no hope of rescue or if you do not wish to be rescued, or even found, for whatever reason. If you decided to find or build a long-term shelter, you will want to make the shelter as comfortable as possible. In cold weather you will need to be warm and snug, whilst in hot weather you will need to be sheltered from insects and the sun.

Caves are ready-made shelters and can make excellent long-term homes – there are communities that still live in caves with all 'mod cons', TVs, fridges, etc. Invariably caves are dry, even if water runs through them, and they only require the building of a screen or barrier to close off the entrance. Check the cave before moving in for the possibility of rock slides inside or out. The last thing you want is to be trapped inside.

Like turf shelters, sod houses can be made by cutting sods and building them up as one would do with bricks. Sods can be used where there is a shortage of wood or other building materials. Cut turf in long strips, taking about two inches of soil with the turf topping. Roll up the strip as you cut.

Fig. 58 Cutting turf

Log Cabins

Everyone at one time must have watched an old cowboy film where they build a log cabin and thought to themselves 'I could do that' or 'I wish I could do that'. If you do find yourself building a log cabin, scale it to house the people you have with you. You can always expand it later on if the need arises. Square or rectangular rooms are the easiest to roof.

Choose a flat site for your cabin. If you wish to make doors and windows all well and good, but these are not really necessary, a blanket pinned over the doorway will keep out the cold. Build fireplaces out of stone but remember that some stones explode when hot. Fill in the gaps between the logs with mud and wood chips. Get your mud from the floor inside the cabin; this will increase your space and interior height.

When building log cabins, strip bark from logs before using; this will stop it falling off at a later stage when the wood dries out. It will also stop insects from infesting the walls of the cabin.

If the log cabin is to be permanent it must be lifted off the ground by use of a stone plinth in order that the wood does not rot.

A Selection of Shelters

Hollow covered with logs

A hollow covered over with logs and then turf is good enough for a quick shelter just to get you out of the elements. Plastic sheets can be laid between the logs and the turf to make it water resistant.

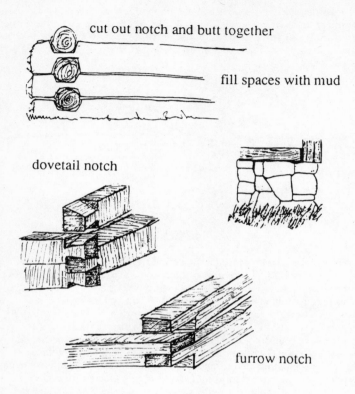

cut out notch and butt together

fill spaces with mud

dovetail notch

furrow notch

Fig. 59 Joints for log cabins

Stone barriers

The gaps in between the stones are filled with mud to make it fairly wind resistant.

Poncho shelters

In a survival situation, anything you can get your hands on will help you build a shelter. Tarpaulin is an excellent material for long-term tent-like constructions or teepees.

Teepees

Best known through the North American Indians in cowboy films. Easy to construct and easy to dismantle if you need to move on. This type of shelter is better for long-term survival and would need to be made beforehand. (Instructions for making a teepee are given in Fig. 79.)

Natural tree shelter

In heavy snow some trees like the pine or fir will make a natural shelter because no wind or rain can get in through the thick foliage. Small cooking fires can be used in this kind of shelter if you are careful.

Bivvy

Use a plastic sheet opened out on the leeward side of a wall (or build a wall). This can hold one or two men comfortably.

Turf

Only used in area devoid of any other types of material or other forms of ready made shelters. Perfect for moorland terrain.

Lean-to

This is the simplest form of shelter and can be refined by adding a floor, end walls, etc.

Tree bivouac

Chop a small pine, fir or spruce tree five feet up the trunk, until it tips. Then remove all the inner branches until an area is cleared under the trunk. Add side branches to outside to help waterproof it.

Parachute shelter

Build the central post no higher than 5 ft (1.5 m), raise wall to about 3 ft (91 cms). Tie a parachute (or tarpaulin) over the post and walls and secure with blocks.

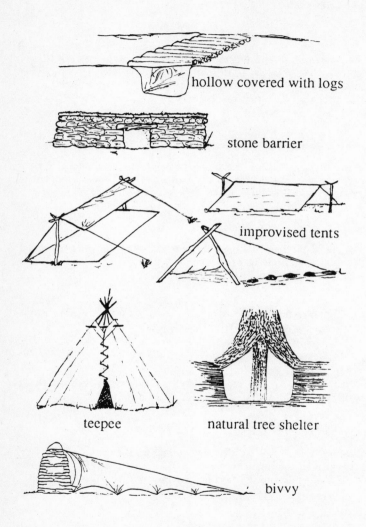

hollow covered with logs

stone barrier

improvised tents

teepee

natural tree shelter

bivvy

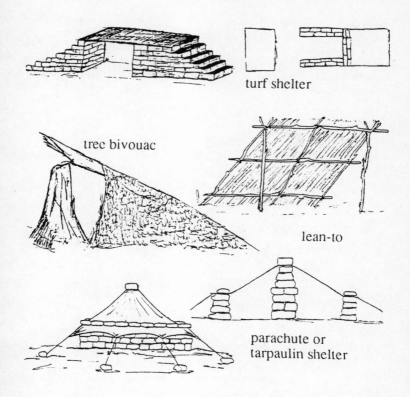

turf shelter

trec bivouac

lean-to

parachute or
tarpaulin shelter

Fig. 60 Shelters

Snowdrift shelter

Find a deep snowdrift that is fairly firm. Establish which is the leeward side and dig inwards and upwards. Build in a sleeping shelf if for long-term shelter.

A snow trench is very similar to the hollow described first in this section except that it is dug in snow rather than earth. Snow walls can be built even with soft snow. Roll a snowball as one would do for a snow-man and stack and trim to make a solid wall or structure.

Whilst living in a snow house, you must make sure you have a plentiful supply of wood and liquid inside your shelter. Just because your shelter is built of snow, does not mean you don't treat it like a house. In very cold conditions, do not leave the shelter even to relieve yourself. If you have to move your bowels, try to time it for when you leave the shelter to throw away accumulated rubbish and collect fuel. Remember though, still do your toilet inside – a frost-bitten backside is not nice and very hard to treat.

Fig. 61 Snow shelters

Keep the fire going at all times and keep shovels inside, in case you have to dig yourself out. Mark the entrance clearly so you will not lose the entrance to your shelter when you do move away from it to dump refuse, collect wood, etc.

Fig. 62 A tyre igloo

Tyre igloo

This can be made in inner city areas from scrap tyres or in farming areas where tyres are used to hold down silo sheets.

145

The tyres are arranged in a circle, as Fig. 62, and the insides of the tyres are filled with soil to provide sufficient weight and strength. A doorway can be made from two upright pieces of wood. As the structure gets higher, use planks as cross struts for additional strength.

A sleeping platform can be incorporated into the design at the outset and any draughts found in the finished igloo can be filled with mud.

Fig. 63 An Iron Age house

Iron Age house

Many lessons can be learnt from the way Iron Age man built his shelters. Unknowingly, modern man is going back in time when he constructs a shelter in a survival situation. In many cases, he is 'roughing it' whereas Iron Age man lived quite snugly.

Bedding

Use ferns, bracken, hay or grass to make a good thick bed. Change the bedding regularly. A blanket can be made into a sleeping bag with a little ingenuity (see Fig. 64).

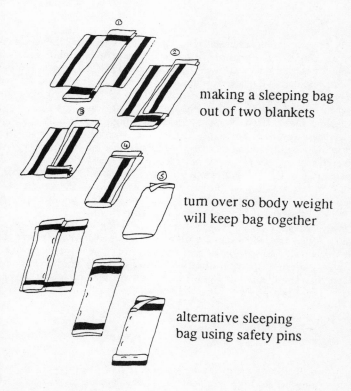

making a sleeping bag
out of two blankets

turn over so body weight
will keep bag together

alternative sleeping
bag using safety pins

Fig. 64 Adapting a blanket into a sleeping bag

17   Permanent Camp

Many survivalists put themselves in a position where to survive is their only option left as a form of challenge; other people actually drop out – you see them every year at Stonehenge trying to get to the Summer Solstice festivals. They are not hippies, they are not drop-outs, they are the people who have chosen that way of life and therefore have something to offer every survivalist who wishes to sit down and share a can of ale with them. These people are the travelling people, unlike gypsies.

Gypsies nowadays invariably live in fancy caravans on sites or drive tarmacing wagons and a lot of their life has become 'civilized' in that sense. Travelling people – young travelling people – do what the old gypsies used to do and that is pull up, camp, set up a fire and get a community going and they are the people who know about the countryside. They are often criticized because they are travelling people, but it is well worth gleaning any information you can from them.

It is because of these people that we are going to cover permanent camps. A permanent camp is set up by any survivalist or travelling person who decides to get out of the rat race. I have heard stories of people selling up everything in Manchester and going up to the Dales and selling fossils and making a good living out of it, living in a tent or a knocked up shelter and living off the land.

Permanent Camp

If you do decide to drop out, or if four or five of you want to start up a community and you get permission to camp up or you decide to pick one area where you will go, then there is a need for a permanent camp and there is also a need to provide some of the comforts you have supposedly given up.

This can be done fairly easily – you can make settees, tables, chairs, wet pits, dry pits, etc. Try to get hold of a Scout or Cubs handbook at a book sale because you will find pioneering projects in here. The pioneering concept is very common in the Scout movement where they go away to 'Camp' and build themselves a complete camp site with a fence and a gate and tables, chairs, dressers and racks for drying pots and pans, etc. They make all the home comforts out of things they find about them, twigs, reeds, sticks, etc., much in the same way as Robinson Crusoe survived. These books also contain games which will help to while away the evenings.

If you decide to set up a permanent camp you need some kind of order within the system. You need to try and build a table where you can eat as a community instead of having to crouch round a camp-fire and make chairs or stools you can sit on to keep off the wet grass and any number of other ideas can come to mind when you start tying sticks together. See Appendix II for a scenario.

Simple furniture can be made using basic materials and a few ideas are given in Fig. 65.

Camp Hygiene

It is imperative that camp hygiene is maintained in order to lessen the possibility of disease and infection, and these simple guidelines should never be neglected for any reason.

It is so easy, when in a survival situation, to throw waste from food around the camp site, albeit out of the immediate vicinity of the shelter. Scrap food will attract flies and insects as well as rats and other scavengers. Flies carry many diseases, and it can be a nuisance if the camp is infested with mites and flies buzzing around. All waste should be burnt or buried. Bury waste away from your main water supply and make sure that the site you have chosen to bury your waste will not drain into or wash away into the water supply and contaminate it. If possible, bury waste between 1-2 ft (30-60 cms).

Toilet Areas

These should always be sited well away from the main camp. The wet pit should have pebbles or stones for waste to drain through. Ash from the fire and more pebbles should be thrown in every other day until the pit is half full, when it should be filled in completely and a new one started.

149

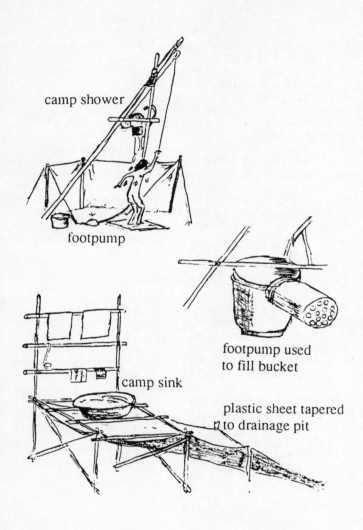

camp shower

footpump

footpump used
to fill bucket

camp sink

plastic sheet tapered
to drainage pit

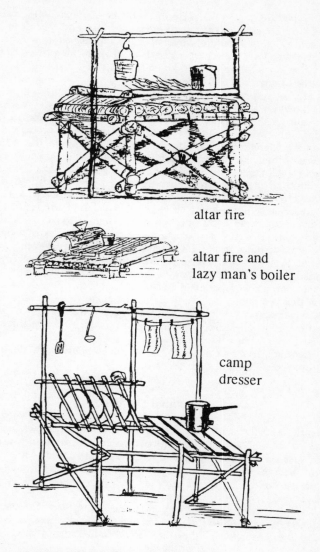

altar fire

altar fire and
lazy man's boiler

camp
dresser

Fig. 65 Simple furniture

Dry pits are dug in the form of a hole or a trench. The excavation should be covered with soil after use to prevent flies from being attracted. The pit should be covered with branches or some other form of cover when not in use. Spread ash from your camp-fire into the pit every day. As with the wet pit, when it is half full, it should be re-filled with the original soil and a new pit dug.

You must empty your bowels regularly if you are to keep healthy, and even though it is not pleasant crouching over a pit it is very necessary. This calls to mind a problem I had – enforced constipation I called it. During July 1989, I had the good fortune to run in the Saunders Mountain Marathon, a two-day event taking place in the wonderful scenery of the Lake District, which involved fell running whilst carrying all your equipment. There is a mid-camp if you can make it, and, after arriving tired and exhausted, pitching my tent and having a meal, I felt the need to empty my bowels. On seeing the trench with ten men crouching precariously over this steaming smelly pit, my body refused to co-operate until I could sit on a proper toilet. I wanted to go – after all I didn't want to run around the remaining course carrying extra weight, but my body would not respond. On reaching the end of the event, I walked into the local pub and almost before I took off my rucksack my body decided I should empty my bowels. I only just made it to the toilet.

You should always scrape your boots clean before entering your shelter so that you do not tread any animal waste inside. Try not to stand in your water supply when collecting water. Pick three points on the river, one for water collection, one for utensil washing and one for washing yourself when camped (see Fig. 66).

Check at least a mile upstream for possible pollution, i.e. fields draining into the river, dead animals, etc.

Personal Hygiene

Keep clean at all times. Many people forget this basic rule when in a survival situation. Disorientation can cause forgetfulness. Your priority aim, to be rescued, can cause personal hygiene to be classed as a minor priority. Wash every day and keep your hands clean, especially when preparing food. Treat cuts and scratches promptly because minor injuries can turn septic very quickly.

Wash your feet every day and let the air get to them. Sweaty feet get blisters very easily, which should be treated as soon as you see or feel them.

Do not sleep in wet clothes and wash your clothing often in case fleas or ticks get into the seams of the clothing.

A high standard of personal and camp hygiene must be maintained at all costs.

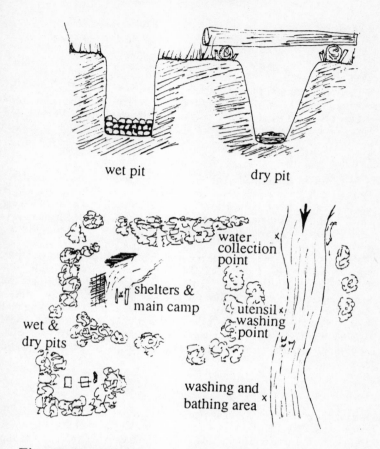

wet pit

dry pit

water collection point

shelters & main camp

utensil washing point

wet & dry pits

washing and bathing area

Fig. 66 Wet/dry pits and camp layout

Tips and Tricks

Salt

Boil up a quantity of sea water. Be careful about where you collect the water – do not collect from near sewer outlets and obvious pollution. When the water has boiled away, a deposit of salt will be left. Continue doing this until you have sufficient salt for your needs. Store the salt in an airtight container and keep it dry.

Improvised water filter

Water can be filtered through a clean sock using an inch of gravel in the bottom, then a layer of sand or ash on top of that. Pour the water in so it filters through these layers. Always boil the water after filtering. See Fig. 97 for a more refined water filter.

Candles

There are two traditional materials used to make candles, tallow (animal fat) and beeswax. Beeswax has always been more expensive and is usually reserved for church candles. With modern methods of honey extraction it is difficult to get, and so paraffin wax distilled from coal is used. Tallow candles smell as they burn but they give a better light than rushlights.

Thick cotton yarn is used for the wick. Render the fat down and then take several lengths of wick, twice the length of the finished candle, plus 4 ins (10 cms). Take a stick and hang wicks over the stick so they are the same length. Dip the wicks into the container of melted fat to within 2 ins (5 cms) of stick. Withdraw and leave to set. Continue dipping and leaving to set until the candle is thick enough, then cut between the two candles leaving a length for a wick on each candle. Suspend the stick holding the drying candles over a tray so the drips can be collected and re-used.

Snowshoes

If caught out in heavy snow or you are forced to travel on foot through thick snow, make yourself snowshoes by breaking some bushy branches from a conifer tree and tying them on to the base of your shoe with the stem facing to the back. This will spread your weight over the snow and make walking easier.

Curing skins

Soak skin in several baths of tepid water for about three hours until soft and pliable. Lay skin out and remove all flesh and fat, together with a thin layer of surface tissue with a blunt knife, keeping an even thickness all over. Rinse in lukewarm water several times and squeeze to remove all the grease. Stains can be removed with a little white spirit. To dress the skin, dissolve 4 oz (120 g) alum in 2 pints (1.1 l) water and mix

1 oz (30 g) washing soda and 2 oz (60 g) salt in another pint of water. Pour the alum solution slowly into the salt and soda solution stirring vigorously. Mix ½ lb (225 g) plain flour with a little water, then add the alum mixture to make a thick paste, stirring thoroughly. Pin out the skin on a board (see Fig. 88) and paint a thick layer of the paste on to it without getting any on the fur.

After twenty-four hours, scrape off the paste and put on another coat. Leave again for twenty-four hours and repeat the paste coating. Leave third coat for three days before scraping. Rinse the skin in water to which borax has been added (1 oz (30 g) per gallon). Then wash skin in clean tepid water until all traces of paste are gone.

Squeeze out pelt but do not wring. Pull it into shape before tacking it out, flesh side up, on a clean board. Paint a coat of neatsfoot oil all over skin and leave to dry. When almost dry but still pliable, unpin it and work it, by pulling it repeatedly over the back of a chair until it is supple, which takes a lot of work. Once it is soft all over, put it into a shallow receptacle and cover with dry, hardwood sawdust. Work it about in the sawdust, pulling gently then hang it in a cool, airy place to dry out completely before use.

Never heat skins at any time as this just hardens them.

Dowsing rods

Take a couple of lengths of coathanger wire, and bend into 'L' shapes or else use the more conventional 'Y' shaped hazel twig.

Hold the twig or wire firmly in front of you with a section in each hand. Walk slowly over the area where you hope to find water, carefully quartering the area by walking north in two or three places along one edge of area and then east over two or three places so you cross the area several times. Mark any places where you feel a movement then go back over these.

The movement when over water is unmistakeable; the twigs will jerk or the wires move across each other. Twenty per cent of people have the ability to dowse. Once water is found all you have to do is dig a well!

Baskets

Hard baskets can be made from twigs and one-year-old materials without shoots. Brambles (thorns rubbed off with a handful of rags), elm bole shoots and peeled willow rods, can be used immediately but most other twigs should be collected in autumn, tied into bundles and left in the open to weather until they become leathery. Do not let them dry out completely or they will be brittle. Weathering takes from one to three months depending on the weather.

155

Grasses for soft basketware made from rushes, reeds, sedge and thick grass should be cut in July and allowed to dry without bleaching, then gathered into bundles and stored in a dry place. They must be damped before using.

Coiled baskets and mats

Grasses, straw, even bracken, can be coiled easily to make a variety of useful items, by wrapping it round a core of grass, straw, string or rope. The core must be dried after collecting but be damped before using. It is easier working with damp grass but all the natural inner moisture must have been removed first and just the outside damped.

wrapping the core

starting a circle

starting an oval

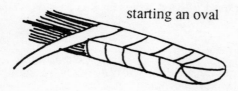

Fig. 67 Starting off basketwork

Wrap the grass round the core until the bound piece is big enough to turn into a circle or oval depending on the shape of the finished item.

Round baskets or table mats start with a circle and oval baskets, floor mats and sandals, etc., start with an oval. You then continue going round the base using one of the stitches shown in Fig. 68.

Lazy squaw stitch. This consists of long and short stitches alternately. First the short stitch is passed round a single piece of core, then the second stitch goes round top core and the one below.

Navajo stitch

lazy squaw stitch

Fig. 68 Stitches

Navajo or Figure of Eight. A very strong stitch. Work a figure of eight over top core and the one below (see Fig. 68).

Keep stitches together and upright. Fasten off loose ends by threading into finished work. Keep grass flat without any twists. New lengths are joined by laying the end along the core and working over it to secure it. To add a new length of core, cut the end of the old core so it tapers, lay the tapered end of new piece on top and carry on stitching.

This technique can be used to make a simple sandal. Once the sole is made to the required size, sew an elastic strap over the top by way of a row of stitches along the middle of the sole, and then cover the top of the sandal with a felt insole which should be stitched into place.

Baskets start with either a circle or an oval; the sides are then gradually curved up until high enough. Handles can be worked by looping the coil away from the main work, binding the core and working extra stitches either side to strengthen it.

157

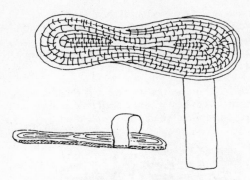

these sandals can be made from grass,
reeds or rope. The strap can be made from
cloth or even old inner-tube rubber.
There is no set pattern to the stitching

Fig. 69 Stitching a coiled sandal

Rushwork

Gather rushes when they flower in July. Cut them as long as possible
and keep in straight bundles in an airy, dark, dry place. Turn regularly
whilst drying which takes about three weeks. Before using, soak for
about a minute and keep wrapped in a damp cloth until next day. Do
not use broken reeds.

Choose three rushes and fold them roughly in half so the ends are
not level; this avoids a weak joint at the point where all three run out
together. Tie a piece of string in the fold and attach the string to a strong
base. Divide the six strands into three pairs so each set has a thin and
thick piece and plait them. Each pair is twisted before bringing outer
strands over centre. As the rush gets short, a new one is worked in until
it is secure. The plaited rush is then sewn into the required shape using
strong thread and keeping the work flat.

Rushlights

These are made from rushes with soft, white, spongy centres. After gathering, soak for a few hours and then dry them in the sun. The trick to
making a good rushlight is to peel away a strip of green outer skin down

one side of the rush, leaving enough skin still in place to support the soft inside. When a number of the rushes are ready, heat some mutton fat, tallow or wax in a narrow container until just melted – don't overheat. Dip the rushes one at a time into the fat or wax and allow the fat to set. Repeat three or four times allowing the rush to dry between each dip.

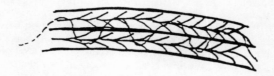

Fig. 70 Sewing plaited reeds

Cutting peat

Peat can only be dug by hand in the summer. The peat is cut in strips, each cake being 10 × 4 × 4 ins (25 × 10 × 10 cms). The diggings are layered so the deeper peat can be cut as well. The peat is set to dry, first in loose walls and then into beehive-shaped 'ruckles' to allow the air to get through. Drying is a slow process, made slower if the summer is wet. Once dry it can be transported by sled or cart and stored in a stack protected from the rain.

Rope

Rope making has lost much of its craft now with the introduction of nylon and machines. However, I once watched two men twisting straw with the aid of a carpenter's brace. As one man twisted the brace and walked backwards, the other man grabbed handfuls of straw and twisted it into the length of rope. They later coiled the finished rope to make a target for archery.

The method they used was the same as the one used to make rope years ago using hemp. Unfortunately it is now illegal to grow hemp (hence the saying – smoking old rope); however, out in the wilds in a survival situation, who would know?

A simpler way to make a rope is to use the stems of a tough trailing plant like ivy, clematis or brambles (minus thorns). Old plants are best. Soak them until they are pliable and then plait or twist them together.

To make a tow rope, take six long stems of varying lengths and tie the ends together and fix firmly to a branch of a tree. Walk backwards away from the tree twisting the roots, adding new strands as one strand finishes.

Besom brush

Cut yourself a pole 3-4.5 ft (90-137 cms), long according to your height, from ash, lime or hazel. Gather a bundle of birch twigs, preferably in autumn to be left over winter to season. Cut the birch twigs from the crown of the tree so they are pliable. They should be between 2-3 ft (60-90 cms) long. Arrange a good armful of twigs with the longest in the middle. Bounce the non-sweeping end on the floor to level off ends, then use thin strips of willow, hazel or oak to bind in two places. You can use pliable wire to bind if you prefer. Put the first tie 6 ins (15 cms) down from the levelled end and the second 4 ins (10 cms) below that. Make a point at one end of the handle and drill a hole through the handle 6 ins (15 cms) from the pointed end. Force the pointed end of the handle through the middle of the bound end until it is beyond both sets of bindings. Push a 4-in (10-cm) peg through the twigs and into the hole.

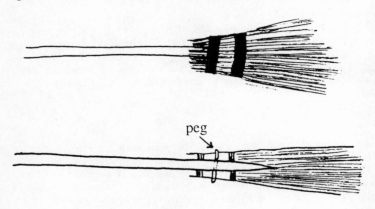

peg

Fig. 71 Making a besom broom

Soap

First make a lye solution by running rainwater through wood-ash as in fig. 72. Then boil this lye solution until it thickens. Mix 1 pint (500 ml) of the lye with 2 pounds (900 g) of clean melted fat and simmer gently for 3 hours. Cow, pig or sheep fat can be used or vegetable oils.

When the mixture cools a pound (450 g) of salt is added, which will fall straight through to the bottom, but will harden the soap. When the salt has settled, pour the liquid soap into wooden moulds lined with damp cloth or leaves, leaving the brine in the container. Empty tins can be used if both top and bottom are removed.

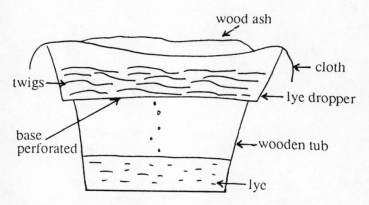

Fig. 72 A lye bath

Colouring and scent can now be added. Herbs like lavender, rosemary and lemon balm can be added, and colour is added by using carrots, beetroot, spinach, etc. This soap improves by keeping in a cool airy place. The soap block can be cut into cakes with a wire or knife after twenty-four hours.

Roll-up mats and screens

Use stiff grasses for your first attempts as they are easier to handle. Softer grasses can be used when you are more adept. Take a length of string which, when folded in half, is a third longer than the required length of the finished mat. Slip the doubled string around the first straw, twist the string and add a new straw. Continue in this manner until the required length is reached. Items like mats or blinds will need several strings running down their length.

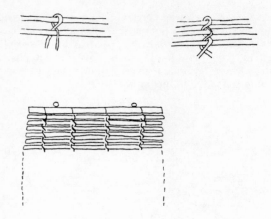

Fig. 73 Making mats or blinds

Simple clay pots

Clay can be found in heath areas and at the foot of hills. The vegetation is usually thick and there are often oak trees. It can also be found on river banks. The quality varies from area to area. Leave the clay to weather for a few days (the longer the better – a year won't hurt it) and then break off the amount you need and put it to soak. It will be ready after a few days. Adding fine sand at this stage helps to prevent it cracking when it is fired.

Before starting, roll and bend the clay in your hands. If it cracks it needs more water. If it feels sticky it is too wet. Knead the clay well to remove air bubbles, which will make the finished item crack when firing. Keep unused clay damp by spreading damp leaves over it. If the clay does dry out it can be re-used by breaking it up and leaving it to soak.

Roll the clay into sausage shapes, and then coil it to make the base. When the base is big enough, start to build up the sides. Moisten the outside and rub with a stone to smooth it. Leave to harden and then put to fire.

To make a simple firing kiln, lay twigs on the ground, put the pots rim down on the twigs and then pack brushwood all round. Set fire to the brushwood and cover with grass, moss and turves of earth. When it burns away the pots will be ready. These pots will crack easily, so make more than you need.

A diagram for a more sophisticated kiln is shown in Fig. 74.

Small pieces of clay can be formed into spoons and a sea shell pressed into the bowl to finish it off. Bricks can be made from clay as well using a brick mould (shown in Fig. 75), and tiles can be made from cutting through a few bricks. A hollow pressed into a few tiles will make plates.

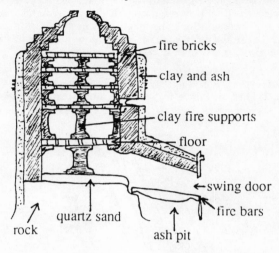

Fig. 74 A more sophisticated kiln

Fig. 75 A brick mould

Preserving food

Salting. Hand-salted food generally tastes better. To make it, cut the meat into pieces and rub thoroughly with dry salt. After a couple of days, put into a brine solution. The meat is left in the solution for three to six weeks. To use the meat, soak for twenty-four hours in fresh water. This method can also be used for vegetables and fish.

Drying. Either by the sun or by the wind. To dry meat, cut into thin slices and dry by fire. For vegetables, fish and fruit, sun or wind drying is more usual. Slice and hang up so the elements can dry them thoroughly.

Fig. 76 A drying rack

Smoking. Meat is usually salted before smoking. Build a sealed container and light a fire at the bottom. Hang the food to be smoked in the top half. Oak chips are best for the fire, and pine should be avoided at all costs because it is too resinous and will taint the food.

Weaving grass

You can weave long grasses or plant stems (like Rose Bay Willow Herb) into a thick mat, which you could then put on top of a roof to insulate and waterproof the shelter or use as a mattress.

Set up a frame as shown in Fig. 77 with two sets of strings running top to bottom across the required width. Lay bunches of grasses across one set of strings (the lower set B) but below other set (A). Reverse positions of strings by raising B and lowering A and set another bunch of grass in place. Reverse strings again. Continue like this until required length is reached. Tie off strings A to B across the width.

Hot water system

If you can find an old oil drum and clean it out thoroughly, you could set up a hot water storage system as shown in Fig. 78. This would, however, use a lot of wood to keep the fire going to keep the water temperature constant.

Teepee

This is a project which ideally is made before leaving home. The diagram (Fig. 79) gives instructions for a 16 ft (0.5 m) high teepee. You will need 4-6 poles, 17-18 ft (0.5-0.54 m) each to support the structure, and you would then carry these poles with you if you move camp.

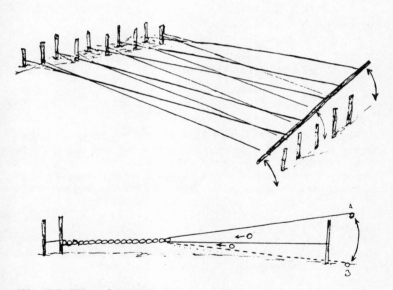

Fig. 77 Weaving grass

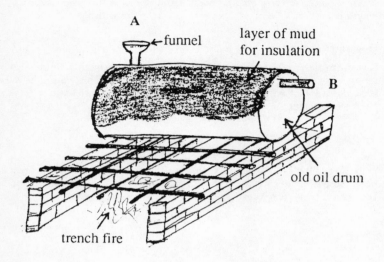

Fig. 78 A hot water system

The teepee is made from four 32 × 2 ft (0.97 × 0.6m) strips, sewn together with double flat seams to help keep it waterproof. If it will be moved frequently, all edges need to be reinforced. Make metal eyelet holes around the base so it can be pegged down. Use scrap pieces to make door flaps and lacing strips. Waterproof the outside if possible.

Moccasins

Moccasins can be made from leather, canvas or even an old inner tube. Cut pieces as shown in Fig. 80 to fit your feet, and then sew them together.

To adapt to make boots, instead of sewing the small top shown in the diagram on to the base, sew a tube round the whole of the top opening. Grease the outside sole to waterproof it.

166

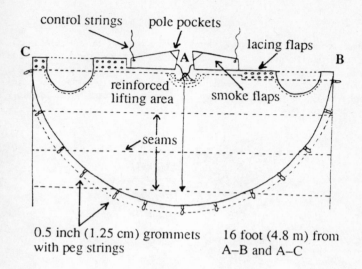

control strings   pole pockets

lacing flaps

C   A   B

reinforced
lifting area

smoke flaps

seams

0.5 inch (1.25 cm) grommets
with peg strings

16 foot (4.8 m) from
A–B and A–C

Fig. 79 A teepee

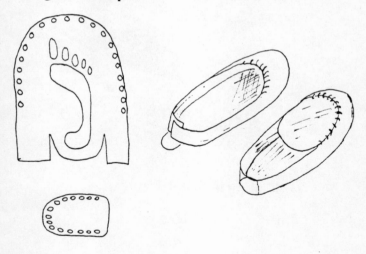

Fig. 80 Moccasins

Fishing nets

These can be made with strong rope, twine or rope made from creepers, etc. Once the net is made, it can be used for any of the types of fishing nets shown. If hanging net is used rather than bag-type which is pulled through water, you will need to attach floats to top edge and weights to the bottom edge, so it will hang in the water like a curtain.

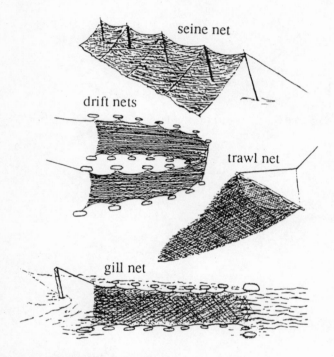

Fig. 81 Fishing nets

168

18   Wild Food

Water

Water is your greatest need. The Greek philosopher Miletus once declared 'The first thing is water', and he couldn't have been more correct. The simple thing to remember is that without water you will die. The human body needs at least 4 pts (2.2 l) of water each day. Any less amount reduces efficiency.

When water is scarce, drink sparingly. Never drink untreated urine because the waste material in it will make you sick, which will dehydrate you even more. It is possible to purify urine and a still is shown in Fig. 96.

Do not drink impure water, no matter how thirsty you are; always try to purify it first. Never drink from stagnant water. Waterborne diseases can kill: these include dysentery, cholera and typhoid.

Dysentery

Symptoms – severe prolonged diarrhoea, with bloody stools, high fever and a general feeling of weakness. If you catch dysentery, eat frequently, try drinking boiled water or the juice of boiled bark. Boil all muddy, stagnant and polluted water for at least two minutes.

Running water may have slight impurities in it but more often than not, the rocks and gravel will clean the water. Before drinking from a stream, check upstream for dead sheep lying in the water.

Collect morning dew by digging a small hole before settling down for the night and placing a container at the bottom, then cover the hole with a plastic sheet and weight the edges with rocks, placing a small stone in the middle of the sheet.

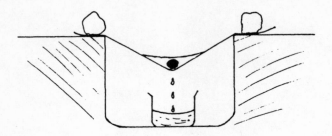

Fig. 82 Condensation trap

Food

Before pre-packed food, frozen TV dinners, southern-fried chicken, takeaways and monosodium glutamate, mankind lived on natural resources. Survival is all about living on natural resources. It is just a question of learning what you can eat and how to cook it.

Plant Food

Catching game is an art in itself. Therefore the first lesson must be in plant food. The world is full of plant food and Britain is no exception. There are four main food sources from plants:

1 Roots
2 Leaves
3 Stems
4 Fruit and nuts

Wild food often has quite a bitter taste, but this usually goes when it is boiled or dried.

Roots only need washing rather than peeling. In autumn roots are larger and possibly tougher, whilst in spring, although smaller, they are sweet and tender. Young roots will only need to be cooked for about ten minutes in boiling salted water, whereas older roots need to be cut into small pieces and cooked until they are soft. If they won't soften after an hour – give up.

Leaves are better eaten young. Like spinach, they should be cooked in a pot with only a few spoonfuls of water. Ten minutes should be enough for a pot full of leaves, which will boil down a lot in quantity. Large tough leaves should be shredded.

Many books cover the subject and a full list of useful books is given at the end of this book (see p. 303).

Always carry some food with you; but if you run out there are many types of food at hand, such as roots, berries, all sorts of edible plants and many types of game, including rabbits, hares and pigeons.

First let us cover the edible plants:

Alexanders. Flowers April to June with yellow/green flowers. Grows up to 4 ft (1.2 m) and is widespread in hedgerows and wasteland, especially near the coast. The flower buds can be added to salads as can the young leaves but the stem provides the main food. Cut off the leaf stems near the plant base and you should get about 6 ins (15 cms) of pinkish stem; discard greener parts. It has a very heavy smell but this goes when it is cooked. Cook in boiling water for ten minutes then eat like asparagus in melted butter.

Beech. Picked in spring, the leaves make a fine salad vegetable with a mild cabbage flavour.

Bilberry. Found on heather moors and mountains, often growing low to the ground beneath heather. It is rich in Vitamin C and makes delicious pies. Can be dried and stored.

Blackcurrants. The berries are rich in Vitamin C when fresh.

Blackthorn. Rich in Vitamin C. When berries (sloes) are dried they can be used to help cure diarrhoea. The berries are very sour but make good wine.

Borage. Fresh young leaves can be eaten raw.

Bracken. Roots can be roasted but have a strong taste. Young shoots can be picked as they are unfolding and should be boiled for thirty minutes. It has a strong flavour.

Bramble/Blackberry. The young tender shoots can be boiled for ten minutes to make a tasty dish or take a teaspoonful of fresh or dried leaves and pour boiling water over them to make a tea substitute. Leave to draw for five to ten minutes. Bramble is abundant in the UK and blackberries are of course edible and delicious. The fruit is best picked from August to October.

Bulrushes. The early shoots of the flower heads can be cut when they first appear, then can be boiled and eaten with salt and butter, rather like sweetcorn.

Burdock. Burdock leaves can be boiled and when cooled make an invigorating drink. In winter the roots can also be boiled and have a nutty taste, although it is mainly picked for its leaf and flower stalk which can be boiled or eaten raw in salads. Peel the stalk like one would do with rhubarb. Older leaves can be added to the stewpot. Burdock grows at the edges of woodland and can be mistaken for rhubarb except in summer when it produces large thistle-like flowers.

Chicory. Found alongside roads. Its leaves cluster at ground level and it has a carrot-like root. The leaves resemble dandelions but are thicker and rougher. You can eat the tender young leaves without cooking them or grind the roots as a substitute for coffee (see dandelions for instructions). The roots can also be boiled like carrots but are not very palatable being rather bitter. Changing the water twice whilst cooking helps reduce the bitter taste.

Chickweed. This common weed can be mixed with other vegetables to complement taste or it can be boiled on its own. Don't pick individual leaves but bunches of the whole plant as the stems can be eaten too. Wash well and put in a pan without additional water. Add butter, seasoning and chopped spring onions, simmer for ten minutes, turning all the time. Add lemon juice.

Chives. Grows mainly on limestone near fresh water. Can be used to give a mild onion flavour. The roots can be eaten boiled or raw but it is easier to cut the long stems and leaves. Using the leaves will also leave the plant alive to use again.

Clover. Most people try to find four-leaved clover, but it can be eaten raw. Usually found in abundance.

Comfrey. One of the weeds that people try to get rid of in their garden, but it is high in nitrates and can be used to feed the garden. Grows best in damp places, especially near running water and is widespread in ditches and on river banks. Flowers June to October with white, creamy or mauvish-purple bells. A bushy perennial plant, growing up to 3 ft (91 cms) high, with dark green, glossy hairy leaves. Comfrey is also known as knitweed because it is good for knitting bones together after a break. One of the few wonder herbs with many uses. It can be used as a poultice to draw splinters, is good for healing ruptures and makes a refreshing drink. The root can be eaten. Although the leaf feels furry, all the fur disappears when it is cooked. Older leaves have more taste and the best way to cook them is like spinach with a little water and plenty of seasoning. There is no need to add butter because the leaves are glutinous. It can be fried, boiled or eaten raw and is rich in Vitamin B12. To the inexperienced eye foxglove can be mistaken for comfrey so be careful as foxglove can cause anything from palpitations to massive heart attacks, depending on how much you eat.

Corn Salad. Very common plant which grows virtually anywhere. Found all year round on arable land. Leaves can be eaten raw or boiled like spinach.

Crab Apple. Abundant in old hedgerows. Best left until they turn rich red and yellow when they lose a lot of their bitterness. Can be added to other cooking or made into cider by pressing the juice out.

Dandelion. Dandelion leaves can be found anywhere, all year round because of its long growing season from February to November. Grows to about 1 ft (30 cms) high and has yellow, many petalled flowers with rough-toothed leaves growing from base of stem. Dandelion roots can be used for making a substitute coffee which tastes like shop-bought coffee without the caffeine. The roots are best picked in the autumn when they are at their fattest. Scrub roots clean and do not peel; then dry or roast until brittle before grinding fairly coarsely. The root can also be used as a vegetable chopping it into thin rings, boiling and eating it like cabbage, or it can be sauteed before boiling in a little water with salt added. Boil until most of the water has gone. The flower can be used in making wine and the leaves used in salad by adding olive oil, lemon juice and garlic or served in sandwiches with a dash of Worcester sauce. Dandelion leaves are rich in iron as they take up three times as much as cultivated garden vegetables do from the soil, but do not eat it to excess as it is a diuretic, hence its local name 'piss the bed'.

Dock Leaves. Docks have wide leaves and are usually found growing close to nettles. Young leaves should be picked in spring and cooked until tender. Water must be changed several times to reduce the bitterness. Has a medicinal use for relieving nettle stings if it is rubbed over the sting.

Elder. Purple berries are edible raw or cooked. Flowers can be coated in batter and baked into cakes. Leaves can be eaten but have no nutritional value and very little taste.

Fat Hen. Grows profusely on waste ground. Reaches about 3 ft (1 m) high and has a coating of white powder on the leaves. Small green flowers appear in summer at the top of the plant. Seeds can be collected and ground to make flour for bread. The young leaves and stems can be used in salads. They can also be boiled, chopped and added to frying onions but it does boil down considerably, so cook plenty. Rich in iron, protein, calcium and vitamin B1.

Fennel. A very popular herb used for flavouring stews and soups. Leaves can be eaten raw. Young roots and shoots can be boiled like parsnips. Old roots are chewy and taste strong.

Flowering Rush. Tall stemmed plant with inch-wide (2.5 cms) rose pink flowers which grow in fresh water. The bulbs are edible.

Good King Henry. This widespread plant has been eaten for many centuries. It flowers May to August and is a valuable spinach substitute. Leaves and young shoots can be eaten raw or boiled. Remove stringy parts and peel shoots.

Goutweed. Another name for ground elder and part of the parsley family. The young leaves can be eaten and should be treated in the same way as nettles, i.e. don't eat the fully developed leaves only the young shoots. Fully developed leaves will make you nauseous. Cook as for spinach.

Hawthorn. The young shoots when picked in spring can be eaten raw and have a nutty taste as do the leaves, which make a good addition to salad. Later in the year, the haws can be picked and eaten. They are juicy and meaty and taste very good.

Heather. The flower can be eaten raw or dried, and it can be used to make a tea.

Hops. Part of the hemp family – no, it is not like smoking cannabis! Common all over. Young shoots used to be eaten regularly about a century ago and these are still eaten in Belgium and other European countries. You can peel them and then cut and boil the shoots until they are tender.

Juniper. Ripe berries can be eaten but do not use in large amounts as it can cause kidney complaints.

Lady Smock (or Cuckoo Flower). This is part of the cabbage family and common in deep meadows and woods and the edge of rivers. Flowers April to June. Young leaves are good raw, old ones taste slightly peppery but are good for flavouring stews and soups.

Lesser Celandine. Alternative name Pilewort. Part of the buttercup family and the leaves can be eaten raw or cooked like greens.

Lime. Leaves of the lime tree make a delicious sandwich filling with butter, lemon juice or Worcester sauce. Can also be eaten raw just as they come off the tree. Flowers can be gathered whilst in full bloom in June/July and laid out to dry in a well-ventilated room. After two to three weeks can be used as tea. Drink without milk.

Mallow (Common). Purple-pink flowers found June to September. Boil the leaves and the liquid makes a nourishing, if thick, soup. The leaves can be eaten although they are an acquired taste. The seeds can be eaten raw like nuts.

Marshmallow. Unlike the modern-day version of marshmallow, which is made up of starches, gelatine, sugar, monosodium glutamate and other chemicals, marshmallow root was what the sweets were originally made from. The root contains everything except the chemicals they use to make it now. Very common on the east coast where it grows in clumps in ditches and dykes.

Marsh Marigold. Leaves and stems can be boiled like spinach, although it is said to taste superior to spinach. The flower can also be eaten. Treat carefully as marsh marigold is sometimes listed as a poison.

Marsh Samphire. Found in salt marshes. In summer they look like small cactus plants only a few inches high. Pick in May or June when young and tender. Wash and slice and add to salads or bottle and add spiced vinegar. Keeps fresh for months when pickled. Fresh shoots can also be boiled for ten minutes, *in unsalted water*, before being tossed in melted butter and garlic. Never leave to stand in water as they will begin to decay. If you wish to keep it, find a dry place in the open. To cook, boil in a little water for ten minutes, drain and simmer with butter.

Mountain Sorrel. A succulent plant with watery fat leaves. It has an acidy taste but it can be eaten raw or used as a pot herb to add flavour to soups and stews.

Nipplewort. Very high in calories. Can be eaten raw or boiled. If boiling, this must be done for about ten minutes to remove bitterness. Part of the daisy family and widespread and common on shady banks and roadsides. Flowers from June to September.

Parsnip. Grows wild in chalk and limestone areas, on waste ground. Look for abundant small, yellow flowers in July to October. Grows to about 18-24 ins (46-61 cms) in the wild. Plant is hairy and there are about eight or nine leaves. Ideally they should be dug after the first frost but you may need to mark their position as they are unremarkable when the leaves begin to drop. Roots of wild parsnip are a lot thinner than cultivated ones. Wash and scrape them and boil until tender, about three-quarters of an hour. Remove flesh from core and shape resulting mash into flat cakes, which can then be fried in suitable fat.

Pignut. These nuts can be eaten raw or scraped and washed. The plant is common June to July in woods, meadows and heaths. Care must be taken when collecting that it is pignut because it is part of the parsley family. The root must be dug with a knife to find the tuber.

Pineapple mayweed. Found on rough ground. Edible but with a bitter taste.

Plantain. Great plantain has green flowers and broad leaves with what seem like ligaments in them. Can be cooked as greens but has a very sour taste, especially the smaller plants. Eaten a lot in America and China.

Poppy. Both field and corn poppy. The leaves are not in the least narcotic although people tend to think they are. Gather the young leaves before the plant flowers and boil in salty water. They have a nutty taste and are tasty if mixed with herbs – sorrel is good. The flower comes June to August. Poppy seeds can be sprinkled on bread before cooking.

Ramsons. Have a pungent garlic smell, which only adds a mild garlic taste to food. Chopped leaves are added to food.

Reeds (Common). Grows to 5-8 ft (1.5-2.4 m) in dense beds in shallow or brackish water or marshes and swamps. Flowers are long and have purple spikes. They fade to brown in autumn and stem goes hard. While stem still green, if it is punctured it gives out a sugary gum. North American Indians used to eat the gum as sweets. They also used to cut the reeds whilst green, dry them and grind to powder. When this is placed near a fire it swells, browns and can be eaten like marshmallow.

Rose Bay Willow Herb. Large plant standing anything up to 6 ft (1.8 m) tall, with a pink flower showing from July to September. Very common plant found growing all over. Numerous uses from building shelters to making arrows but the young stems and leaves can also be boiled as greens. Mature stalks should be peeled. The interior is sweetish and should be eaten raw. The leaves should be dried and you can make a substitute tea from them.

Rough Hawkbit. Common in meadows, roadside verges and grassy places. Flowers May to September. Yellowish flower, the sort of thing you feed to rabbits.

Rushes. Grows along the sides of river banks, lakes, ponds and marshy ground. Usually found growing in a few inches of water. It has a fleshy rootstalk and should be peeled and boiled like potato. It can also be roasted.

Salsify. Rarely eaten today, mainly because of the belief that it tastes fishy. Found mainly around estuaries in the south-east of England. Flower is similar to a dandelion but purple in colour. The tall straight stems are best when boiled. The roots should be peeled and boiled or steamed with butter and lemon juice.

Sea Beet. Common in shingle by the sea except in Scotland. Flowers June to September with tiny green spiky blossoms. Grows up to 3 ft (91 cms). Pick the leaves between April to October, both the big fleshy ones

near the base and the thinner spear-shaped ones nearer the top. Strip
out central spine of bigger leaves and wash the leaves well before cooking. The small leaves can be used in salads. Boil the larger leaves in a
large pan in half an inch (1 cm) of water with the lid on for a few minutes. Chop and press down the leaves at intervals. When the leaves go
dark green, remove the lid and simmer for five minutes. Strain as much
liquid as possible off (saving it for adding to stews, gravy, etc.) Return
to pan and cook over a low heat with a knob of butter.

Sea Kale. Looks like grey-green cabbage. Find in early spring when just
starting to grow and cover with pebbles or seaweed, marking the spot.
Keep doing this and it will produce long white stems which you can cut
in June or July. Wash the stems, cut into small pieces and boil for twenty
minutes, drain and serve with butter.

Sea Spinach. Found on sand and shingle banks. Harvest in early summer.
Remove central spine, wash well and boil for ten minutes. Add a knob
of butter and serve.

Silverweed. Found in abundance in damp grassy areas and waste land.
Predecessor of the potato but not often used today. The undersides of
the leaves are matt grey, which gives the plant a withered appearance,
whilst the tops are silky green. Like the potato, silverweed can be boiled,
roasted or even eaten raw. It can be ground down to make a substitute
flour to use to make bread. Silverweed is underestimated as a food. The
taste is similar to parsnip.

Sorrel (Common). Young leaves can be picked in early spring and used
as a 'tarty' lettuce substitute. Sorrel leaves are a good addition to the
stewpot or they can be eaten alone as a vegetable, in which case they are
cooked in a little water like spinach.

Stinging Nettles. Can be boiled to make tea. Young shoots can be eaten
and should be prepared like spinach. Available all year round. Very high
food value in young shoots. Tea, beer and wine can be made from the
leaves. A lot of people believe that the formic acid in nettles is poisonous. It is poisonous or irritating if you are stung, but not if it is eaten
because cooking destroys the formic acid, but there is, in any case, insufficient to harm you. One of the commonest plants in the country and
one of the most useful. In the eighteenth century, Scandinavians used to
cultivate nettles and make cloth out of them. Should not be picked for
eating after beginning of June because in high summer the leaves
become coarse in texture, bitter in taste and make a very good laxative.
Remove the leaves from the stem before cooking and wash very well.
Can be eaten as straight vegetable by boiling in a closed pan for about
fifteen minutes in a little water. Strain off water and add a good knob of

butter and seasoning or add chopped onions then simmer for further five minutes turning all the time. They can be cooked by frying in a little butter with onion. Soups and purées can also be made. When picking if you grasp firmly they are not supposed to hurt (that's where 'grasp the nettle' comes from).

Sunflower Seeds. These seeds, loved by birds, contain lots of important minerals, such as phosphorus, magnesium, iron and calcium as well as vitamins B and E.

Sweet Cicely. Has a mild aniseed taste. Leaves used to sweeten food. Found on grassy edges in the north of England. Roots can be boiled. Sweet Cicely has an abundant usage.

Thistle. The thistle has a small nut in the centre of the flower. This nut is high in protein and is best eaten when the flower is fully open. Pull off the flower head and the soft nut is found at the base of the flower. It can be eaten raw and is very nutritious and filling. Thistles cannot be mistaken with their blueish-purple flower with lots of prickles.

Watercress. Rich in Vitamin C. Young leaves can be eaten raw or older ones added to soups. The leaves are bitter tasting, but the bitterness is reduced by cooking in several changes of water. Watercress is a green vegetable found growing abundantly round running water in the British Isles but never pick from stagnant ponds or streams flowing through pastureland as they can be infected by lungworm. Flowers June to October with small bunches of white blossoms. The stems are hollow and it is a creeping plant. Silky green colour to leaves. Now used mainly as a garnish but was once a respected side vegetable. Most of the watercress eaten today is commercially grown but it can be found growing wild. Land cress is very similar with a tangy strong flavour. Pick the older leaves which have a slight shine on them rather than the tasteless young leaves. Just cut the tops off the plant, do not pull whole plant up. Wash well and use in salads. Can also be stewed as a green vegetable. Tastes better if salt added.

Wild Cabbage. Probably the ancestor of the garden cabbage. Numerous species grown all over Western Europe and can be seen growing at side of rivers. Wild plant is very tall and has little yellow flowers. Smells like turnips and cabbage when leaves are crushed. Bitter if eaten raw but after a couple of good boilings, they are good to eat. Filling but do not eat too much as it is a laxative.

Wild Rose. In high summer, the petals of the wild rose are delicious to eat but avoid the white part at the base which is bitter. The berries can be collected in autumn to make drinks.

Wild Strawberry. Looks like the garden variety but tends to be smaller, often no bigger than beads but much tastier.

Wintergreen. An evergreen plant, which is fairly abundant mainly round conifer woods and moors in North of England. Has firm red berries hanging on stem in winter. Game birds love the berries so where the plant is found there is usually plentiful game. Leaves and fruit are spicy. Young tender leaves are popular in salads or as vegetable and can be made into tea. A liniment is made from this plant.

Various vegetables and fruits which we consider to be cultivated vegetables grow wild in the countryside. They may not be as big as shop bought varieties, but they are the same species. These include cranberry, wild onion, raspberry, wild carrot, wild celery, wild radish, gooseberry, redcurrant, and the herbs, chervil, parsley, mint and angelica.

With the abundant plant life available in this country you should not go hungry but if you were really desperate, there would be crops growing in the fields; however, the farmer will not be too happy if he catches you!

There are many books on the market on this subject which can inform you of herbs and the medicinal properties of plants. One of the best is *Food for Free* by Richard Mabey, which covers many types of plants which can be eaten.

Plants should be collected before dark if it seems likely you will have to sleep rough whilst out walking.

Butter and Cheese

You could produce your own butter and soft cheese if you can get milk either by buying or helping yourself from a cow in a field. (This is not recommended, however, because quite apart from irate farmers, most cows are milked by machine these days and may not accept hand milking.)

Leave the milk to separate overnight then put the thicker cream into a jar with a lid and shake it for ten to fifteen minutes. You will hear it change from liquid to solid. Pour off liquid buttermilk, which you can drink, and work (lightly knead with cool hands) the butter with plenty of clean water to get rid of remaining buttermilk before salting lightly (1 oz to 1 lb butter; 25 g to 250 g butter).

To make a soft cheese the separated cream from the milk is put into a piece of muslin and left to hang and drip for twenty-four hours. The resulting soft cheese can be mixed with herbs, garlic or even some of the butter to give a tasty soft cheese.

You can get milk from cows, goats or sheep. If you were making permanent camp, you could get a goat but it would need to be milked twice a day. You should get between one to two gallons (4.5-9 l) of milk per day from a goat.

Taste Test

Just because birds and animals eat something doesn't mean it is safe for humans. One person should test one plant at a time and choose a plant that is plentiful in the area. Don't experiment with fungi. If you eat fungi you must *know* what you are doing. When you select a plant to eat, look for colour of sap, by squeezing leaf or stem between fingers. Discard any with creamy or milky sap. The only exception to that rule is the dandelion, all of which is edible. Once crushed, rub juice around inside bottom lip and at same time, place small piece of plant, about fingernail size or smaller, on tip of tongue. Wait about four or five minutes, and if you detect any stinging or burning or putrid sensation throw it away.

If there are no sensations, take a larger piece of plant, about 2 ins (5 cms) square and chew it and swallow. Wait about two hours. If you experience any stomach upset or feeling of nausea, discard plant.

If no symptoms appear, take a piece about 6 ins (15 cms) square, chew and swallow and wait further two hours. If there are no symptoms at all, it is probably safe to eat.

Having identified the plant as safe, boil it and throw away the juice and then boil it again before eating. Don't eat a great amount of a new plant at a time. What is safe in small doses may not be in large quantities.

Try the same procedure with other plants, nuts, berries and flowers so that you can build up a varied diet, but only try one new taste a day, so you will know which you reacted to and which one is safe to eat.

Eating to Survive

To stay healthy the body needs certain foods. These are:

Proteins. To renew tissue and help growth. As we cannot store protein we need to eat protein-rich food each day. This is found in meat, eggs and fish and if none of these are available, comfrey leaves are high in protein.

Carbohydrates. These give us energy and are found in sugar, flour and potatoes. A wild source is dried roots and fruits.

Fats. These help to keep you warm. Collect any fat floating on the stewpot for later use.

Minerals. Keep bones, teeth and blood healthy. Calcium found in milk and cheese is needed for healthy teeth and bones. Iodine is needed by your thyroid gland and is found in sea salt. Iron prevents anaemia and is found in eggs, meat, vegetables and plants like dandelions and nettles.

Vitamins. Vitamin A helps you fight infection and is found in dairy food, eggs, meat and fish oils. Dandelions have a high content of vitamin A. Vitamin B is found in cereals, liver and eggs and keeps skin, nerves and blood healthy. Vitamin C fights colds, flu, gum infections (e.g. scurvy) and is found in fruit and green leaves. Vitamin D keeps teeth and bones strong. Sunshine is best source, but it is also obtained from fish and eggs.

Herbs and plants can be dried to provide winter food by picking fresh green leaves on a warm sunny day and hanging in the shade in small bunches. Ensure they are not diseased or covered in insect eggs first.

Dried foods should be reconstituted by soaking overnight. They will still absorb a lot of water, so take care they don't boil dry. Dried elderberries don't need soaking and neither do herbs which are being used as seasoning or to make tea.

If food is in short supply, stay as still as possible so as to use up fewer calories, or better still, sleep.

Fungi

This is a very difficult area to cover because there are deadly fungi growing in the UK as well as some which will just make you feel very ill, and a positive identification is very difficult to describe.

Obviously the safest solution would be to avoid fungi completely, but I appreciate that wild mushrooms taste delicious, so I would advise you to get a book on fungi with colour drawings or better still photographs and study it well. Be very sure before you pick any fungi.

Mushrooms which are safe to eat will have a white top, pink gills beneath and no sheath at the bottom of the stem. All three identification factors must be found before eating any mushroom you find. You cannot apply the taste test (see previously) to fungi because some symptoms take days to appear whilst others can be lethal in very small doses very quickly.

Nuts

Many of our native trees bear nuts – hazel and walnut being the best known but you can also eat sweet chestnut and beech mast. Nuts are the major source of protein available in the wild apart from game. Do not overpick nuts as wild animals eat them too. Nuts sweeten when stored, but they must always be stored in dry conditions.

Acorns. The raw acorn is very bitter, but chopped and roasted it tastes a little like almonds. The acorn can also be ground to make a coarse meal but the bitterness has to be removed first. This can be done by burying the acorns in ash or charcoal and watering from time to time until they become sweet. They can also be used as a coffee substitute by chopping the kernels, roasting to a light brown, grinding and roasting again.

Beechmast. Widespread in the British Isles, especially on chalk. Nuts appear in September to October with four nuts in a prickly brown husk. The husk opens when the nuts are ripe. They can be eaten raw, roasted or salted and taste like young walnuts but the nuts are small and a lot are needed. Each tree fruits every four years but there is rarely a shortage. Can also be used as animal feed, especially for pigs. If you have access to a press and a lot of beechmast you can make beechmast oil which can be used for cooking.

Hazel. Common throughout the British Isles except in damp areas. Found growing in hedgerows, woods and scrub in August to October. Half an inch to an inch (1-2.5 cms) long ovals in a green husk. Late September is the best time to collect and if they are ripe, they fall easily. If the ground below the bush is fairly clear, give the bush a shake and collect from the floor.

Sweet Chestnut. Common in England, scattered in Scotland. A tall straight tree which carries two or three nuts in a case covered with long spines, in October and November. Nuts begin to fall in October and a few sticks thrown into the tree should help them on their way. Break the husk by standing on them and remove the nut. They can be eaten raw by removing the brown, bitter tasting husk. To roast them, slit the skins and put in the hot ashes or close to live coals. Leave one with its skin unslit and when that one explodes, the others are ready to eat.

Walnuts. Not common but highly prized as one tree can yield 150 lb (68 kg) of nuts in a year. Best when ripe and dry in late October to November. If you wish to pickle them, they should be picked in July while still green.

Game

Game has to be stalked, caught, skinned, gutted and cooked. This all takes up valuable time – time which could be put to better use moving back to civilization unless you are camping out and can spare the time.

If you do see any game or fish, by all means try to catch it, but do not be too disappointed if you fail. Remember rescue could always be just over the next hill in the form of roads, railways, farms, villages, towns or even other ramblers. The section on hunting will give more information on hunting and fishing methods if you need it.

Stewing is the easiest way to deal with game. Skin the animal, cut into pieces and put in the stewpot with salt, herbs, roots and other leaves, etc. Cover with water and simmer until the meat is tender and comes away from the bone easily. Game can also be spit-roasted over your fire or it can be cut into fairly large pieces, covered with leaves and then covered with clay. A small rabbit will take about an hour to cook in the fire in this way and the meat will be very tender. Small pieces of meat can be spitted on a piece of wood (be sure you can identify the wood, although there are few poisonous trees in this country) and cooked by toasting over a fire. A good fire for cooking gives off little smoke and has red embers.

Seaweed

In the unlikely event of becoming lost on a beach it is a good idea to know about survival in these types of areas. Therefore this section is about food which is easily collectable and can bring in an abundance of edible foods by simple foraging.

Seaweed is under-rated as a good food source, although in the Far East it is eaten in large quantities. All seaweeds are edible and rich in vitamins and minerals. They can be eaten raw or cooked, however all seaweed should be eaten in moderation until unaccustomed stomachs get used to it. There are four types of seaweed: red, blue, green and brown.

Brown seaweed tends to be tough but all the other types are palatable. The plants should be freshly gathered and feel firm and slippery but still be firmly attached. If they smell fishy or putrid or are withering or in a state of decay they should be avoided. Always wash thoroughly to remove sand and debris and be very particular about where you pick the seaweed, avoiding sewer outfalls and other signs of pollution.

Carragheen (Chondrus Crispus). A purplish-brown seaweed, which is found growing on rocks on the Atlantic coast, in the middle shore area. Its short stalk is 3-6 ins (7-15 cms) long with a wide, flat, branching, fan-shaped frond. Best gathered in late spring or early summer. Collect fresh, clean plants and wash well to remove sand and grit. Cut off the stalks and dry. Store in a dry place until needed. Wash carragheen in fresh water and then boil in three times its own weight of water, adding sugar and seasoning. Simmer slowly until carragheen dissolves leaving a liquid which becomes a jelly when cold. This can be used to thicken soups and gravies to which it adds a lot of flavour. To dry it, wash it well and lay it out on a wind free surface outside. Wash from time to time with fresh water. It becomes bleached and creamy white. Trim off tough parts, dry thoroughly inside and store in bags. Dried seaweed is used the same way as fresh.

Dadderlocks (Alaria Esculenta). This is very common on open and exposed shores. Recognized easily by its long slightly wavy, yellow/brown edged fronds. The middle is yellowish and it has a sweet taste when eaten.

Dulse (Rhodymenia Palmata). Dulse is the commonest seaweed and is found in great abundance around the coast. Its colour is dark purplish/red and the size varies from 4-12 ins (10-30 cms) and it can be found on rocks and by the shore line. It may be branched or have single blades. It tends to be very tough unless cooked for four to five hours.

Laver (Porphyra Umbilicalis). This is common all round Britain. Often found on rocky shores clinging to rocks. It has a wide irregular shaped frond. When wet it is a purplish-red but changes to a greenish-brown when it starts to wither and finally turns black when dry. This seaweed is eaten worldwide and is very tasty. Wash well and then simmer in a little water until it forms a mush. Pour off excess water and form into balls. Coat with fine oatmeal and fry in hot fat.

Sweet Tangle (Laminaria Saccharina). This grows in abundance worldwide. It is a flat plant which grows up to 8 ft (2.4 m) in length. Found attached to small stones and rocks on muddy shores. The name implies that it has a sweet taste, and it tastes similar to peanuts. It can be dried and crushed to a powder to make a type of bread or boiled in a soup or eaten as a vegetable.

Although all seaweeds are edible, apart from the odd stomach ache, gathering seaweed can be dangerous. Watch the tide and make sure you neither drown nor get cut off by the tide whilst collecting food.

Shellfish

Shellfish is plentiful around the coast and there are many varieties: winkles, mussels, razorshells, cockles, limpets, oysters and scallops. All you need is a container to hold them and a lever to lift rocks.

Shellfish breed during the summer months and this period should correspond with the warm weather. The bacteria pumped through the shellfish as they feed can increase greatly during the summer. For these two reasons, it is best to avoid shellfish when there is no 'R' in the month (May, June, July and August).

Always follow these rules when gathering shellfish:

1 Never gather near habitation or anywhere where sewage or other refuse is pumped into the sea
2 Always wash thoroughly inside and out
3 Always check the shellfish is alive before cooking because they decompose rapidly. Try to force open the shell. If it shuts again quickly it is alive. If it comes open fully or doesn't shut again, it is dead and should be discarded

Clams. Common in sand and mud on middle to lower shores. They have an oval shell similar to a mussel. Up to 5 ins (13 cms) across and grey or brown in colour. They burrow deeper than cockles and recognition is by the trunk (siphon) which they can protrude from their shells to feed. Rinse the shells as for cockles then scald in boiling water for ten minutes. Remove fish from shell and cut off siphon. Fry or bake the remaining meat for half an hour or boil until tender.

Cockles. These can be dug up from sandy beaches where they are common in the sand or sandy mud on the middle shore area. They grow up to 2.5 ins (6 cms) across in two halves, both of which are heavily ribbed and pale brown to blue-grey. Use a lever or knife to dig them up. Usually found 2-3 ins (5-7.5 cms) under sand. Look for mud veins in the sand or veils of plankton, but the best way is just to dig about. Gather them carefully, don't throw them into your pail as the shells break very easily which kills the shellfish. Only collect those bigger than 1 in (2.5 cms) across. Wash off the mud and sand and leave to soak overnight in clean fresh water. Check that each one is alive before dropping into a pan of boiling water. Discard any which are dead. Cook for five minutes after which the shell will open. The cooked cockles are delicious fried in bacon fat and served with bacon on toast.

Limpets. Found attached to rocks. Shaped like flattened cones. Grows up to 2.5 ins (6 cms) across. Usually smaller than this however so you need to collect a lot. Do not pick from piers or jetties. Prise the limpets off the rocks with a knife. Soak and boil like cockles until the meat floats free. They are tough and will need considerable further simmering before being ready to eat.

Mussels. Found clinging to undersides of rocks. Prise off with a knife. Care must be taken when picking mussels because they are one of the major causes of shellfish poisoning because they pass at least ten gallons (45 l) of water through their shell each day and, with our polluted seas and beaches, the poison they retain can lead to stomach problems. Make sure you follow the general safety outlines carefully when gathering mussels and gather from clear stony shores at low tides, outside summer months. Stand mussels in fresh tap water, changing water at least twice and check each is alive before cooking. They can also be baked in hot ashes in their shells. They only need to be cooked for a couple of minutes.

Razorfish. Also dug up from clean sandy beaches at the edge of low tide. Will disappear into the sand at the slightest noise. You can either dig them out or pour water into escape holes. Cook as for clams. The meat is tough and needs cooking for a long time.

Scallops. Found in rock pools at the bottom of the beach on low tides and on lower shore at very low tide. After washing and scalding for ten minutes in boiling water, cut away the white and orange meat from the shell, dust with flour or breadcrumbs and fry for about four minutes.

Winkles. Found clinging to the undersides of rocks and weeds on the middle shore, usually in large colonies. They are ½-1 in (1-2.5 cms) high with a pointed spiral shell and usually dark grey in colour. Prise loose with a knife. They should ideally be soaked for about twelve hours in fresh water to remove grit and sand. This can be done overnight but, as they will still be alive, they will try to escape and they make a strange noise whilst trying. Plunge winkles into already boiling water to cook for about ten minutes, then allow to cool. You have to winkle meat out of their shell with a pin. The whole winkle is edible except for the shell and the tiny plate at the mouth of the shell. A lot are needed to make a meal and they are not as tasty as whelks or mussels.

Fish

All fish found in British waters, whether they be in river, lake, canal or sea are edible. Some however taste better than others.

Fish are divided into three categories, game fish, coarse fish and sea fish. There are fishing seasons for game and for coarse fish to allow the fish time to breed. For these seasons see p. 230.

Game Fish

Game fish need oxygen-rich water containing no pollution. All go through a series of changes during their lives and have various names at each stage.

Brown Trout. Markings and colouring change with the various stages the trout goes through. Adult fish have irregular spots on the back which are darker near the backbone. Size varies. Young fish swim in shoals whilst adult fish are more solitary and live near the bottom. They are also more predatory. Bait: live fish, natural and artificial insects, spinning lures, worms, small crustaceans.

Char. Dark back with pale spots. Red underbelly. Body thins before tail begins. Has white edge to fins under belly. Does not grow very big. Found in very few places in England (mainly Lake District), two or three lakes in North Wales and various Scottish lochs. Lives in deep cold water. Bait: artificial flies and spinners.

Grayling. Found in clean rivers and streams with a fast current. Can usually be found where there are brown trout. A very sleek fish with an extra large back fin. Does not grow very big – 4 lb (1.8 kg) would be good. They spawn March to April and are consequently thought of as a coarse fish. They are good fighters. Bait: flies and trotted worms. Will also take maggots.

Rainbow Trout. Thrives in still waters. Resembles brown trout except for colour, the rainbow having a vivid band of pink/purple scales along middle of side. Spots continue on to tail and fins. More tolerant of pollution than most game fish and can be found at various depths throughout water. Bait: natural and artificial flies, lures and worms.

There are various sub-species of trout which are found in only a few lakes. These include: powan, vendace, gwyniad, pollan, houting and schelly. All look more like herring than trout and have very fine scales. They live in still waters, mainly in the north and north west of the country. The fish eat plankton and other small life.

Salmon. Goes through a variety of names during its life cycle. Born upstream, travels down to sea where it lives until ready to breed, then it travels back upstream. Usually will not feed when travelling to breed. Bait: artificial flies, metal lures, plugs, worms, prawns, trailed live bait. A more unsporting but reliable way to catch salmon is netting. This is of course illegal, as most salmon waters are privately owned.

Coarse Fish

Barbel. Lives in running waters. Has long, slim, powerful body and four barbels, two from top lip above mouth and one from each corner of bottom lip. A bottom feeder which roots around in river bed for aquatic animals, weeds or worms. Only lives in very pure water. Bait: bread baits, cheese, worms, grubs, tinned meat.

Bleak. Also used as bait fish but can grow up to 8 ins (20 cms). Bait: single maggot or bread pellet close to surface.

Bream. Bronze or common bream. Deep bodied, slab-sided fish found in sluggish rivers and still waters. Found mainly from Midlands to North. Has huge appetite. Lives and moves as a shoal. Heavy ground baiting will bring the shoal. Feeds mid-water and bottom. 5 lb (2.25 kg) fish are common.

Carp. Lives in still waters of all kinds, ponds, lakes, etc. Can also be found in slow running rivers and drains. Three varieties: common which is fully scaled, mirror which has a number of large scales along centre line and leather which has no scales. Two species of common carp: the deep-bodied type introduced from the Continent to many still waters and the slimmer fish thought to come from the original fish bred in monasteries for food. Can grow up to 50 lb (23 kg). Has four barbels, two from upper jaw and one at each corner of mouth. Mainly solitary. Prefers soft muddy bottoms where they search for food and where they lie in cold winter months. They rise as water temperature rises to eat minute invertebrates. Surface feeders in summer. Often found in weed beds. Bait: worms, maggots, grubs, bread, luncheon meat, tinned animal food, boiled potatoes.

Chub. Wide distribution in England. Not found in Ireland or Scotland or in extreme west of Wales or South-West Cornwall. Prefers slow running rivers but will live in still water. Grows up to 9-10 lb (4-4.5 kg) but 3 lb (1.3 kg) is good. Mainly solitary. Basks at surface. Feeds mid-water but lurks in weed beds. Good fighter towards end of season. Bait: cereal and ground bait, but will also take flies and live bait.

Crucian Carp. Resembles larger carp but no barbels on upper jaw. Fully scaled and resembles its close relative the goldfish. Bait: small bread pellets, tiny worms and grubs.

Dace. Lives in fast water. Fond of shallows and rapids where water aerated. Swims in shoals. Often mistaken for young chub when caught. Average weight 8–12 oz (225–340 g). Bait: bread or small grub baits but will also take small flies.

Eels. Found all over the British Isles in slow running rivers, ponds and canals. Can live for up to twelve years in the same water and big specimens are common. Must be pulled out of water quickly, otherwise they will wrap themselves around rocks or roots and escape. Be aware that eels have sharp teeth and treat them with respect. Mainly solitary, eels are bottom feeders and nocturnal but will sometimes feed during day, especially during storms. Can be found under stones and rocks, in holes in river beds and near weed beds. Bait: lob worm, small fish, small eels.

Gudgeon. Similar to barbel but much smaller. Has two barbels only from top lip. Prefers running water over sandy or gravel bottoms. Can withstand high level of pollution. A shoal fish feeding on bottom of water. Bait: small worms and maggots.

Millers Thumb or Bullhead. Two back fins but all fins are spined. Has broad, flat head. Found in gravelly runs of clear water in small streams. This mainly solitary, bottom feeder can be found under stones and around weed beds.

Minnow. Usually used as bait fish. Silver in colour with dots or black stripes. Usually found in shoals in shallow running water. Average about 3 ins (7.6 cms) in length.

Perch. Striped predator. Two big back fins, the front one of which is spined and which it can erect into your hand. Found all over the British Isles. Prefers slow running stretches of rivers and streams, preferably with overhanging cover but can be found in ponds and canals. Colours more brilliant at breeding. Mainly solitary. 4 lb (1.8 kg) would be a specimen. Basks at surface. Feeds mid-water and can be found round weed beds. Bait: almost anything, insects, freshwater shellfish, worms, grubs, bread. Will also take fly and spinning lure.

Pike. Wide distribution throughout Great Britain. Found in slow running rivers, lakes, canals, gravel pits and even small farm ponds. Has long, sleek, bony head and has needle sharp teeth which it will use and as these slant backwards it is difficult to get yourself free. Will eat any type of fish as well as frogs, ducklings, etc. Maximum weight 40-50 lbs (18-22 kg) but 10 lb (4.5 kg) is a good fish. Solitary fish. Basks at surface and feeds midwater. Often lurks in reeds and weed beds. Bait: livebait, herrings, sprat and mackerel as dead bait, spinning lures.

Roach. Most common coarse fish. Widely distributed in the British Isles. Shoal fish found in still and running rivers, canals and ponds. Feeds in midwater on water creatures, worms and plant life. 2 lb (900 g) fish is a specimen. Bait: bread in most forms, grubs, seeds, berries, cereals such as spaghetti; larger roach will take worms.

Rudd. Similar to roach but deeper bodied with redder fins and a bright red eye. Prefers still water and slow running rivers. Often found in backwaters. 2–3 lb (900 g–1.3 kg) a specimen. Bait: all baits taken by roach but will also take small dry fly on warm summer evening.

Ruffe or Pope. Similar to perch but less deep bodied and with two back fins which are joined together. Small fish only a few ounces in weight. Lives in shoals in deep water preferring coloured or shaded areas. Bait: small worms, fry and insect larvae.

Silver Bream. Small, more silver than relative the bronze bream. Mainly found in eastern Britain. Slab sided like bronze but more rounded.

Feeding pattern is similar but shoals are not so big. I lb (450 kg) would be a specimen. Bait: as for bronze.

Tench. Thick bodied with muddy colour. Rounded back fin and stubby tail. Powerful fighter found in still and sluggish rivers and ponds. Bottom feeder. Skin has very small scales and slimy texture. Has two barbels at the corners of its mouth. Mainly solitary. As water cools with winter frosts, it disappears into the mud where it stays till spring. Bait: worms, bread bait of all kinds, grubs, water creatures.

Zander. Also called pike-perch because of resemblance to both. Introduced from Continent. Some fish have stripes on flanks but are more streamlined than perch. Found mainly in East Anglia where 1 lb (450 g) would be a good weight. Two back fins, front one of which is spined. Bait: live or dead baits, small spinning lures.

Crayfish

About 4 in (10 cms) long and found in rivers in chalk areas. They like clean oxygenated water. They are nocturnal and spend the day beneath rocks and in burrows. Cook crayfish by dropping them into boiling salted water. Cook for ten minutes, drain and eat when cold.

Sea Fish

There are two main ways of sea fishing around the British Isles – from the shore or from a boat. Both will provide you with fish virtually wherever you go, provided you continue for long enough. All the fish caught off these shores are edible but there are too many to go into details.

Beachcasting. The ability to cast long distance (100–150 ft; 30–45 m) is most important. You need to use the correct weights and hooks to carry your line out far enough to where the fish are. Bait will depend on what is available locally. Be careful of obviously polluted areas.

Boat fishing. There are two ways of fishing from a boat, either with a rod and line or with a net.

Cooking Fish

Gut the fish as shown in the section on hunting (see p. 226) and clean out the entrails. Rinse well in clean water. Wrap the fish in leaves and place on stones beside the fire. Ideally the stones around the fire should be flat enough to cook on. Turn the fish round after five minutes, then turn over. After a further five minutes, open a leaf to see if it is cooked. If it isn't wrap it up again and leave a little longer.

Campfire Bread

Bannock is the traditional bread of the traveller. A simple bannock can be made with a mixture of oatmeal or white or wholemeal flour, salt to taste and enough water to make a thick dough. The mixture is then baked or fried.

Corn pone is made the same way but with yellow corn meal. The flavour of corn pone is flat and rather gritty.

The recipes used here are a little more complex, using baking powder, but the mixtures can be combined before leaving home and sealed into a plastic bag. The mixture will add little weight to your pack and will keep virtually forever. The plastic bag can be used as a mixing bowl when you add the milk or water to make the dough.

When griddle cooking camp-fire bread, it is important that the fire is at the right heat before mixing the dough. Generally it takes at least fifteen minutes for a fire to burn down to the glowing embers that makes the low heat a griddle bread requires. Pre-heat the frying pan or griddle before adding the batter and protect the frying bread with foil set to the windward.

Camp-fire breads can also be baked in a camping oven but these are cumbersome to carry with you. A simpler variation is to cook on a hot rock or make an oven as part of your fire if you will be using the camp site for a while.

Bannock with Baking Powder

5 oz (150 g) plain unsifted flour
2 teaspoons baking powder
2 teaspoons sugar
1 teaspoon salt
2 tablespoons powdered milk
1 tablespoon melted fat or corn oil
5 fl oz (150 ml) milk or water
butter or bacon fat

At home, measure the dry ingredients into a medium mixing bowl, mix well. Add melted fat and work with a spoon until mixture is fine and crumbly. Seal in a large sturdy plastic bag. At the campsite, when you are ready to make the bannock, open the bag, stir the ingredients to form a well for the water, and gradually stir in the water and work the mixture to a stiff dough. You may need to use a little less or a little more water for a dough stiff enough to hold its shape. Work the dough with lightly floured hands on a piece of floured foil, placed on top of a flat rock, patting the dough into a flat cake the size of the griddle. Grease griddle lightly, heat it and set bread on it. Protect the griddle to windward with foil. Cook ten minutes on one side, flip bread over and cook ten minutes on the other side. Makes four to six servings.

Corn pone

4 oz (100 g) yellow corn meal
4 oz (100 g) sifted plain flour
1 oz (25 g) sugar
4 teaspoons baking powder
1 teaspoon salt
2 oz (50 g) powdered milk
1 fresh egg
7 fl oz (200 ml) water
2 oz (50 g) melted fat or butter

At home, measure the dry ingredients into a mixing bowl. Seal in a large sturdy plastic bag. At the campsite, mix ingredients together in the bag lightly. Corn meal tends to settle to the bottom of the bag. Add the egg (dried egg can be used with more water). Then add the water and half the fat and mix thoroughly in the bag to make a semi-liquid dough. Heat the remaining fat in the griddle. Pour the corn pone dough on to the griddle and cook until the top of the batter is as dry as a pancake and ready to flip, which takes about ten minutes. Flip the corn cake and cook another ten minutes.

Beer and Wine

Nettle Beer

2 lb (900 g) young nettles
2 lemons
1 gall. (4.5 l) water
1 lb (450 g) demerara sugar
1 oz (25 g) cream of tartar
¾ oz (20 g) brewers yeast

Put nettles in pan with thinly pared rind of lemons. Pour on the water and bring to the boil. Simmer for fifteen to twenty minutes. Strain on to sugar and cream of tartar. Stir well, add juice of lemons and yeast mixed with a little liquid. Cover and keep in a warm place for three days.

Remove to cool place for two days. Strain and bottle. Keep a week before drinking.

Birch Beer

½ lb (250 g) black birch bark
1 oz (25 g) hops
¼ lb (100 g) pimento
¼ lb (100 g) ginger
6 pints (3.5 l) golden syrup
½ pint (28 ml) yeast

Boil bark in 3–4 pints (1.7–2.3 l) of water and when reduced, strain and boil rapidly until thick and treacly. Meanwhile boil hops, pimento and ginger in 12 pints (7 l) of water for twenty minutes then strain over birch bark extract. Stir until it boils adding syrup and when dissolved strain into cask. Add 10 gallons (45 l) of water which has been boiled and cooled. Stir in yeast. Leave bunged for two to three days until fermentation ceased. Strain into bottles. Seal and store in cold place.

Nettle Wine

4 lb (1.8 kg) nettle tops
4 lemons
2 lb (900 g) sugar, preferably brown
1 oz (25 g) cream of tartar
2 galls. (9 l) water
1 tbs dried or brewers yeast

Put nettles and cut up lemons in water and boil for twenty minutes. Strain liquor out and add cream of tartar and sugar. When cool enough, add yeast and ferment for three days in warm place. Then let it settle for a couple of days in a cooler place before bottling in screwtop jars. You can drink it within a week of bottling and it doesn't keep long. Very refreshing.

19   Poisons

Poisonous Plants

Autumn Crocus – whole plant
Baneberry
Bittersweet (or Woody Nightshade) berries often show red, green and
    yellow together
Black Nightshade – berries especially before ripe
Bluebell
Briony (White and Black) – berries
Broom
Buckthorn (Common and Alder) – berries
Buttercup (all species)
Caper Spurge
Caster Oil plant – seeds
Cherry Laurel – seeds in berries, foliage
Christmas Rose (house plant)
Columbine
Cowbane – all plant
Cuckoo Pint (Wild Arum or Lords and Ladies) – berries
Daffodil – bulbs, sap, leaves if eaten
Daphne Mezerium – berries
Darnel Rye Grass
Deadly Nightshade – berries
Dog's Mercury
Fools Parsley
Foxglove – all plant
Fritillary (very rare)
Giant Hogweed – sap
Green Nightshade
Guelder Rose
Hellebore (Stinking and Green)
Hemlock – all plant

Henbane – all plant
Holly – berries
Honeysuckle – berries
Horse Chestnut – nuts (conkers)
Hyacinth – bulbs
Ivy
Laburnum – seed pods
Lily of the Valley – berries
Lupin – seeds, seed pods
Mandrake
Marsh Marigold
Meadow Saffron
Mistletoe – berries
Monkshood – all plant
Oleander – all parts, even smoke from burning wood
Poinsettia (house plant)
Pokeweed
Potato – leaves, stems and sprouting tubers and green potatoes
Privet (Garden and Wild) – berries, foliage
Ragwort
Rhododendron
Rhubarb – leaves
Scarlet Pimpernel
Snowberry – berries
Spindle Tree
Spurges (all species) – all plant
Spurge Laurel
Thornapple
Water Dropwort (Tubular, Hemlock and Fine-leaved) – all plant
Water Iris (or Yellow Flag)
Wood Anemone
Yew – berries

Reaction to Poisonous Plants

***   Extremely poisonous, possibly fatal
**   Very poisonous, rarely fatal
*   Extremely unpleasant but not fatal

Assume all parts of plant are poisonous unless otherwise stated.

Black Briony. ** Symptoms: vomiting, diarrhoea, blisters on the skin, berries burn the mouth

Castor Oil Plant. *** Symptoms: vomiting, sweating, rapid pulse, weakness and collapse

Cherry Laurel. ** Symptoms: headaches, vomiting, dizziness, low blood pressure, dilated pupils, unconsciousness

Cow Bane or *Water Hemlock.* *** Symptoms: dizziness, vomiting, unconsciousness, violent convulsions and coma

Cuckoo Pint. ** Symptoms: sore throat, diarrhoea, irregular pulse, coma

Deadly Nightshade. ** Symptoms: vomiting, diarrhoea, convulsions, coma, rapid pulse, dilated pupils

Death Cap Mushrooms. *** Symptoms: (start after 6–24 hours) pain, vomiting, intense thirst, weak pulse

Foxglove. * Symptoms: nausea, weakness, rapid pulse, perception of yellow haloes round objects

Hemlock. *** Symptoms: dilated pupils, lowered temperature, difficulty in moving, fluctuating pulse, rapid breathing and stupor

Henbane. * Symptoms: nausea, difficulty breathing, dizziness, confusion and rapid pulse

Holly. * Symptoms: stomach pain, vomiting, diarrhoea

Laburnum. ** Symptoms: stomach pain, vomiting, drowsiness, fever, rapid pulse, coma

Leopard Lily * (houseplant). Symptoms: extreme swelling of lips and tongue and a lot of pain

Lily of the Valley. *** Symptoms: stomach pains, vomiting, cold clammy skin, delirium, coma, possibly death

Monkshood. *** Symptoms: burning mouth and throat, stomach pains and vomiting, intense thirst, headache, coldness, paralysis, convulsions, delirium and coma

Oleander. *** Symptoms: stomach pain, vomiting, diarrhoea, rapid pulse, dizziness and coma

Pokeweed. * Symptoms: stomach pain, vomiting, diarrhoea, dizziness, exhaustion

Rhubarb leaves. * Symptoms: stomach cramps, vomiting, weakness, reduced blood clotting, liver and kidney damage

Thornapple. ** Symptoms: dry mouth, nausea, dilated pupils, loss of co-ordination, drowsiness, delirium, coma

White Briony. * Symptoms: diarrhoea, copious urine, also skin irritation

Woody Nightshade. ** Symptoms: vomiting, stomach pains, distressed breathing, hot flushes and exhaustion

Yew Tree. *** Symptoms: vomiting, stomach pains, fever, drowsiness, stiffness and often death

Snakes

There are only three kinds of snake found in Great Britain, the Adder and the Grass Snake, both of which hibernate in the winter, and the very rare Smooth Snake. The Slow Worm is also regarded as a snake because of its appearance but it is actually a lizard and quite harmless as is the Smooth Snake. It is very unlikely you will come across any snakes in the British countryside, mainly because they are more scared of you than you are of them and will try to get away rather than attack.

Adders, which are the only poisonous snake in Great Britain, are mostly seen in spring and have a dark zigzag line down their backs. They grow to about 24 ins (60 cms). Females are usually duller and browner than males. Adders live in any dry place and prefer sandy heathlands and rough commons.

Grass Snakes live in damp grass and near slow moving water. No markings. Can grow up to 42 ins (106 cms) making them the largest snake in the British Isles but they are quite harmless.

If you are in an area where snakes are likely, keep to the paths and wear boots. The feet are the commonest target of snake strike.

Snakes are relatively timid and only attack when startled or cornered. The Adder will usually hurry away before you reach it. If you see a snake stay about 20 ft (six metres) away. If you do get bitten, clean the wound and get it bandaged. Keep the injured limb held low. The bite will only make you feel nauseous.

Weever Fish

Lives on sandy sea beds and whilst it only grows to about 2 ins (5 cms), it has poison glands on its dorsal fin and gill cover that can give a painful sting. Generally, the fish lies hidden in the sand during day coming out to feed at night.

20　Herbal Remedies

Preparation of Herbal Remedies

Herbs used for medicinal treatment are usually safe but there are pre-cautions that should be taken.

1　Only treat minor ailments – if you are unsure, see a doctor
2　Make sure you have identified the plant correctly
3　If it is a new remedy to you, try to cross-check before using
4　Do not use the same herb over a long period. Change to another herb after a while
5　Certain conditions – such as pregnancy – may mean that an appro-priate herb becomes unsafe

The quality of herbs varies, so exact doses cannot be given.

An *infusion* is the commonest way to administer. Use 1 tsp of dried herb leaf or flower to a cup of boiling water. For roots and seeds, a *decoction* is made by simmering them for about twenty minutes in water.

Tinctures are herbs which have been steeped in alcohol – cheap white wine is suitable. Use one part herbs to four to five parts wine and leave to steep for two weeks before straining.

A *compress* is a bandage soaked in an infusion or decoction and applied to sprains and inflammation. A *poultice* is a paste made up of dried or fresh materials mixed with hot water and flour or bran to form a paste. Spread the paste between thin lengths of gauze and apply to affected area.

Macerations are plants put into water, oil or vinegar and sometimes wine and left to steep for anything up to three weeks.

Oils are used for massaging and made by steeping herbs in oil. Almond is the best but vegetable oil can be used.

Ointments can be made by infusing herbs in melted lanolin.

Gathering and Drying Herbs

Leaf and stem. Gather before 9 a.m. before the sun is high but after the dew has dried. Hang upside down in dry, dark, warm space with good ventilation. Check daily to see they are not going mouldy. Throw away any parts which are mouldy.

Seeds. Pick when ripe (usually when brown and shrivelled) but before they fall. When seed pod develops, you can tie a paper bag around the pod so the seeds fall into the bag. Put seeds near hot water heater to dry.

Roots. Pull up entire plant at end of growing season. Wash and break root into small pieces. Dry on a screen keeping root pieces separate. Turn the roots so they dry evenly.

Bark. Peel in vertical strips, without encircling the tree because the tree will die if you do. Pick in autumn before tree becomes dormant or in spring before sap starts to rise. Strips can be hung up to dry.

Flowers. Pick daily when open after the dew has dried but before sun is hot. Lay out on a screen to dry.

To Extract Essential Oil

Pound one cupped handful of leaves in a pestle and mortar until it is a green mulch. Scrape into a large preserving jar and cover with 18 fl. oz (500 ml) of any vegetable oil. Sweet almond oil yields best results but corn oil and ground nut oil are cheaper. Add one tablespoon cider vinegar. Close tightly or, if using a preserving jar, vacuum seal. Make sure jar is only about three-quarters full so jar can be shaken. Once sealed, put outside in strong sunlight. Shake the jar whenever you pass. In about a month the oil should be ready for straining through a nylon sieve. Mash the herbs well into the sieve to extract every last ounce of oil. Strain and re-bottle in a clear dark jar once it smells strong enough. Test smell by dabbing on pulse spots. If not strong enough, add fresh herbs to strained liquid and start again.

Several remedies are given to treat each problem because all the plants may not be available to you, either because of where you are or the time of year, and different plants work better for different people. Some of the remedies can be used instantly, others require days or even weeks to prepare. Your circumstances will dictate what you can use. Some of the remedies can be stored or the herbs carried with you after drying. If you do this, label the plant clearly with what it is and don't keep longer than a year. Gather fresh supplies when available and discard old stock. It is not necessary to gather huge stocks of any remedy, unless you know you are going to need it.

For a standard dose, use 1–1½ oz (25–35 g) of plant material to 20–25 fl. oz (560–700 ml) water. Take a cupful three times a day. If you need to sweeten the mixture use honey. Remember many herb remedies are slow to work.

If you have trouble taking an unpleasant tasting herb, pound the herb well and mix with cornflour and honey. Roll the paste into pellets which will be easy to swallow.

Remedies

Anaemia

Nettle soup can be used to treat anaemia. It is also mildly laxative. Gather half a pound of young nettle tops, 2 oz (50 g) butter, 1½ pts (850 ml) milk, salt and pepper. Melt the butter in a pan, add the nettles and stew gently for about ten minutes. Add milk, bring to boil and simmer for further ten minutes. Allow the soup to cool slightly then purée in blender.

Appetite and Digestive Problems

A tea made of watercress restores appetite and is believed to purify the blood. Pour ¼ pint water (150 ml) over a handful of watercress and allow to stand for a few minutes before straining.

Wormwood in small quantities acts as a tonic. *In excess it can damage the heart and induce hallucinations.*

Hyssop tea and peppermint tea, made with leaves or flowers, will encourage poor appetite.

Chewing raw fennel leaves reduces appetite.

A digestive tonic can be made by adding a handful of basil leaves to a bottle of medium dry white wine. Tastes like a very herbal vermouth.

Tea made from dandelion leaves cleanses the blood and aids digestion. Drink two cups of strong tea daily.

Small quantities of tansy flowering stems, either fresh or dried, aids digestion. *Do not take in excess and should not be used by expectant mothers.*

Fennel tea soothes an upset stomach and aids digestion. Use 1 teaspoon of dried or two teaspoons of fresh feathery leaves to a cup of boiling water. Leave to stand for ten minutes.

Asthma

Elecampane roots can be candied and eaten to ease coughing and asthma.

Thornapple has narcotic properties (datura). The leaves can be blended into a suitable mixture which can be ignited to make a vapour to relieve asthma.

Make an infusion of thyme with a few fresh leaves to a cupful of boiling water. Leave to stand for ten minutes then drink to relieve asthma.

Angelica tea, elder tea and chamomile tea, all made as thyme tea, can also be used.

Bad Breath

Chew fresh parsley to remove bad breath. Especially good after eating garlic.

Bleeding

A decoction of the root of salad burnet stops bleeding as does a pad of moss or lady's bedstraw or fresh yarrow leaves.

Garlic taken regularly reduces cholesterol and encourages blood to clot if you cut yourself.

Roman soldiers used goldenrod to staunch bleeding.

Bruises, Wounds, Sores and Cuts

Comfrey roots and leaves have an important healing effect on damaged tissues, cuts, bruises and strains. Use a poultice or compress or an oil if the wound is not open. Comfrey root lifted in the spring and grated can be used as a modern plaster. The mash will set hard enough to hold broken bones in place.

Arnica ointment relieves bruising as does a comfrey compress.

Promote healing with cabbage leaves – the greener the better. Smear the area with a crushed cabbage leaf. Leave as long as is practical (even a few minutes helps) and then rinse away. Then regularly treat the area with a cabbage compress. Put a handful of chopped cabbage leaves between two pieces of damp, hot muslin or gauze and press it on to the wound.

Marigold ointment for scratches, grazes, etc. 3 oz (75 g) dried marigold flowers, 1½ pts (850 ml) boiling water, lanolin. Make a balm by infusing dried flowers in boiling water for about one hour. Then strain the liquid through clean muslin and squeeze out as much moisture as possible. Mix one part of strained infusion to 4 parts lanolin. Keep cool. Use liberally on arms and legs.

Marigolds also help stop bleeding and are mildly antiseptic and therefore are good for cuts. They will also reduce skin inflammation. Use the flowers to make a poultice, compress, oil or ointment.

Take a large basal leaf from an aloe vera (house plant) and peel away the outer green rind to reveal the shiny clear gel. Apply this gel to a sore or burn. Alternatively, cut two ins (5 cms) off a leaf to reveal gel and apply the cut side to injury. Aloe provides a protective covering and aids immediate healing. Because it works so quickly the sore must be absolutely clean before the gel is applied. *Do not use greenish brown juice from rind as this will irritate the wound.*

Bruising around the eyes can be treated with hyssop. Crush a handful of fresh leaves into a clean handkerchief. Dip quickly into boiling water and apply locally, as hot as can be tolerated. Repeat until swelling subsides.

Honey can be used as an anaesthetic for small sores and wounds.

Thyme can be used as a disinfectant for washing wounds.

Burns

Marigold and egg white will soothe and prevent scarring. Immediately after burning area, moisten a clean linen cloth with egg white and dab on to burn. Then to prevent scarring in the following days, make an infusion with marigolds and dab it on to the wound with cotton wool. Pour 1 pt (560 ml) boiling water on 1 oz (25 g) of marigold flower petals and cool before straining and using to bathe area.

Honey eases pain from burns.

Cold compresses of chamomile or just cold water will bring relief from burns.

St Johns Wort used as a poultice between gauze quickly eases pain of burns and cuts.

Catarrh, Bronchitis, Asthma, Sinusitis

The flowering root of catmint, fresh or dried, can be used to make a tea to relieve colds, catarrh and bronchitis.

Menthol can be extracted from mint leaves during June to August. Just pour 1 pt (560 ml) of boiling water over 1 oz (25 g) dried mint or six fresh leaves. Leave to brew for fifteen minutes before inhaling vapour.

Garlic and onion make an expectorant for catarrh on the chest. Make a syrup by cutting an onion and some garlic cloves into slices and sprinkling with sugar. Leave overnight and take 2 tsp of syrup three times a day. Prepare fresh syrup each morning and evening. Take for about a week.

Marjoram was once used as an ingredient in sneezing powder.

Mix three crushed cloves of garlic with a tsp of cider vinegar. Add 1 pt (560 ml) boiling water. Cover head and jug with a towel and inhale for ten minutes.

Bergamot vapour helps to relieve bronchial catarrh and throat infections. Pour boiling water on to a large handful of leaves in a bowl and inhale vapour.

Crush a clove of garlic and mix with a dessertspoon of honey and cup of hot water. Drink three times a day.

Circulation Problems

Horseradish increases blood flow to counteract the feeling of chill in illness and is good for poor circulation and chilblains. Use the fresh root only in the amounts you can eat, as horseradish sauce or as a tincture of the fresh root in vodka. *Do not make a tea or decoction or use in cases of stomach ulcers or high blood pressure.*

A strong cup of thyme tea in the morning gives the circulation a boost.

Hawthorn tea encourages good circulation in cold weather. Put a heaped tsp of hawthorn leaves and blossoms in a cup. Pour hot water over it and leave it to stand for 1–2 minutes before straining off. Sip two cups a day.

Garlic increases blood flow; good for varicose veins. Also lowers the blood pressure and the level of cholesterol in the blood, so it is helpful to those with high blood pressure. Dose is anything up to three cloves a day.

Colds, Fevers and Influenza

Fresh or dried flowering pennyroyal plant is used for treating colds when used as infusion. *Do not use where kidney disease is present or for pregnant women.*

Elderflower reduces fever; good when chestiness is also a problem as it will help relieve congestion. Use normal strength tea as required – very safe.

Marigold tea made with petals raises temperature and induces sweating.

Dried leaves, stems and flowers of yarrow made into an infusion to reduce temperatures is especially good for fever and stomach problems as it has a calming effect. *Large doses of yarrow however induce headaches and giddiness. Use with caution in pregnancy.*

A sponge can be improvised with a ball of grass dipped in tepid water to bathe away sweat caused by fever.

Borage tea reduces temperatures.

Angelica tea, lime flower tea, agrimony tea, sage tea and rosemary tea, all help fight colds and coughs.

A tisane made of the light-pink blossoms of mallow helps coughs and colds.

At the first shiver, brew up some elderflower, peppermint leaf and yarrow flower tea. Add one tsp of each to half a pint (280 ml) boiling water. Cover and infuse for 20 minutes. Drink a warm glass at bedtime, spiked with cinnamon, ginger or cayenne pepper and sweetened with honey. Drink plenty of water. *Large doses of yarrow cause headaches and giddiness.*

Cold Sores

A strong infusion of cornflower petals patted on cold sores will help them heal.

Coughs

Thyme will counteract infections of throat and lungs and also calm the muscles there – particularly good for a dry cough and for asthma. Add a few leaves to a cupful of boiling water. Leave to stand for ten minutes, then strain, store and use as necessary. Use normal strength tea or gargle three or four times a day.

An infusion of borage leaves relieves coughs.

Make garlic honey as cough syrup. Peel garlic cloves and put into jar. Add honey a little at a time over a couple of days until the jar is full. Set in a warm place for two weeks to a month until garlic has turned opaque. Add honey slowly to jar to give honey time to fill all the spaces. The honey will become liquid and the garlic limp and tasteless. Take a teaspoonful of strained liquid every couple of hours or whenever necessary. Dilute with water for children.

Sage tea relieves coughs.

Mullein will clear the lungs by stimulating a cough but because it contains mucilage, it will also relieve any soreness. The flowers are more effective than the leaves. Use normal strength tea as required.

Marshmallow milk is used for relief of hoarse coughing and inflammation of the mouth, pharynx and stomach. 1 oz (25 g) grated marshmallow root, 1 pt (560 ml) milk, 1–2 tbs honey. Put all ingredients in a saucepan and bring slowly to boil. Then simmer gently for thirty to forty-five minutes. Take one tablespoon three times a day for hoarse coughs and for relief of gastric ulcers.

Elecampane root can be candied and eaten to relieve coughs.

A decoction made with linseed seeds can be used to ease coughs.

Cystitis and Urinary Infections

Crush a clove of garlic and mix with small carton of natural yoghurt. Eat one carton every morning and evening.

Madder root is used as a diuretic and is of help with kidney troubles.

Borage is diuretic. A syrup can be made to help kidney and bladder inflammation. Puree ½ lb (225 g) of fresh flower plant, strain through muslin cloth and make into cordial with 1 cup of white sugar. Take one tbsp every day.

Parsley eaten fresh helps ease water retention.

Goldenrod made into an infusion and taken three times a day before meals helps treat cystitis as does an infusion of blackcurrant leaves.

Dandelion tea is beneficial for kidney and liver problems.

Elder tea is of value for treating cystitis.

Diabetes

Sweet cicely leaves can be used by diabetics to replace sugar.

Ear Ache

Pierce a garlic oil capsule with a sterilized needle and squeeze the oil into a teaspoon warmed under a hot tap until the oil is warmed; after checking temperature, drop warmed oil into ear. Plug ear with cotton wool.

Emetic (To Cause Vomiting)

A tablespoon of ground mustard seed in lukewarm water will cause vomiting.

Eye Problems

Compresses made from fennel infusion soothe tired eyes.

Pour a little witch hazel on to a cotton wool pad and dab it round the eyes to reduce redness and swelling.

Hyssop can be used to treat bruising round the eyes. Crush a handful of fresh leaves into a clean handkerchief. Dip quickly into boiling water and apply locally, as hot as can be tolerated. Repeat until swelling subsides.

An eye lotion to remove grit from eyes is made by soaking some clary seeds in clean warm water until they swell. Carefully introduce into the corner of the eye on a cotton bud. Particles of grit will adhere to the seeds and come away. The strained liquid makes an eye lotion.

An eye compress for cleaning and soothing tired inflamed eyes can be made by infusing 1 tbsp of chopped vervain leaves in ¼ pt (150 ml) boiling water. Allow to cool and strain into a screw top bottle. Soak cottonwool pads with the infusion and place over each eyelid. Leave for ten minutes before repeating the process. Finally clean eyes with fresh cold water and pat dry.

An eye wash can be made with ¼ oz (5 g) rue to 1 pt (560 ml) water to make a tea. This tea is then diluted to parts 1 to 10 with sterile water and used externally in eye bath. *Not used much now and never by expectant mothers.*

Marigold ointment (see cuts) can be used externally to treat conjunctivitis.

For tired, itchy eyes, use cold, used tea bags, either ordinary tea or chamomile, as compresses.

Fainting

Oil of lavender will relieve someone feeling faint.

If you feel giddy, lie down with your knees bent and head to one side, then if you do pass out, you will not come to any harm. For a slight feeling of faintness, sit with your head on or between your knees.

Foot Problems and Athletes Foot

Tired feet can be eased by soaking in an infusion of marigold flowers.

Roman soldiers used to line their boots with silverweed to give a cool lining to ease aching feet.

Honey smeared on the feet helps ease athletes foot.

A tea made from a few leaves of thyme in boiling water, which is left to soak for ten minutes before cooling, makes a good wash to ease athletes foot. Can be stored in a jar. Red clover can also be used in place of thyme.

Hangover

Borage leaves added to hot water and inhaled are a hangover cure. Can even be drunk if desperate.

Sip a glass of warm water with lemon juice or drink hot peppermint tea or take three to four capsules of oil of evening primrose.

Hayfever

Drink an infusion of thyme, marjoram, hyssop or lavender, sweetened with honey to soothe the irritated mucous membranes in your nose. For streaming eyes, use compresses of witch hazel.

Headaches

These often start out as digestive problems; if so, sip hot water with the juice of a lemon added.

For headaches caused by nerves or tension, a few drops of oil of lavender massaged into temples will help.

For severe headaches, drink an infusion of lime or chamomile flowers, or suck a sugar cube with two or three drops of oil of lavender rubbed in.

Elizabethans used to chew tarragon root to relieve headaches.

Oil of basil applied to the temples relieves migraine.

Use an infusion of pennyroyal, either fresh or dried for treating headaches. *Do not use where kidney disease is present or when pregnant.*

Thyme mixed with rosemary in a tea relieves headaches.

Rosemary tea, lime flower tea or marjoram tea are remedies for nervous headaches, or try inhaling rosemary oil.

Meadowsweet can be used as a painkiller to support another herbal remedy.

Feverfew used as meadowsweet for headaches in particular and may be more effective for some people than others. Use normal strength tea, made with fresh or dried flowers or leaves, one or two cups a day or two small leaves in a sandwich. Believed to relieve migraine as well.

Heat Stroke

When suffering from heatstroke, lie down in a cool place. Bathe yourself with water. Sip cool water slowly. Don't gulp down cold water. If you've been sweating a lot, you will have lost salt. Add some salt to water and drink it – not too much or you will be sick. Take salt tablets or some salty food.

Indigestion, Sickness, Constipation, Diarrhoea and Stomach Upsets

Chamomile has a calming effect on the digestive system, thus is particularly good for nervous indigestion. Use normal strength tea made of flowers, as required – a very safe remedy.

Fresh caraway leaves, roots and seeds have digestive properties and are used to relieve colic, griping and flatulence.

Meadowsweet counteracts stomach acidity, moderates diarrhoea and has a soothing action. Use normal strength as required.

Peppermint is an immediate comfort for all stomach pains and nausea. Use normal strength tea as required, leaving it to brew for fifteen minutes, but do not use continuously for long periods.

Fennel tea is a mild laxative and diuretic.

Crush one clove of garlic into a cup of warm milk and drink the mixture after meals.

An infusion of coriander or lemon verbena can be used as a digestive for colic, griping and flatulence.

Fresh basil leaf is antiseptic and mildly sedative and used for stomach ache and sickness.

Tea made from bergamot relieves stomach troubles, nausea and vomiting. 2½ cups of boiling water to 1¾ cups of leaves. Mildly relaxing.

Dandelion tea is a mild laxative and diuretic.

Fenugreek water is useful for treating dyspepsia and diarrhoea. Simmer 1 oz (25 g) seeds in 1 pt (560 ml) water in a covered pan for fifteen minutes. Allow to cool and drink a wineglass full. Also helps flatulence.

The dried leaves, stem and flowers of yarrow are used as infusion to help relieve dysentery and diarrhoea.

Hops have a relaxing effect on the digestive system and their bitterness stimulates the appetite. Use normal strength tea, one cup twice a day but *do not use for long periods or in cases of depression*.

Pennyroyal can be made into an infusion to treat nausea and flatulence. *Should not be used where kidney disease present or when pregnant*.

Fennel and dill are carminatives, particularly good for indigestion and colic (they are the basis of gripe water used for babies). Use the seeds to make a normal strength decoction and take one tablespoon three times a day. *Do not use stronger doses and avoid during pregnancy*.

Sage, garlic and thyme have an antibiotic effect when an infection is the cause of the trouble.

Insect Repellent

Rub bruised elder leaves on skin to keep flies away.

Essential oil of thyme mixed with essential oil of lavender repels insects.

Any of the following can be used as insect repellents: cotton lavender, pennyroyal, southernwood, feverfew, oil of lavender, marjoram, growing basil, tansy and fresh nettle leaves.

Marjoram, mint or mugwort, stood in a vase or hung from a door frame repels insects.

Pennyroyal is a flea repellent.

Insect Stings

To relieve stings or small cuts, wash a handful of plantain leaves, then crush with pestle and mortar or a rolling pin and board. Apply the pulp to the affected area and leave for several minutes. Leaves are best picked when in flower.

Use a cabbage leaf to rub over insect bites and stings. Acts in the same way as a dock leaf for nettle stings.

Use a compress of ice-cold witch hazel (keep bottle in fridge or running water) or cool marigold lotion. Otherwise apply neat oil of eucalyptus or oil of lavender.

Use infusion of pennyroyal or lemon balm to relieve insect stings.

Apply witch hazel to relieve insect bits, or rub in some crushed parsley leaves.

Insomnia

Make an infusion of chamomile flowers, hops or catnip and drink it hot at bedtime. Catnip is especially good if you can't sleep because of emotional problems.

Woodruff made into a herb pillow helps insomnia.

Lemon balm is one of the best relaxing and tranquillizing herbs and one that is very safe. Use normal strength tea as required.

Flowering tips of catmint, fresh or dried, made into tea makes a soothing drink to relieve sleeplessness, stress and irritability.

Thyme tea taken at night is said to prevent nightmares.

Sage tea, chamomile tea or hop tea are beneficial for nerves and sleeplessness.

Valerian dried rootstock is a sedative and tranquillizer for a variety of nervous troubles and for insomnia. *Should not be taken over a long period.*

Tea made with pale green lime flowers is a remedy for insomnia, tension headaches and exhaustion.

Inhaling oil of basil helps insomnia sufferers to sleep.

Laxatives

Dandelion tea is a mild laxative.

Leeches and Ticks

These are picked up around marshes. Dogs also pick up sheep ticks from pastures. They cling on to their victims with their mouths and if pulled away sharply, the head remains and sets up an infection. If you put a lighted match or cigarette to them they will let go. Bathe area with antiseptic.

Mouth Ulcers

Rose honey is used to treat mouth ulcers.

Chamomile tea can be used as a gargle for mouth ulcers.

Cut a clove of garlic in half and squeeze the cut end and apply to ulcer.

Nose Bleeds

Hold head back, apply an ice-cold compress to back of the neck and pinch nostrils gently together. After a few minutes plug the nostrils with cotton wool, soaked in either lemon juice or witch hazel.

Powdered nettle leaf used as snuff stops nose bleeds.

Pregnancy and Menstrual Problems

Raspberry leaves ease period pains. Good to take during pregnancy as well. Two small cups a day of normal strength tea is the dose.

Lady's Mantle may help any menstrual disorders. Use normal strength tea twice a day.

Fennel stimulates menstrual flow.

Chamomile tea helps ease painful periods.

Fresh borage leaves eaten in a salad will increase milk flow in nursing mothers.

Rheumatism

A compress or poultice of lavender oil or a hot compress of marjoram will ease rheumatism.

Soften a handful of fresh or dried mint leaves with warm water and apply as a poultice to relieve rheumatism in joints and muscular pain.

Angelica tea, elder tea, chive tea, dandelion tea made with fresh flowers or nettle tea made with either young green leaves or dried nettles are all beneficial for rheumatism.

Take a couple of large cabbage leaves. Place between two pieces of hot muslin and apply to sore areas for as long as possible, twice daily.

Sedatives

Lemon verbena in an infusion is a mild sedative, as is fresh basil leaf. Dill seeds are mildly sedative. Cowslip flowers can also be boiled to make a mildly sedative tea.

Valerian dried rootstock is a sedative and tranquillizer for a variety of nervous conditions and for insomnia. *Should not be taken over a long period*.

Vervain flowering plant, either fresh or dried, can be used for nervous exhaustion and depression.

Skin Problems

An infusion of vervain or flowering honeysuckle can be used to bathe skin infections.

Heartsease (or pansy) and parsley are internal cleansing herbs particularly useful for skin complaints that are caused by toxins in the body. Use normal strength tea as required.

Reduce inflammation with a violet poultice. Pour ¼ pt (150 ml) of boiling water over 2 oz (50 g) fresh violet flowers or leaves. Leave to infuse for a few hours then dab on to the inflamed area.

Soften skin with comfrey. Add a teaspoon of comfrey to hand cream or Vaseline and rub into sore skin.

For sore, dry skin and chilblains, break up 6 flower heads of marigolds and stir into 4 oz (100 g) of melted petroleum jelly. Simmer on low heat for two hours and strain into a jar. Cool before use.

Fenugreek seeds can be used as a poultice for skin inflammations.

An infusion made by steeping 2 oz (50 g) dried clary leaves in 1 pt (560 ml) vinegar for two weeks can be used as a compress to treat boils.

Chamomile oil can be used to soothe allergic skin rashes. Made by tightly packing flower heads into a preserving jar, covering with olive oil and leaving in the sun for three weeks. The oil can be used after decanting and straining.

Dab the white juice of a dandelion stem on any hard to heal spots.

Take a couple of fresh, large cabbage leaves. Place between two pieces of hot muslin and apply to sore areas for as long as possible, twice daily.

Grind mustard seeds to a flour to make a poultice for chilblains.

Cook cabbage in milk and, when cool, apply as compress to blisters.

Garlic honey (see coughs) can be used for external application to treat acne and herpes.

For athletes foot, boils, ulcers and other skin infections, cover the surrounding area with Vaseline and crush a clove of garlic on to a square of sterile gauze. Place on the infected area and leave for fifteen minutes. Apply four times daily.

Sore Throat

Sage acts as a disinfectant in the mouth and throat and reduces catarrh. Use half normal strength, ½ oz (10 g) leaves to 1 pt (560 ml) water as a tea or gargle two or three times a day.

Rose honey is used to treat sore throats.

Blackberry leaves soothe and heal mouth ulcers, bleeding gums and sore throats. Normal strength decoction as a drink or gargle when required.

Gargle with a strong infusion of thyme, sage, flowering tops or leaves of hyssop or clary leaves. Add a little vinegar for extra help.

An infusion of marjoram, leaves or flower of lovage or lime flowers will relieve a sore throat.

211

To relieve a sore throat use syrup of honeysuckle. Made with 3 oz (75 g) fresh honeysuckle petals, ½ pt (280 ml) boiling water and 4 oz (100 g) sugar. Lightly crush honeysuckle petals before pouring boiling water over them. Leave to cool then strain liquid into a pan. Add sugar and slowly bring to boil. Leave to simmer gently until mixture syrupy. Cool, then pour into bottles and seal.

Splinters and Thorns

A long thorn can be used to probe for splinters. Make sure it is from an edible bush and sterilize first by holding in a flame or soaking in salt water.

Strains, Sprains and Sore Muscles

Make a compress with witch hazel, oil of lavender, comfrey leaf tea, bay leaves or marjoram to relieve the pain from a strain.

Arnica ointment brings relief to strains.

Take a couple of large cabbage leaves. Place between two pieces of hot muslin and apply to the sore areas for as long as possible, twice daily.

Make a peppermint tea with a pint (560 ml) of boiling water and 1 oz (25 g) dried mint or six fresh mint leaves. Leave to infuse for three hours. Add to bath water to relieve sore muscles.

Oil of wintergreen is used for liniment.

Sunburn

Boil a handful of plantain leaves in ¼ pint (150 ml) milk for five minutes. When cool, dab over skin to relieve sun or wind burn.

For mild sunburn, bathe in witch hazel. Use an infusion of chamomile tea as a compress. If you have capsules of vitamin E, burst these and squeeze on to burnt area.

Make an infusion of salad burnet leaves with 1 pint (560 ml) boiling water to a handful of slightly bruised leaves. Cover bowl and leave to stand for ten minutes. Strain and cool. Soak gauze in liquid and apply to sunburn until relief felt.

Toothache

A dab of oil of cloves will ease toothache because it acts as a local anaesthetic, although it doesn't taste very pleasant. Alternatively, chew a clove.

Chewing peppermint leaves eases toothache and whitens teeth.

Sage tea also helps toothache.

Oil of marjoram dabbed on sore tooth helps relieve pain.

Chamomile poultice is used to soothe toothache; chamomile tea can be used for teething babies.

Travel Sickness

5–10 drops of tincture of ginger (2–3 drops for children) in a small glass of water should put paid to this problem. Take half an hour before start of journey and carry extra mixture with you in a bottle.

Worms

Tansy flowering stems, either fresh or dried can be used to treat round-worm. *Large quantities however are harmful and it should not be used by a pregnant woman.*

Southernwood flowers and leaves are used as treatment for worms. Mix with treacle for children.

Toiletries

After sun lotion

Any of the following can be used: gin, cold tea, milk, cider vinegar, liquidized cucumber.

Antiseptic

Garlic juice. Chamomile. Rosemary oil. Savory leaves fresh or dried and dried flowers. Lavender oil. Lovage. Madder. Marjoram. Fresh basil leaf. Thyme. Peppermint. Southernwood.

Burning bay leaves purify air.

Clary leaves in an infusion make an antiseptic skin wash.

Add salt to boiling water and use to bathe wounds or sterilize vessels.

Deodorants

Liquidize lettuce leaves and brush liquid under each arm.

Rub watercress between fingers and then under your arms to diminish odour.

Dilute two tbsp of apple cider vinegar in ¼ pt (150 ml) distilled water. Soak cotton wool in solution and dab under each arm.

Three drops of lavender oil in ½ pint (280 ml) distilled water. Apply with cotton wool pads.

Mouthwash

Infusion of chamomile used as mouthwash for sore gums.

Peppermint, marjoram or thyme infused in boiling water, cooled and strained.

Gargle with 1 tsp vinegar to 8 tsp water.

Strong tea of thyme or sage – both natural disinfectants, swished through mouth night and morning will relieve mouth infections.

Shampoo

An infusion of red clover can be used as a wash for an itchy scalp.

Pour a pt (560 ml) of boiling water over 2 tbsp chamomile flowers and 2 tbsp soapwort. Leave for half an hour, then strain and massage into hair. Rinse out thoroughly. Soapwort produces natural lather.

Dandruff treatment. Use a decoction of sage (3½ oz (100 g) to 1¾ pt (1 l) water) rubbed into hair.

Soap

Soapwort root produces really soapy lather. Simply chop 1 oz (25 g) of root and boil in 1½ pts (850 ml) water. Simmer for half an hour, strain when cool. It can be kept in the fridge.

Toothpaste

Use salt or rub a couple of sage leaves over the teeth.

Chew a twig of wood, oak is good, until it is fibrous.

Rat Deterrent

Catmint strewn around or hung up is a rat deterrent.

21   Hunting

Traps and Snares

Anything that swims, crawls, runs, jumps or flies, is a possible source of food and prey will always leave signs of their presence, either as tracks, droppings, or noise, etc.

It is not easy to catch game. Only practice, patience and perseverance will feed you and you must be prepared for the fact that there are going to be days when you will go hungry.

Baited Snare

As game eats the bait, it loosens the trigger and sets off the snare (Fig. 84).

Duck Snare

Fishing for duck is very simple. Fasten a line to a sharp peg and then wrap it with bread and throw to the duck. When the duck swallows the bread, pull the line. The peg gets caught in the duck's gullet and you can reel the duck in.

Spring Snare

When the game runs through this snare, it sets off the trigger.

All snares must be checked regularly to avoid causing unnecessary suffering.

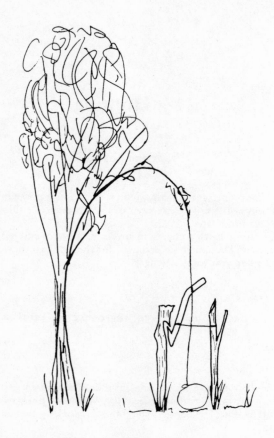

Fig. 83 Spring snare

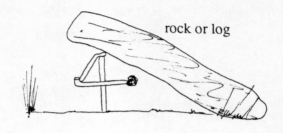

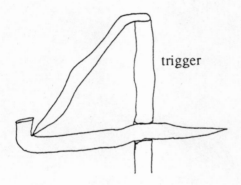

Fig. 84 Trigger snare

Nets

Nets can also be used to catch rabbits. Wait until they are in the field feeding and then cover the nearest entrance to the burrow with netting. Go to the other side of the rabbits from the warren and make a noise. The rabbits will run to the warren and get caught in the net. The nets can either be similar to those used in fishing, i.e. drift-type net, or you can make a larger version of a child's fishing net by attaching the mesh to a briar handle.

Fig. 85 Traps (1)

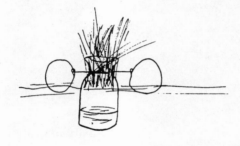

Fig. 86 Traps (2)

Where to Set Traps

Animals are elusive and very wary, which makes hunting no easy task. However they often leave indications of their presence by leaving tracks or signs of where they were feeding in crops, etc.

Ring Barking

Ring barking is a common name given to the action of animals on trees. Look for trees that have been stripped of bark around the base, especially young saplings. Rabbits often leave teeth marks in the bark. Deer tend to tear the bark from the trees with an upward movement when food is in short supply. The tears tend to be long, about 3–4 ft (91–122 cms) up the trunk of a tree. Squirrels often eat bark as they try to get to the sap. Bare areas in the trees, which can often be seen from the ground, are usually caused by squirrels. These areas are mainly found at the junction where a branch protrudes from the trunk, where the squirrel can sit quite at ease, whilst gnawing away at the bark. Badgers scratch the base of trees in order to clean their claws. Often muddy areas are left round the base of the tree by the badger and mud will be embedded in the scratches. These marks often indicate that the sett is nearby.

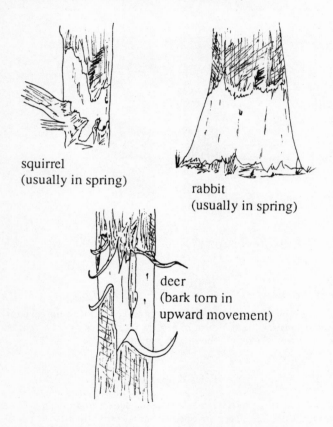

squirrel
(usually in spring)

rabbit
(usually in spring)

deer
(bark torn in
upward movement)

Fig. 87 Ring barking

Signs like these are often used by the hunter when setting traps and snares. Rabbit runs and diggings seen in bankings, all indicate to the hunter that food is nearby.

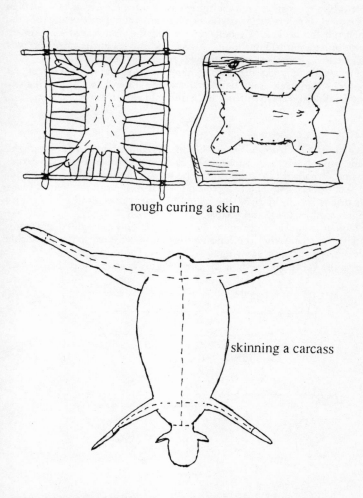

rough curing a skin

skinning a carcass

Fig. 88 Curing a hide and skinning a carcass

Skinning Game

Hang the dead animal upside down and allow it to bleed by cutting the throat. This does not need to be done with small game.

It is best to skin the animal immediately after the kill as this is when it is easiest. It is less messy if you skin the animal before gutting. Slit the skin from the neck to the belly, cut round the crutch and slit skin on inside of leg joint to knee joint. Cut around the leg at the knee and peel the skin away from the rear until you reach the neck.

For small game like rabbits and hares, remove the head and feet, slit from crutch to neck. Slide hand in between skin and coat and pull away from back legs. Peel skin from back and pull skin from front legs.

Rough Curing

Wash skin and clean away any blood, fat and scraps of fat from the inside using fine gravel, sand or the back of a knife. Stretch skin across a frame or nail or pin the skin to a board and leave it in the open with the skin uppermost. The longer you leave it in the sun the better. Once it is dried, lay the skin on the ground or on a tree and beat it with a branch until it is soft and pliable.

If you scrape it thoroughly and leave it long enough to dry completely, the smell from the hide will lessen. Always wear the fur inside unless it is raining or snowing.

A more thorough method for curing skins is given on p. 154.

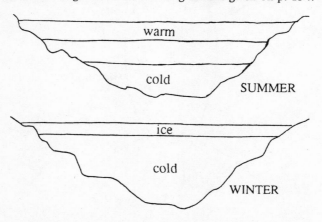

Fig. 89 Water temperatures

Fishing

In summer a lake or pond is warmest at the top and coolest at the bottom. Fish seek the temperature and feeding conditions that suit them best. In winter the surface may be iced over. Temperature stratification disappears and the location of the fish is less predictable. Cold makes fish less active.

Fig. 90 Fishing traps

Fishing through Ice

In a severe winter you may have to try ice fishing. Local people will usually provide helpful information about the best spots to try from and will also warn you of any hazardous places. But, even with the best of advice, every ice fisherman needs to stay on the alert against thin spots in the ice. If there is nobody to ask, check the thickness of the ice by throwing stones on to the ice in front of you before actually going on to the ice yourself. If you leave the stones there, they will mark a safe pathway back. It is unsafe to be on a lake alone. Make sure the second man has the rope and never let children go ice fishing alone.

Fig. 91 Fishing through ice

Equipment is simple and inexpensive. The first requisite is a chisel or similar tool to cut holes in the ice. This is extended into a 'spud', which is a pole with a chisel attached firmly to one end. A skimmer is also needed to scoop out bits of floating ice. To carry the bait, you will need a bucket of some description. A sledge is useful for carrying the gear, which should include several fishing lines and a vacuum flask of something hot to drink. The sledge will also serve as a place to sit and to which a windbreak can be fixed.

An easy way to find a good fishing spot is to use a hole left by someone else, even if it is slightly blocked. It is easier to clear out ice than to open a new hole.

Bait should be changed frequently – mealworms, grubs and minnows are good bait. Where the water is deep, try using a small shiny spoon as a weighted lure.

Fishing Techniques

Fishing spears
Remember that fishing spears must be made from very strong, supple

224

wood because of the type of use they are put to. They must also be very sharply pointed, with either a flint tip or the wooden point fire hardened.

There is an art to spear fishing. Most people presume that a fishing spear is thrown – it is not, it should be poked or thrust at the target. It would be better if a barb was carved on to the shaft near the point. In shallow water, a barb is not necessarily needed if you can pin the fish to the river bed.

Spear fishing is best done at night with a torch. Fish are attracted to the light or the use of a mirror on a river bed. The mirror reflects the moonlight and attracts the fish and as the fish swims over the mirror it makes an easier target.

Netting

Arrange the net to lie in the water with one end tied securely to a tree. Wait by the other end and when a group of fish swims over it lift the net clear of the water and the fish will be caught up in the mesh. Tie the end you were holding up out of the water and out of your way while you collect the fish.

Another way to use a net is as a drift net, vertical in the water. To do this you will have to attach floats to the top side. The fish will swim into the net and get caught. If your net is long enough to span the river, secure each end to a tree, and you could then leave it to fish for you.

Night Lines

Night lines are easy to use and require no real effort. This is an excellent way of fishing if you are trying to conserve your energy in a survival situation.

The bait must be securely fixed on to the hook. Worms and maggots can be picked off a hook without the fish being caught if they are not secure. Small fish or pieces of meat are the best bait for this job.

The line should be strong so that it can hold a number of fish at one time. A night line therefore can be either one line or many lines attached to one strong line if you wish.

Tickling Trout

The trout is the only fish that can be tickled with any real success. It is often found in clear running water, hiding under river banks, under rocks and under jetties and bridges.

When tickling, put hands into water quietly and smoothly, behind the fish and keep stroking up the body until you reach the gills, then grasp the fish by the gills and toss it on to the bank.

Try not to jump when you first feel the fish, because this will startle the fish and you will lose it. Remember there is nothing in British waters that can cause you any harm, other than the freshwater pike, and this fish does not hide or attack. Some fishermen claim pike just sneer at you from the middle or deeper sections of the river!

Eel Baskets

Eels can be caught in torpedo-shaped withy baskets, baited with such things as fresh chicken guts, shrimp heads or almost any meat or fish waste. A fine meshed wire cage could also be used. These baskets are sunk below the water surface and left overnight.

Gutting Fish

The secret to gutting fish is to use a really sharp knife.

1 Remove the hook and kill fish with a sharp blow just behind head
2 Cut off head behind gills
3 Cut off tail
4 Use a sharp knife to slit along belly
5 Remove internal organs carefully
6 Extend slit and open fish out flat
7 Place a finger under the base of the spine and pull upwards and the spine with bones attached will come away from the flesh

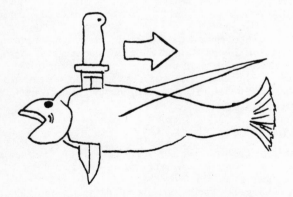

Fig. 92 Filleting a fish

226

Shooting

Safety rules for shooting are best expressed by the following poem:

A Father's Advice to his Son

If a sportsman true you'd be
Listen carefully to me
Never, never let your gun
Pointed be at anyone
That it may unloaded be
Matters not the least to me.
When a hedge or fence you cross
Though of time it cause a loss
From your gun the cartridge take
For the greater safety's sake.

If twixt you and neighbouring gun
Birds may fly or beasts may run
Let this maxim e'er be thine
Follow not across the line.

Stops and beaters oft unseen
Lurk behind some leafy screen,
Calm and steady always be
Never shoot where you can't see.

Keep your place and silent be
Game can hear and game can see.
Don't be greedy, better spared
Is a pheasant, than one shared.

You may kill or you may miss
But at all times think of this
All the pheasants ever bred
Won't repay for one man dead.

Commander Mark Beaufoy

Wildfowling

A winter sport involving long hours at dusk or dawn in all weathers. A good knowledge of the local area is required if the wildfowling is done on mud flats and saltings, etc., because ignorance of the local conditions can be dangerous with areas of quicksand or quick changing tides cutting you off.

227

Anyone may shoot along the tide line below the normal spring high water mark between 1 September and 20 February. Nevertheless the same areas are open to the public and as one is not allowed to carry a firearm in a public place, you could technically be prosecuted. However BASC (see address section in Appendix III) have arranged immunity from prosecution for members (or members of affiliated clubs) with the Crown Commissioners.

It should be borne in mind that many areas of saltmarsh and estuary around the coast are now bird sanctuaries and shooting is not allowed at all.

Wildlife

The Wildlife and Countryside Act 1981 makes it illegal to:

- Kill, injure, disturb or take away any Protected Species, such as badgers, red squirrels, etc.
- Pick or uproot Protected Plants or uproot any wild plants

The list of Specially Protected Species is long and ranges from moths right through to dolphins. Birds are divided into four groups: Pests, Sporting Birds, Specially Protected Species and Others.

The Pest species are as follows:

Collared Dove
Crow
Feral Pigeon
Herring Gull
House Sparrow
Great Black Backed Gull
Jackdaw
Jay
Lesser Black Backed Gull
Magpie
Rook
Starling
Wood Pigeon

Only the Pest Species and the Sporting Birds may be killed. All other birds are protected and it is illegal to kill, injure or possess one or to damage, destroy or steal from their nests.

Lists of Protected Birds, Animals and Plants are very long, and more details can be found in Appendix V.

Official Hunting and Fishing Open Seasons

Game

Pheasant	1 October – 31 January
Partridge	1 September – 31 January
Grouse	12 August – 10 December
Black Grouse	12 August – 10 December
	(31 August in Somerset, Devon and New Forest)
Blackgame	20 August – 10 December
Ptarmigan	12 August – 10 December
Woodcock (England & Wales)	1 October – 31 January
Woodcock (Scotland)	1 September – 31 January
Capercaillie	1 October – 31 January
Snipe	12 August – 31 January
Wildfowl (inland)	1 September – 20 February
Wildfowl (foreshore)	1 September – 20 February

Grouse, pheasant, partridge and ptarmigan must not be killed on Sundays or Christmas Day.

Deer

Red and Sika Deer	stags	1 July – 20 October
	hinds	21 October – 15 February
England and Wales		
Roe and Fallow	bucks	21 October – 30 April
	does	1 November – 28 February
Scotland		
Roe and Fallow	bucks	1 May – 20 October
	does	21 October – 28 February

It is illegal to kill any deer from one hour after sunset to one hour before sunrise on any day.

Rabbits

May be killed at any time of the year but not at night.

Hares

Hares may be killed at any time except on moorland and unfenced cultivated land. In these areas, open season is:

229

England and Wales	11 December–31 March
Scotland	1 July–31 March
Northern Ireland	12 August–31 January

Hares must not be killed at night. It is also illegal to sell hares between 1 March and 31 July.

Foxes

No legal close season, but fox hunting is regarded as 1 November to mid April.

Game Fish (Each area has minor local variations in the actual date)

England and Wales
Salmon	1 February–31 October
Brown and Sea Trout	1 March–30 September
Rainbow Trout	No close season

Scotland
Salmon	November–January
Brown Trout	15 March–6 October
Rainbow Trout	No close season

Coarse Fish

| Close Season | 15 March–15 June |

Sea Fish

No restrictions on sea fishing

22 Knots

The scouts call it pioneering, some people just call it tying knots. There are knots suitable for most occasions, e.g. timber hitch, clove hitch, even a highwayman's hitch. No one can be expected to know all of them, but, to be honest, no one is even really sure how many types of knot there are.

The most commonly used knots are:

Bowline

Used to lift and lower people in rescue situations because it won't tighten round their chest and cause crush injuries to their rib cage. To make the knot, form a loop in your left hand, very much like a figure six. Use your right hand to feed the end of the rope through the loop and around the back of the rope which is leading away from you and then back down between the loop.

A common way of remembering this is class the loop as a rabbit, out of the hole, round the tree and back to bed.

Bowline in the Bight

This is a bowline without access to the ends of the rope which is carried out in the same way as above but with a doubled over length of rope. It is often used to make lifting straps. The two loops that this knot provides are often used when a rucksack strap breaks.

Timber Hitch

Ideal for tying long logs together to build a scaffolding or for dragging materials. The Bowline in the Bight is often used with this knot when dragging. If an extra half hitch is used, the timber hitch becomes a killick hitch and makes the knot more useful.

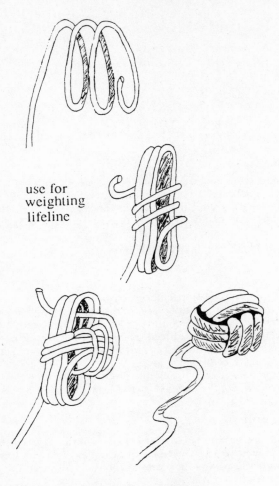

use for
weighting
lifeline

Fig. 93 Monkey's fist knot

Butterfly Knot

Also known as Alpine Butterfly Knot and used to make rope ladders.
Drape any section of rope over your hand in the form of an upside-
down U. Twist a loop into the left hand section of this length of rope as

close to the top as possible. Pull the top of this loop up behind the top
of the rope until you have a loop the size you need. Form a second loop
in the same way as the first loop making it so that it sits on top of loop
one. Pull down the top of the rope and push it through both loops
together. Pull both ends of the rope to tighten both loops. This will trap
the larger loop. Complicated to describe and make, but when making a
rope ladder, practice makes perfect as well as all the difference to a
sturdy rope!

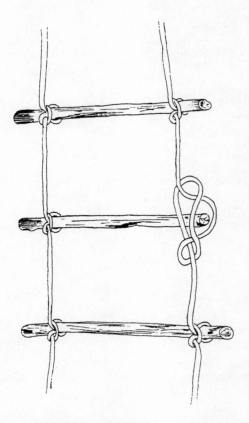

Fig. 94 Marline hitch

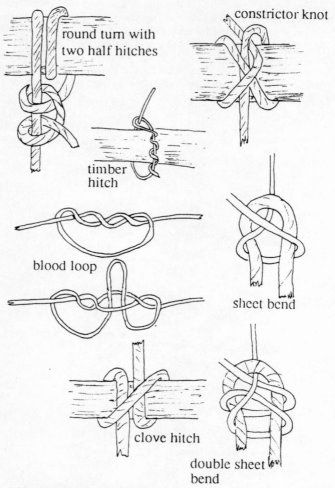

Fig. 95 Various knots

Blood Loop

Used by fishermen to attach hooks and swivel lines to fishing lines. Start with a multiple over hand knot, left over right, three times. But only in

234

one piece of line. Pull the loop through one of the twists before pulling the ends tight and trapping the loop.

Clove Hitch

One of the most basic knots with the most uses. Form two loops by folding the rope over itself twice. In the same way, place loop two behind loop one and place them together over the end of the pole.

Part Four

23   Air Crashes

With the ever increasing amount of aircraft and people flying upon these airlines around the world, one of the major causes of people finding themselves in a survival situation is undoubtedly the air crash. It is unlikely that an air crash or crash landing in Great Britain will ever tax your survival skills to the limit, because no sooner would the plane go down than the rescue services would be beating a path to the plane. If however you did find yourself lost in some desolate area after a crash landing there are many things you can do to ease the situation until the rescue services arrive.

It is standard practice that in most types of survival training, especially with the armed forces, the scenario for the survival training begins with a plane crash. A plane that has crashed or been forced to land in difficult terrain is one of the most difficult of disaster scenarios. It could actually happen anywhere and therefore a keen survivalist would undoubtedly learn about desert regions, arctic regions, tropical plants, etc., which this book does not aim to teach. Standard rescue procedure and survival procedure however, will hold you in good stead. Later chapters in this book will cover these subjects.

Airline cabin staff on most aircraft are trained for such emergencies and in the situation which occurs in a crash they would be the best people to listen to. Contrary to popular disaster films, the cabin staff are usually heavily into survival. Standard procedures inside an aircraft preparing for a crash landing are explained to passengers at the very start of the flight, i.e. tightening the seat belt, head between knees, use of oxygen masks, etc.

When the aircraft finally stops moving, it should be evacuated as would have been explained in the pre-flight briefing. If it is on the ground then quickly get away from the immediate area of the plane. Many times on *Tomorrow's World* we have seen the implications of an aircraft fire and the steps they are taking to lessen the danger. However, there is always the possibility that the aircraft will catch fire. Assume this will happen and get away as quickly as possible. Don't push or panic, but listen to what the cabin staff instruct you to do.

If you ditch into water, dinghies will automatically inflate. These are usually anchored in the wings. Don't inflate the life jacket whilst in the plane as this makes it harder to walk down the aisles. Wait until you get into the water and then inflate it before getting into the dinghy. If the plane is sinking, release the dinghies from the wings and as soon as the passengers and equipment are on board, get away from the plane.

However self-disciplined you believe you are, to find yourself in this kind of survival situation will be dramatic, it will be abrupt, you will be confused and most probably in a state of shock, if not on the verge of panic. Remember the key word *survival* and try to act as calmly as possible.

If you land in an area which isn't populated, don't just blunder off into unknown terrain. Get the injured to a safe place, try and get a count of all people involved to establish if anyone is missing. Treatment of injured people must be the priority so establish how many are injured and types of injury and get them sorted out. The major problems in an air crash will be bleeding wounds, breaks, shock, etc. Try and separate the dead from the living. It is inevitable that people will die in an air crash. If you take the bodies away from the survivors it will be easier to calm them down and they won't suffer from shock as much.

Once the engines have cooled down, it is amazing how much you can find on a wreck, even after a fire. Investigate the wreckage and salvage what you can. Use anything you find, equipment, food, clothing, but don't take any risks. If there is a chance of the fuel tanks igniting, fumes coming from seats, etc., don't go back in.

While you are waiting to salvage what you can from the wreck, sort the survivors into small parties, keeping together and try to find out more about your location, where you are, how easy will it be to be rescued from the crash position, etc. That should be a priority in a rescue situation. You must decide whether it is more practical to move or to stay at the crash site. There is a good chance that the cabin crew will have radioed the location and rescue services will already be on the way. In that situation, you should not wander off except to get away from impending danger.

If you do move, leave ground to air markers which are shown later in the book. There will always be some type of search and rescue operation so don't despair that they will never find you. As soon as an aircraft goes down and therefore off the radar screen, they will start wondering where you are back at air traffic control and they will start search and rescue operations. Staying where you are will mean you have a better chance of being found along your original logged flight path. Find flammable materials, so you can build a big fire. If you have come down in a dense wood or forest or on a small island among hundreds of others, get a beacon prepared and as soon as you see or hear an aircraft, light it to attract attention but in all probability the flight path logged with air traffic control will be searched first and most probably the wreckage will be noticeable from the air.

There are various reasons why people decide that it is better to move and these are mainly because they are in a dangerous or unprotected position on a hillside where they are at the mercy of the weather or of falling rocks or avalanche.

Always move down slopes, never up. Firstly because if you go down the slope you will be less exposed to the elements and secondly, because you will find a lot more equipment for building shelters, as well as more opportunity for catching game and finding food generally, and it will also help the rescuers if you go to meet them.

If there are insufficient natural resources to build a shelter, skeletonise the aircraft. Let's be honest – if an airliner crashes it is not going to fly again. The rescue services will pick up the pieces and ship it back to some hangar in Farnborough, so don't worry about wrecking an aircraft. If you want to take the side panels or tail plane off the fuselage to build a shelter, then do so.

Get a fire going first and if possible, get a pot of tea going; this can be difficult if there are over a hundred survivors, but a pot of tea and a warm fire will boost morale. Stay together as much as possible in groups to reduce loss of body heat and get yourself prepared to face the tasks that are at hand.

Use sound man management – don't send an injured person to find water, etc., send fit healthy people to find food and water but do give injured or walking wounded something to do, even menial jobs, so that they feel they are doing something to help and are not being a burden. In a survival situation, injured people can quickly feel they are becoming a burden and this gets worse rather than better. Give them a simple job, even plaiting reeds for shelters or something similar will boost their morale. Get other wounded to talk to and comfort the most badly injured. If you do send people out looking for food or water, never let them go alone; always send parties out in groups of two or three.

When a plane crashes in the middle of a heatwave, you tend to think there is no wind or rain and therefore there are no problems. You may not be in danger from hypothermia but you can get sun stroke. It is as imperative that you find or build some form of shelter to protect you from the sun as well as from the wind and rain.

When lighting a fire, don't just have little camp-fires. Have a few small fires for cooking on by all means as this is usually easier, but have a communal fire which you can all sit around because it is easier to see a big fire at night from overhead planes. When a plane is spotted overhead, put some damp grass or wood on to the fire because it will make it give off heavy smoke, which will be noticed more easily.

The same survival techniques can be used in many other scenarios. The shipwreck is another situation in which the same information and routines are used as for the plane crash.

Survival situations can come from an air crash, a shipwreck, or a car crash out on a lonely moor. Be prepared and follow standard rules.

24   Water Still

The amount of water needed each day varies according to the amount of work undertaken and the surrounding temperature. A man on average, needs between 5–7 pts (3–4 l) of water per day to survive.

You can set up a still that will remove the salt from sea water to make it suitable for drinking as follows:

Start a fire. Connect two plastic bags to each other with a short piece of rubber tubing after filling one bag with sea water. Seal the joints with adhesive tape. Place the bag containing the water into a container of some sort and place it over the heat. A tin would make a suitable container but line the bottom with damp grass, so that the heat will not burst the bag. Bring the water, in its bag, to boiling point. The steam will pass into the other bag (which should be on a lower level), where it will evaporate and the resulting distilled water will collect in the bottom of the second bag.

If no other source of drinking water can be found, a still can be set up as outlined above and a drinkable liquid made by removing the salts and waste products from your own urine.

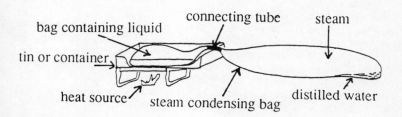

Fig. 96 A water still

25   Survival in the Home

You do not have to be miles away from civilization to be caught in a survival situation. Natural disasters, military action and civil disturbance could cut you off from all the usual services and food supplies. You may find yourself left to your own resources until the services can be re-established.

With no power, central heating, hot water, lighting and refrigeration will all cease. Battery radios and televisions will keep you up to date with the world news for some time until the batteries run out. Taps run dry and toilets cease to work.

In the rural areas there would be natural resources to draw upon. In large cities, shops would soon be looted once any private stocks of food had been exhausted. The population of these empty cities would then move out towards the countryside. Food would become more valuable than any other commodity. Protection of your food stock will become paramount.

Food Storage

Most families have some food in store. It should be rationed and supplemented with whatever can be found.

Storing food is a good habit to get into, especially if you live in an isolated area. If you have the room, stock up a year's supply of food and replace it every time you use it. The stock does not need to be established all at once: it can be built up over a period of time. Make use of special offers in shops and supermarkets. Every time you go shopping buy an extra tin or packet of food and store it away in a cool, dry, dark place, off the ground. Moisture and heat causes bacteria and moulds to multiply, and if stores are left on the floor you will only succeed in feeding insects and rodents. All containers must be insect and rodent proof. Label items with colour-fast waterproof pens, noting contents and date of storage. Rotate tins and packets, using in sequence with the oldest

244

first. Make notes from your experiences of which food keeps better than others, for example, corned beef keeps better than beef stew, wheat keeps better than flour (so it is worthwhile investing in a small hand grinder). Screw-top sweet jars are good for storage and Tupperware type containers are also very good. Use adhesive tape to seal the tops.

Recommended Shelf Life of Foods

Wheat	Indefinitely below 15°C (65°)
Milk Powder	Two years
Honey	Indefinitely
Egg powder	2 years
Salt	Indefinitely if kept absolutely dry
Canned food	3–5 years but replace regularly
Oats	Indefinitely
Cooking oil	2 years but replace regularly

Complete rations can now be purchased in a variety of menus, either freeze-dried or dehydrated. Freeze-dried foods are best both for taste and texture and retain minerals which are lost in dehydration but both need water for re-constitution. Dried fruit and nuts are a valuable source of nutrition. Raisins, sultanas and currants keep well.

Storage Time for Tinned Food

Milk puddings, including evap	12 months
Cream and milk puddings	12 months
Prunes	12 months
Rhubarb	12 months
Fruit juice	12 months
New potatoes	18 months
Blackberries, gooseberries, plums, blackcurrants	18 months
Raspberries, strawberries	2 years
Vegetables (apart from new potatoes)	2 years
Other fruits	2 years
Baked beans	2 years
Pasta products	2 years
Soups	2 years
Fish in sauce	2 years
Ready meals	2 years
Hot meal products	2 years
Solid pack meat products	5 years
Fish in oil	5 years

Suggested Storage List

The items listed below, if correctly stored, would provide an interesting and varied diet.

Wheat
Powdered milk
Honey/Sugar
Salt
If stored correctly these will keep indefinitely

Canned meat (not pasteurised ham)
Rice
Will last for three to five years

Dried fruit
Vegetable oil
Will last 1–2 years

Peanut butter
Tomato juice and citrus fruit juices
Multi-vitamin pills
Lentils
Dry green beans
Dried yeast
Soya beans or soya based meat substitutes
Will need to be rotated

Various dried herbs and spices
Stock cubes, Oxo, Bovril, etc.
Onion flakes
Dry soup mix
Sesame seeds (high in protein, Calcium and Vitamins B and E)
Alfalfa seeds (to sprout for salads)
Dry grated cheese
Garlic
Gravy mixes
Dried vegetables for flavour and variety
Ready-mix powder products, e.g. Angel Delight
Any canned fruit (except fruit like rhubarb and pineapples)
Dried dates and prunes
Vitamin B and C tablets, plus iron tablets
Biscuits, wholemeal/digestive, bran crispbreads, sealed into tins
Muesli – snack bars of muesli are also handy
Spreads – Marmite, Bovril, Vegemite, etc. (These have a high salt con-

tent, so allow extra water – but they also contain Vitamin B)

Tinned meat/fish. They taste better than dried varieties

Ovaltine, Horlicks, Complan, drinking chocolate, etc. to be used as meal substitutes

Fruit juices

Variety of dried foods – Vestas, Pot Noodles, etc., but bear in mind extra demand on water

Nuts – sealed in vacuum packs (Unsalted otherwise they will make you thirsty)

Additional Stores

Milk – tinned and powdered

Coffee, tea and hot milk drinks

Sugar and saccharine

Syrup, treacle, honey, jam, marmalade

Soups – packet, tinned and instant

Brown rice, spaghetti, pasta generally

Oatmeal – stored in tin or sealed jar

Fruit – dried, tinned or bottled

Vegetables – tinned or freeze dried

Creamed rice – tinned

Butter/Margarine in tubs or peanut butter in jar

Tinned meat – corned beef, stews, minced meat, etc

Seasoning – sauces, salt, pepper and relishes

Sweets – glucose, barley sugar, plain or milk chocolate

Baby food – tinned, bottled or powder

Pet food

Also bear in mind the following important items:

Soap, toothbrush and toothpaste

Razor blades, shaving cream

Deodorant

Detergents, bleaches, washing powder

Toilet paper

Disinfectants

Batteries, torch, radio, clock, etc

First aid kit – comprehensive kit made up by yourself, sealed in container

Candles, matches

Camping gas containers

Tin opener

Plates, cups, pans, cutlery, etc

Bin liners (to use as toilet liners and for rubbish)
Water purification tablets (Sodium Hypochlorite or Milton to clean and
    purify water)
Paper and pencils, pens, etc
Blankets, pillows, sleeping bags
Towels
Air beds or camp beds
Old newspapers – for wrapping rubbish, burning, etc
Books and games

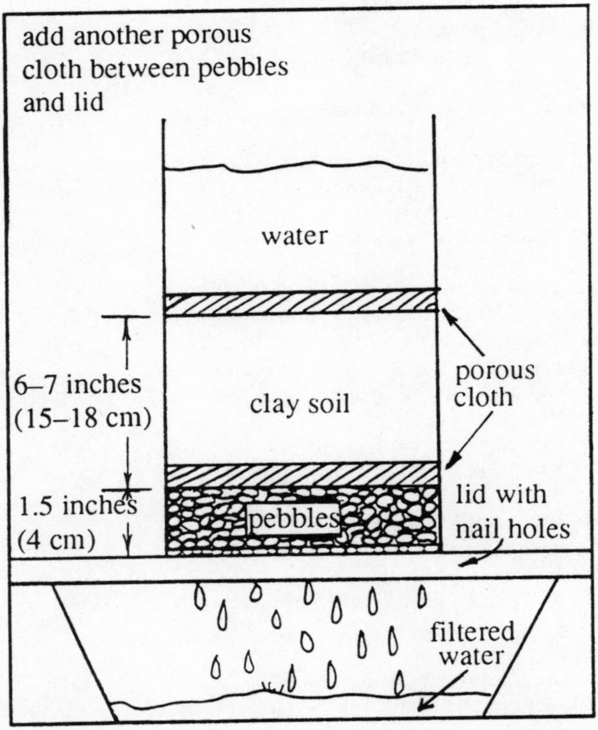

Fig. 97 A water filter

Makeshift Toilet

Use a bucket, preferably with a lid (a camping toilet would be better still), lined with a plastic bin liner. If available fix a chair with a hole made in the seat over the bucket so you can sit in comfort. Keep well doused with disinfectant to keep smells down and reduce risk of infection. When the bin liner is filled, seal and remove as far away as possible. Ideally, it should be buried if it is safe to do so. Keep toilet waste separate from other household waste if using dustbins.

Water Supply

Each person requires 4 pints (2.75 l) of drinking water per day not including cooking and washing.

To Purify Supply

Sodium hypochlorite can be obtained from chemists, but usually only in large quantities, and an additional problem is that it only has a shelf life of one year. Milton and water purification tablets use calcium hypochlorite and as long as they are kept correctly, in dry airtight containers, they have a long shelf life.

Before water is disinfected it must be filtered, especially if it is from streams or ponds. A simple filter is shown opposite.

Another way to purify water is using tincture of iodine – five drops to each quart (1.1 l) of clear water, ten drops if water cloudy. Leave to stand for twenty minutes.

Boiling the water before use is a final precaution. A one-minute boil kills all kinds of disease-causing bacteria, whilst boiling for ten to twenty minutes kills rare infective bacteria. Water must be kept at a rolling boil.

26 Survival and Natural Disasters

It is constantly in the news that rivers flood, volcanoes erupt, earthquakes flatten cities. These are but a few of the natural disasters that befall mankind.

All the rescue services are fully adept at sorting out the aftermath of such catastrophes. The problems arise when it happens to you at some remote camp, or the rescue services cannot reach you with all the services cut, gas, electricity, etc. What can you do to help yourself?

Drought

We all know that drought is caused by long periods of dry weather. This happens only occasionally in Great Britain, and we certainly don't get the sort of problems we see on the television in the Sudan, Ethiopia, Bangladesh and other areas with hot climates. It can get pretty hot in the UK and cause a shortage of water, but fortunately we have a government that can ration water. As this book is aimed mainly at mainland Britain, it would be pointless going into the problems of Africa; after all Bob Geldof brought home the seriousness of their plight. However, in a survival situation, charity begins at home.

Water Conservation

Never waste water. Follow water storage cycles, for example, water used for cooking and water used for washing can be used to water crops and the vegetable and flower garden. Collect condensation and morning dew and use stream water. Do not however re-direct streams because apart from causing problems elsewhere, most of the water will be lost by it being absorbed into the parched soil. See p. 170 and Fig. 82 for instructions on collecting water and condensation.

Collect the water every morning and store it in a shady place to prevent loss by evaporation from the sun. High ground offers the best chance of collecting water by this method.

In the House

If the water is cut off for any reason, do not use the WC unless you have been advised by the water company that it is only a temporary interruption.

Leave sufficient water in the WC to seal the S-bend. This will create a barrier against disease and infection. Build an outdoor latrine away from the house, ideally at the bottom of the garden. After the crisis is over, fill it in and plant a rose bush or shrub; the waste will do it wonders. (For details of outdoor latrines, see Fig. 66.)

Let all the family share the bath water, either one after another or all together. Never drain water away from the bath: use it for watering crops and vegetables in the garden.

Personal Hygiene

Sweating keeps the pores open and free of dirt. However it is important that you clean your hands after going to the toilet or completing some dirty task and especially before preparing food. I know this sounds patronizing, but with the heat and discomfort, these little things are easily forgotten.

Boil all water, no matter how thirsty you are or how clean the water looks. One dead sheep upstream will contaminate your water, your food and you. Cover all food to protect it from flies and other insects and to prevent dry topsoil blowing around the campsite and ending up in your food.

Fire

Fire is closely linked with drought because everything is dry and can be easily ignited. As the fire service always say – 'the best protection against fire is prevention'. Seventy per cent of all fires are caused by careless people with lighted cigarettes and matches, badly managed camp fires, broken bottles, etc. Fire can strike anywhere, anytime. Always have a fire extinguisher at home and/or a fire blanket.

Forest Fires

Forest fires can spread as fast as the wild life that flees before it. The stronger the wind the faster the spread. Man-made forest plantations have fire breaks to prevent the spread of the fires. At these fire breaks and at the entrances to the plantations, fire-fighting equipment can be found to beat out the flames. Make a point of learning how to use them.

If you are present at the start of a fire, try to smother it by cutting off the oxygen supply to the flames.

There are a few tell tale signs to indicate a forest fire.

1 The smell of smoke
2 You will be able to hear the fire before you see the flames
3 Wild life will panic, birds hurriedly leave the area and rodents dig in

If trapped or surrounded by a forest fire and it is impossible to put it out, do not run until you have no choice.

Do not discard clothing, even if you become very hot. The clothes will shield you from the approaching heat. Take notice of the direction of the smoke as this will indicate wind direction. If the wind is blowing the fire your way, do not head for high ground because fire spreads faster uphill. Head for a fire break, a gully, a road or a watercourse as the best escape route. The chances are that the fire will leap over you. If there are none of these options available, try to reach ploughed land or rocky scree or somewhere where there is little or no vegetation. Try to move diagonally out of the path of the fire.

If the fire blocks your escape route, you should get into the middle of the largest open space available. Avoid bracken beds and other areas of dead vegetation. If you are in a car, stay in it – there is less risk of the petrol tank exploding than there is of you being burnt by the fire around you. It is petrol vapour rather than the petrol itself that catches fire. As the heat builds up inside the car, switch on the heaters which will help to cool it down and disperse the smoke.

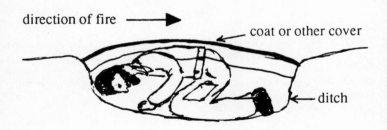

Fig. 98 Sheltering in a hollow

If you are on foot and there is no apparent escape route, try to dig yourself a foxhole or hollow where you can lie up. If there is a pond, get into the middle of it. Cover your head and any exposed skin, such as hands, with a blanket or coat, ideally soaked in water, as this will help prevent you being burned by the hot air. Curl up into a tight ball with your protected head towards the flames. Once the fire has passed, look for a way out upwind where the fire has already been.

Try to go round the fire. If you can't and there are no hollows, etc., it may be that your best escape route is through the flames. This cannot be done if the fire is too intense or the burning area is greater than you can manage to travel through in about ten seconds at most. However in a large clearing, it may be possible if you time your run right and plan your dash carefully.

As the fire moves round the clearing, at the last moment, dash for the far side of the clearing where the fire is burned out. That means when the fire reaches A, run to C and when the fire reaches B, run to A (see Fig. 99).

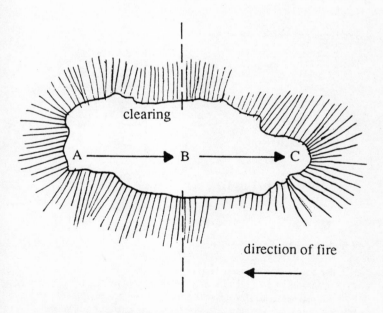

Fig. 99 Crossing a clearing in a fire

Before you make your dash, dampen a piece of cloth or handkerchief and use this to cover as much exposed skin as possible. If you can, soak yourself with water as this will help act as a barrier against clothing or hair setting alight. Cover nose and mouth with a damp cloth and run. DO NOT STOP. Avoid thick vegetation as this will hinder your run and will burn fast and fiercely.

It is possible to fight fire with fire. This can be done by retreating from the edge of the fire to a distance of about a mile or more and lighting another fire along as wide a line as possible. This will burn in the same direction as the main fire, creating a break which you can move into. It is important that you determine the correct wind direction. Winds can swirl and trap the fire and cause it to head back towards you. Use this method only as a last resort. If someone else did the same as you the whole forest could be decimated.

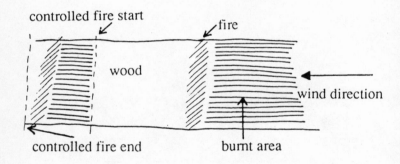

Fig. 100 Fighting fire with fire

Fire and Buildings

Never use water if you are in any doubt about a fire being caused by an electrical fault. If you feel this may be the case, switch off the power at the mains and turn the gas off at the mains also. Television sets and computers must not be sprayed with water because there could still be sufficient residual electrical charge left in them to kill you and cold water is apt to make the tube explode so *handle with care*.

Get injured person on his feet by placing him face down with his head at your feet, and your arms under his. As you straighten up, you will be pulling him up

Once on his feet, hold his right wrist with your left hand. Bend down and let him fall across your shoulder

Stand up carefully keeping your back straight. Transfer his wrist into your right hand leaving your other hand free to steady yourself once moving

Fig. 101 Fireman's lift

255

When evacuating a burning building, do not panic. This sounds easier than actually doing it. Turn off all electrical power and gas and close all doors and windows to try and contain the fire whilst everyone gets out. Keep as low to the ground as possible because there will be more breathable air there.

Never use lifts during a fire and be careful when opening a door; keeping your foot against the bottom will prevent it being blown open by gases which have built up inside. Look for tell tale signs and test the door handle for heat before touching it – do this with the back of your hand close to the knob. Leave doors closed if at all possible. A good solid door can keep a fire at bay for about thirty minutes.

If you find yourself trapped in a room, close the door and fill in the gaps with curtains or carpet or any material that will take time to catch fire and stop smoke getting into the room. Smash a window, using furniture if necessary. If the fire alarm has not already been set off, a chair or coffee table landing in the street should attract someone's attention.

Try to make a rope out of sheets and curtains, but drop out cushions, pillows, mattresses, etc., just in case your make-shift rope is not long enough. Do not just jump out of a window, unless it is on the ground floor. If you have no choice but to jump, protect your head and when you land, bend your knees and roll to the side dispersing the shock on to your back.

If you have to carry an uninjured but unconscious person out of a fire, use a fireman's lift (see Fig. 101).

Vehicle Fires

It has been said many times that cars are deadly. When on fire they become time-bombs. If the petrol tank catches fire, it will explode like an incendiary bomb, spreading burning fuel over a great distance. If a car catches fire in a garage, the main danger is smoke and fumes. These could kill you before the car explodes.

Try to put out the fire with the extinguisher in your car if you carry one. If it is possible to get the car out of a garage *safely*, do so. Having escaped, do not go back into a car for any reason, not even to rescue valuables; let the insurance deal with that later. Attack the fire from the outside through the windows.

If you crash the car, kick the windows out. Doors can jam; don't waste time trying to open them: smash your way out instead.

Flood

Flooding can be caused by any number of reasons, rivers bursting banks, reservoirs overflowing, etc. Water for drinking will become the main problem as dirty flood water mixes with clean drinking water.

If you are in a building, turn off the gas and electricity and move upstairs. Take food with you and try to collect drinking water before it becomes contaminated. Always keep a gas stove or primus handy in case of disaster. Collect a torch, candles, matches and brightly coloured rags to attract the attention of the rescue services. Make sure the matches are kept dry.

If you do not have an upper floor, climb out on to the roof. Erect some form of shelter around the chimney stack using blankets and sheets and await the rescue services. Tie yourself to the chimney stack or any solid structure.

If you live in an area prone to flooding, prepare yourself beforehand. This is easy to do. Build a flood kit (primus and cylinders, food, candles, matches, etc.) and keep it high up. Even a small amount of water can cause a lot of damage, so keep some sand-bags handy to block the door-ways. Better to have a dirty patch on the carpet than have muddy water run round the ground floor and ruin all your expensive carpets and furniture.

If you have a cellar, try and direct the water into the cellar. The fire services will always pump out your cellar after the flood is over. Once again this could save your belongings.

If you have to evacuate your home and you have time, put any loose outdoor items, such as expensive patio furniture, flower tubs, etc., into the house to avoid the risk of them being hurled around outside in the flood and being damaged or of them being washed away and lost or hurting somebody.

If you were trapped in your house, it is unlikely that you would be trapped for very long. As soon as the flood water subsides, the task of cleaning up begins. While waiting, try to get some sleep to conserve energy because the hardest part is the cleaning up.

Avalanche

Avalanches can happen at any time. Invariably if there is a greater risk for some specific reason, there will be warning notices displayed. *Take notice of them.*

There are four types of avalanche:

1 Soft slab
2 Hard slab
3 Airborne
4 Wet snow

1 Soft slab avalanche – snow falling on the slopes, often below a cornice, fails to settle and compact. It may feel hard but the slightest disturbance or loud noise can make it slip

2 Hard slab – looks like a hard surface but is susceptible to vibration. Even walking can cause a vibration and set the whole surface in motion

3 Airborne – this is the most common and is caused by fresh snow falling on a hard icy crust or in cold dry conditions. Usually starts as a slab avalanche which then gathers momentum and more powdered snow, to reach speeds exceeding 150 mph (240 kph). The danger is not so much the avalanche but the chance of drowning from inhaling snow in large amounts

4 Wet snow – these are more common during a thaw or just after a rapid temperature rise. After a snowfall, the new moist snow cannot adhere to the older, less dense layer. It moves slower than the airborne avalanche, lifting trees and rocks as it travels, producing large snow boulders. When it stops, it freezes solid almost instantly, making rescue very difficult

If you find yourself a victim of a wet snow avalanche, discard all your equipment and use a crawl stroke to keep on top of the slide. Cover your nose and mouth. When you come to rest, make as big a cavity around you as you can before the snow freezes around you. Save as much energy as you can for when you hear people approaching.

Avalanches occur most frequently after a snowfall of 10 ins (25 cms) or more, especially on southerly slopes because of the sun thawing the snow. The safest time in warm periods is in the early hours of the day. Slopes at 30° angles or more are the most dangerous. Avalanches are less likely on well-timbered or boulder strewn slopes and windy slopes are usually safe as well because snow is generally hard packed and crusty.

Your first instinct is to run downhill. This is pointless as there is no way you can outrun an avalanche as they can travel at speeds of up to 100 mph (160 kph) and more. It is better to run to the side: you may run out of its path. Discard anything you are carrying, except your rucksack. You can use the rucksack as a pillow under your body to trap air around you, so that if you do get covered, you have an air supply to go at while you dig yourself out.

When it is inevitable that you will be covered, curl up into a ball with the rucksack at the top of your head, covering your head and neck. Keep your mouth tightly shut and hold your breath, because you can drown in snow just as you can in water.

If you start to get swept away by the force of the snow, fight to stay on top of the snow and swim, using a breast stroke or dog paddle just as if you were in water. Use your arms to fend off rocks or slabs of snow. If you come up to any obstacles, rocks, trees, etc., cling to the downhill side.

If you are buried, try and break out immediately the avalanche starts to slow down because as it is newly formed snow, it will start to freeze over immediately it stops moving. You will be able to hear the avalanche rumbling whilst it is moving; when the noise stops, it will start to freeze.

If you have become disorientated whilst you were swept along by the snow and are not sure which way to go to the surface, collect saliva in your mouth and dribble it from your lips. The rules of gravity still apply even though you are buried.

Conserve oxygen by moving slowly and try not to panic. Air will be trapped in the snow surrounding you, which will begin to melt with your body heat and there is the supply you trapped round you as well.

Hurricane

A hurricane is a wind of high speed above Force 12 on the Beaufort Scale (see Fig. 102). Hurricanes develop over the ocean when the sea temperatures are at their highest, especially in late summer. Warm air creates a low pressure core around which winds may rotate at speeds of around 200 mph (320 kph) or more, circulating anti-clockwise in the Northern Hemisphere, clockwise in the Southern. The strongest winds are usually about 10 miles (16 km) from the core or 'eye' as it is better known. The eye is calm and can be anything from 4 to 30 miles (6–50 km) wide. The largest recorded was up to 300 miles (480 km) in diameter.

Hurricanes build up force over the sea and then veer towards the nearest pole, wrecking anything in their path. It used to be that Great Britain did not suffer from hurricanes but since 1987 we can't really count on that!

Satellite surveillance enables meteorologists to see hurricanes developing far out at sea and to track their progress and give warning of their approach. Without a radio to alert you to the weather which is due for your area, nature gives us some warning signs – smells intensify, highly coloured sunsets and sunrises, dense banners of cirrus clouds converging towards the vortex of the approaching storm, abnormal barometric pressure readings, etc.

Safety Precautions

1 Get out of the hurricane's path if you can
2 Hurricane warnings are given about twenty-four hours before it is due to hit. Don't ignore them
3 Keep away from the coast
4 Board up windows and secure anything outside that may blow away

Beaufort number	Wind knots	Speed mph	Speed kph	Seaman's term	Effects observed at sea	Effects observed on land
0	0–1	0–1	0–1.6	Calm	Sea like a mirror	Calm, smoke rises vertically
1	1–3	1–3	1.6–4.8	Light air	Ripples with appearance of scales, no foam crests	Smoke drift indicates wind direction, vanes do not move
2	4–6	4–7	6.4–11.3	Light breeze	Small wavelets, crests of glassy appearance, not breaking	Wind felt on face, leaves rustle vanes begin to move
3	7–10	8–12	12.9–19.3	Gentle breeze	Large wavelets, begin to break, scattered whitecaps	Leaves, small twigs in constant motion, light flags extended
4	11–16	13–18	20.9–29	Moderate breeze	Small waves, becoming longer, numerous whitecaps	Dust, leaves and loose paper raised up, small branches move
5	17–21	19–24	30.6–38.6	Fresh breeze	Moderate waves, taking longer form, many whitecaps	Small trees in leaf begin to sway
6	22–27	25–31	40.2–50	Strong breeze	Larger waves forming, whitecaps everywhere, more spray	Larger branches of trees in motion, whistling heard in wires
7	28–33	32–38	51.5–61.2	Moderate gale	Sea heaps up, white foam from breaking waves begins to be blown	Whole trees in motion, resistance felt in walking against wind

8	34-40	39-46	62.8-74	Fresh gale	Moderately high waves of greater length, edges of crests begin to break into spindrift	Twigs and small branches broken off twigs, progress generally impeded
9	41-47	47-54	75.6-86.9	Strong gale	High waves, sea begins to roll, dense streaks of foam, spray may reduce visibility	Slight structural damage occurs, slates blown from roofs
10	48-55	55-63	88.5-101.4	Whole gale	Very high waves with overhanging crests, sea takes white appearance rolling, and visibility reduced, foam blown in dense streaks	Seldom experienced on land – trees broken or uprooted, considerable structural damage occurs
11	56-63	64-72	103-115.9	Storm	Exceptionally high waves. Sea covered with white foam, visibility reduced even more	Rare on land, usually accompanied by widespread damage
12	64+	73+	117.5+	Hurricane	Air filled with foam, sea completely completely white with driving spray, visibility greatly reduced	Violent destruction

Fig. 102 Beaufort Scale

Do not travel during a hurricane. If you get caught in a hurricane, shelter on the leeward side of any solid structure. Do not move when it becomes calm, wait. After about an hour, sometimes less, the wind will start again blowing in the opposite direction as the other side of the hurricane hits.

Lightning

We all know the dangers of lightning. Lightning takes the shortest route to earth, making it more dangerous on high ground, so keep away from hill tops, tall solitary trees, electricity pylons, flagpoles, etc. Make for low ground and crouch down in a frog-like position. If you are carrying anything, i.e. golf club, gun, etc., put it down well away from you. Don't believe that rubber soled shoes can save you. If you are struck by lightning there is no guarantee that you will be safe.

Stay away from water and boats. If you are swimming, get out of the water and dry yourself and don't put anything on that is wet. If you can find shelter, do so and remember the centre of a large room is the safest. Keep doors and windows closed to prevent draughts which lightning will follow.

Insulate yourself. A dry coil of climbing rope will insulate well, so curl up on it if possible, drawing your knees to your chest. Do not touch the ground or make a contact which could conduct the lightning. If you have nothing to insulate yourself with, crouch down in a frog-like position.

It is said that you can sometimes sense a lightning strike by a tingling in the skin and the feeling that your hair is standing on end. If you are standing up when this happens, drop to the ground at once, falling on to your hands and knees first in case you are struck. This may detract the shock from the torso and possibly save you from heart failure or asphyxiation.

Keep away from and do not hold metal objects. Even being close to a metal object that is struck can cause damage to the lungs, because overheated air moves rapidly as the lightning passes.

27 Signalling

There are various methods which can be used to signal for help, etc.
The main methods are shown here. Even if you do not need to use
them yourself, you may at some time need to be able to read a coded
message.

All the systems use abbreviations for commonly used words. Some of
these are shown but if you don't know them, spell the word out – it will
take longer but you will get your message across.

Morse Code

You do not necessarily need a morse key. Anything you can make a noise
with can be used to transmit morse code.

Heliograph

You can improvise a heliograph from any piece of metal which will give
a reflection on both sides, a piece of tin foil or a tin lid.

Make a small hole in the centre of the metal and look through this
at the place you wish to signal to. Once you are lined up with the target, hold the lid steady and look at your reflection on the back of the
lid. On your face in the reflection you will see a spot of sunlight from
the hole. Tilt the lid until the spot of light on your face disappears
into the hole. This gives the flash. Rock the lid gently to produce a
series of flashes. A group of flashes will be noticed more than a single beam.

Give these flashes in the international mountain distress signal of six
flashes per minute followed by a minute's pause then six more flashes.

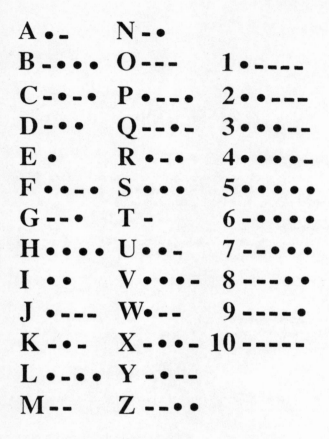

Fig. 103 Morse Code

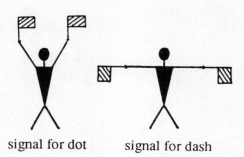

signal for dot   signal for dash

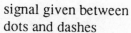

signal given between
dots and dashes

signal given between
letters or words

dual-purpose signal:

by transmitter – erase and start over
by receiver – unclear please repeat

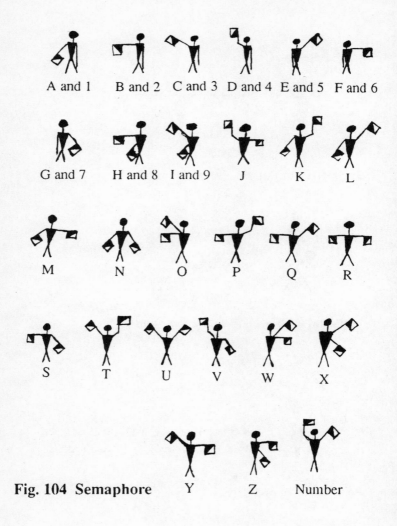

Fig. 104 Semaphore

Fig. 105 Ground to air signals

28   Inner City Survivalism

In the case of a nuclear holocaust or civil unrest, it is fairly obvious that there would be a mass exodus from inner city areas to rural towns and villages. This would take place once most of the major supermarkets and shops had been looted. Martial law would be enforced and perimeter fences would be built to enclose the city dwellers within the mess they have made and in an attempt to control the mass panic.

Food would be rationed and organizations would be set up offering food as payment for work. In the case of war, most of the armed forces would be engaged in conventional warfare somewhere in the world and the job of keeping at bay civil unrest would be in the hands of the local authority. Whilst councillors, statesmen, senior police officers and an assortment of civil servants would be tucked away nice and snug in some nuclear shelter co-ordinating outside rescue services and food distribution chains within the inner cities, the populace would be left fending for themselves. Anybody with a uniform would be given the job of keeping law and order at city perimeters and food distribution centres, whilst the police patrolled the streets, arresting and shooting looters, criminals and any person targeted as a 'radical'.

I say 'people in uniform', because the belief would be that the sight of a uniform would still hopefully hold some form of authority. The major part of the population would, however, probably feel threatened by the fact that some of the policing duties would be carried out by uniformed personnel such as traffic wardens, bus drivers, firemen, ambulance drivers, postmen, etc., and then the only uniformed personnel they would feel an affinity with would be the likes of the Salvation Army or the WRVS.

It is understandable that a mass exodus to rural police-free areas would ensue but here they would come across perimeter guards who would be under strict orders not to let them escape. However, a switched-on survivalist would find no need to leave the inner city areas at that time but would find himself a safe place, out of the way of the authorities, where he could keep hidden until such time as the authorities believed that the situation within the city was under control.

Have you ever studied the railway bankings as you travel by train into big cities such as London, Birmingham and Leeds? There is every possibility that for a limited period of time, trains would cease to run because railway stations would be the perfect place to set up food distribution centres. Railway bankings and sidings would not be patrolled as often as streets, shopping centres and market places. The guards are likely not to notice the odd citizen living rough on some railway banking at one end of some massive siding or yard. There are usually plenty of building materials lying about in such places, like old railway sleepers, sheets of corrugated metal, bricks, stones, girders and any number of other useful items. There are also many deserted buildings tucked out of the way in the middle of woods alongside the track as well as ready-made shelters which are at present used by railway maintenance teams, such as old signal boxes, etc.

The major routes into cities, such as motorways, major roads, railway lines, canals and rivers all seem to converge. These same routes would also be an open corridor for survivalists to escape through once the perimeter guards have been reduced in order to reinforce policing within the inner city areas.

Take a lesson from the Argentinians and keep away from football stadiums. After the rounding up of the radicals, the complainers, the criminal elements and the Greenpeace supporters, who wander the streets saying 'I told you so', the authorities will have to find somewhere to put them, and one of the securest places is a football stadium which is able to house a large crowd of people. Therefore hanging around such places may invite the authorities to throw you in one.

Keep away from crowds because these can usually be steered in directions they don't wish to go. Also the police presence would be greater and would therefore make escape impossible.

There are many areas within inner cities, such as derelict factory sites, etc., which could house and hide a few families. These places would not merit patrols because they look deserted – remember the old saying, 'Out of sight, out of mind'.

Sewerage works are also a good place to hide. These would be unmanned and unused and the smell would probably keep most people away. Most sewerage works have outlets to fast flowing parts of rivers therefore a canoe, boat or raft leaving the city at such a point would have more chance of escaping the perimeter fences and guards because the speed of the river would carry it along.

Old industrial sites and foundries are perfect examples of good hiding places. They are dark and secluded with many little out of the way hidey-holes. Scrap yards are also good and there tends to be an abundance of hiding places in railway sidings as already discussed. City parks could provide cover but would be an obvious place for the authorities to look.

Storm drains and sewers could be used depending on how many people have listened to Jeff Wayne's *War of the Worlds*.

Once the situation has calmed down, escape plans can be made for small numbers of people to leave the area over a number of days or weeks.

From your hide-out you can organize foraging parties to collect news, materials and food, together with intelligence information on the whereabouts of police checkpoints.

If the sewers do run clean after the rains, then half the city would try to get out that way. If however they are still and stinking, it may be possible to find a route out if you are willing to wade waist high through the muck and gunge. It must be remembered that many citizens will be led like sheep and therefore, if the authorities say everything will be in order fairly soon, many will accept that and will stay locked up in their homes and use the last of the water for washing, drinking and flushing the toilet.

An important point to remember is that looters will most probably be shot on sight. Never be caught carrying food; you may be arrested or shot on suspicion of being a looter.

29   Foraging

To a survivalist, foraging is one of the integral parts of collecting the equipment or food he needs. Even while practising, foraging in inner cities or towns can prove to be quite fruitful.

I once had the opportunity to prove this to a group of teenagers who wanted to learn about survivalism. I sent them out to find what they could to make themselves a shelter and make themselves as comfortable as possible in our camp that night. It started to rain and within an hour they were back with next to nothing and consequently their shelters were very sparse.

To prove the point that you don't just give up and get yourself under cover as quickly as possible, I went out to see what I could scrounge. Realizing that the boys hadn't gone far in their own search, because I too couldn't find anything in the immediate vicinity, I travelled a little further afield and finished up at the back of an old foundry. There were a number of skips parked at the rear of the building and I started to wander around, peering into each skip, until I came across one that was full of household items. It looked as if somebody had died and they had cleared the house contents into a skip.

I started to root through the skip and came across a number of useful items. The first thing that caught my eye was an old fishing stool, made of a couple of pieces of wood and a bit of carpeting. I thought to myself that, as there is nothing worse than sitting round a camp-fire at night with your backside getting wet on the damp ground and only your knees getting warm and never being able to sit comfortably because your shoulders ache because you're leaning on your elbows, etc., this was the thing I was going to take back with me, so that I could sit in front of the fire and keep the whole of my front warm and not get damp or wet.

On pulling out this fishing stool, a number of other treasures appeared and on returning to the campsite that we'd picked, the look of amazement on the faces of the young boys at the finds I'd made was enough to prove my point and to get the message over to them. As they lay there that night, in their dug-outs and lean-tos, I slept on a camp bed wrapped in a space blanket under a sheet of tarpaulin, with a Tilley lamp on. All this equipment had been carried back to the camp in the rucksack I'd found. I also found an old kettle, a couple of pans, some old tins and a whole number of other useful little odds and sods. Admittedly I don't think I'll ever be lucky enough to make a find like that again but the equipment I found then I still have and use. Most of it is antique militaria, something that I collect personally anyway, but it is all useful.

In the morning, when I woke up, I collected the morning dew from the old canvas field sink I'd set up and therefore had water to have a wash and make a cup of tea.

The point was proved that if you look hard enough, you will find what you're looking for. Search well and you will always find something that will be of use. It never ceased to amaze these boys that I was only out an hour more than them and yet I slept sound, lying in my bed, knowing that I wouldn't have creepy crawlies wandering all over me, knowing I wouldn't wake up with a stiff neck or a damp back. All these teenagers are now avid survivalists and on the meets that we have, sit comfortably in front of the fire with any amount of equipment ranging from dustbins to old car seats. The stuff they once would have classed as unimportant is now scattered around the various sites we have and this is the basis of survivalism.

Check that any skip you find is not part of a council run re-cycling programme, as you could be prosecuted for trespass and theft. The same rules apply to landfill areas. It would be worthwhile checking the local bye-laws before starting foraging.

Things can be found anywhere in cities, towns, bankings, etc. Buckets are very important and can be found scattered around. It is a fact that almost everything from a DIY shop comes in a plastic bucket, from Polytex-type paint to grout, sand and cement. Once finished with, these are soon discarded and are often picked up by survivalists who think that is just what I need to collect water from the beck, or to store food to stop the mice or insects getting at it. Old ladders, on which a couple or even all of the rungs have broken can be used as roofing struts on shelters.

Old house bricks can be made into a rubbish burner which can also be made into a stove if wrapped with mud. Any number of things can be utilized if you are aware of their possible value and if you are willing to pick them up and carry them back to where you have camped up. All you need is a good pair of eyes and imagination and the time to be able to wander about and look for this kind of stuff.

In any survival situation, the ability to forage is paramount – you forage for food and water, as well as materials for shelters and fires. Many people associate survivalists with Rambo-type psychopaths and maniacs. In effect what they should do, is class them as foragers and resourceful people. People who value the elements, nature, themselves, their abilities and the things that other people throw away.

30　Beachcombing

In a survival situation, equipment is mainly arrived at by scrounging or 'profiteering' – a polite word for 'looting'. The idea is that you wander around and find and pick up what you can. This can often be done by wandering around old railway bankings. Many people dump their rubbish, they won't wait for the council to come and collect it or empty their bins and they throw the rubbish over the nearest siding. The same thing happens on the sides of rivers and canals.

However, one man's rubbish is another man's gold, which is proved by beachcombing. There are actually people who are professional beachcombers, who earn a living by beachcombing.

Many things can be found on the beach. You can beachcomb now, you can beachcomb in a survival situation, it can even become an absorbing and profitable hobby. Ships have been wrecked all around our coast over the years and cargo is washed overboard even today and it's only natural that the tide will eventually bring goods on to the beaches, where it can be picked up and used either to help you survive or provide an income. Even today, many things are still being washed up that actually sunk hundreds of years ago. Over the centuries, people have spent time on the beaches around our coasts for a variety of reasons and naturally have left or lost all manner of items.

In addition to suitable footwear and clothing to cope with summer heatwaves and freezing weather in winter, the only vital equipment is a good pair of eyes, although a stout crowbar would be useful to shift boulders. Metal detectors can be used if you own one and will certainly increase your chances of finding valuable non-ferrous scrap metal or rings and coins. Lead is the most common non-ferrous metal found on the beach and is usually in the shape of fishing weights. You can either melt them down or make them into sets of various sizes for re-sale to the fishermen who lost them.

If you visit those areas where beach fishermen fish at low tide and search round, you will find all sorts of tackle that has been lost.

Around tidal estuaries, especially on industrialized rivers, the greenish tinge of corroded copper stands out plainly and a surprising amount can be found on the beach.

Quite substantial amounts of money can be found on the beach if you wander around after the day-trippers and tourists have left.

To collect sea coal in the north-east of England, you need a flat shovel, a couple of heavy duty sacks and a sturdy old bike to carry away the coal you collect. The coal appears on the beach after high tide, as patches of black pebbles, each pebble measuring from the size of a pea down to a pin head and these patches can cover several square yards, sometimes a couple of inches deep. Simply scoop it into piles and shovel it into your sack. You can either sell it or use it yourself.

The east coast is a good area to search for fossils, which have been washed out of the rocks by erosion. All sorts of fossils are to be found, from common ammonites which look like a coiled snake to rarer fossils and bones which can be sold to collectors and museums. Amber is fossilized tree resin from ancient forests that grew in the Baltic regions. It looks like dull yellow glass but is much lighter in weight than glass. Chunks have been deposited on our shores for centuries and one lucky man, whilst walking his dog, found a piece which he later sold for £3,000.

On the coasts of Scotland, Cornwall and parts of Wales, you can find a variety of semi-precious stones in rough pebble form. You could find agates, cornelians and garnets and if you invested in a tumbling machine (available from craft shops) these pebbles could be polished up and sold. On the coast of Yorkshire around Whitby, you can find jet.

Seaweed makes a fertilizer and soil conditioner and can be found in quantity around our beaches. Bag it in polythene sacks, take it inland and sell it to the suburban gardeners.

Digging up rag worms and other baits used by fishermen is another profitable sideline.

All sorts of things will be washed in by the tide and deposited on the beach. All you need to do is keep your eyes open and grab any opportunity that floats in. This is the attitude of mind that marks a successful beachcomber and a survivalist.

31 Cars

Almost everyone, sooner or later will be in a car that breaks down. In most cases, this is just a simple matter of pulling on to the side of the road or motorway and wandering down to the nearest service station or telephone and calling out the RAC or AA. However, in the remote parts of Scotland and England, high on the fells of the Lake District, the Brecon Beacons or the Yorkshire Moors and Dales or the Highlands in Scotland, you may have quite a walk to get back to civilization.

During the day this never really seems like a problem. You get out of your car and you wave down a passing vehicle of some sort and ask for a lift to the nearest town or petrol station. If you are travelling through these areas late at night however, the possibility of someone passing you on the road is very slim – not many people travel about at two or three o'clock in the morning. If you were to break down in the Highlands of Scotland for example, late at night, it is not really going to be worth your while to get out and leave the car and head for the nearest town hoping for a lift, because a lift is unlikely and the nearest town is going to be a long walk.

Cold Weather

Let's set a scenario. You are travelling through the Highlands of Scotland, your car breaks down, it's pitch dark and you don't really know where you are – all you know is that you are headed in the direction of a town on the map. The car has broken down, there is no way you can get it started. Later on that night, heavy snow comes down and blocks the road you are on.

The fact that your car is broken down and the fact that it is now snowed in, makes the survival situation even worse. In a situation like that, what can you do?

First of all, the car is going to become like a fridge. If it is a breakdown to the wheels or prop shaft rather than a mechanical fault, try and get the engine running and leave it to tick over.

It's a lot easier to travel in snow during the day – it is much harder during the night. At least during the day you can see where you are going. Leave the heater on if you can and keep the car warm. Keep blasting on the horn, blasting in groups of three, as this is the commonly accepted distress signal. Three blasts on the horn and then pause for a while, then another three blasts. Keep this signal going and stay awake.

If you happen to have old blankets or carpets in the car, put them over the car and try to ensure that as little heat as possible escapes. Remember to keep the exhaust pipe clear of snow or any other obstructions – the last thing you want to do is die from carbon monoxide poisoning. Whatever happens, take no risks at all. If you start to feel drowsy, there is a possibility that there is carbon monoxide seeping into the car. Turn off the engine and open the windows. Whatever you do, don't go to sleep with the engine running. If the heater works, switch it on. Leave it on for about ten minutes in every hour, switching it off as soon as you are warm and let the car cool down. Keep repeating this procedure.

If you have run out of petrol or during the night you do run out of petrol, wrap yourself up in anything available, extra clothes, rugs, newspapers, etc., and keep your hands and feet moving in the car. If you can, listen to the radio, tap your feet, clap your hands. Stay awake and exercise gently to keep your blood circulating and prevent hypothermia.

There might be a period of time when you feel you have to leave the car, mainly to go to the toilet. If you feel rescue is going to come soon, leave a sign on the car, so that anyone passing will know you need help. A signpost with a flag will make anyone passing look for you if you are not visible. They won't just drive on thinking that it is another abandoned vehicle, plus, if you put a sign up, it will help you find the car again.

Once daylight comes, if the snow has stopped, you can usually find a clear route. Follow telegraph poles which usually run alongside the road into the nearest village.

You may find yourself trapped for a while, too far out in the wilds to walk back to civilization or the nearest village. Your car might be buried. If this is the case, it is simpler to get out of the car and build yourself a snow shelter on the lines of those shown earlier in this book. Snow will insulate you better than the car will.

Once you are free to wander about in the daylight, if you are still stuck miles from anywhere, scrape or tread big letters into the snow just in case a plane passes over. If you have any potassium permanganate, use that to stain the snow or you could collect wood to make a fire because smoke attracts people's attention.

More and more people are starting to use diesel engines nowadays because they are cheaper to run. If you have a diesel car, you have to remember that diesel is a mixture that contains water and in cold temperatures and freezing conditions, the water in the fuel will freeze, so always cover the front of the engine. Try and wrap the engine up if you are going to leave the car for some time. Talk to lorry drivers if you get the opportunity. Lorry drivers usually drive diesel engines and they may tell you ways they have discovered to stop the water in the fuel from freezing. Some even start small fires under a frozen tank. That is a risk that you must decide about for yourself. You may set fire to the car, but if you do that, somebody may find you.

Unless you are driving a Robin Reliant, don't touch any bodywork in freezing weather. In cold temperatures, the body of the car will be freezing cold and if you touch it, you will freeze the skin on your hand and rip the skin off. When handling metal in freezing conditions, wrap your fingers in adhesive tape from the first aid kit before starting.

General Techniques

To make starting off in the morning easier, always try to park on a hill, then you can bump start the car if the ignition won't turn the engine over. Once you get it going, put the engine into neutral, put on the handbrake and pull the choke out and leave it to heat up properly before driving off.

If your windscreen is frozen, don't try to drive looking through the little hole you managed to de-mist with your hand. Raw potato and onion wiped over your windscreen on the inside will stop it misting up. All these ideas can be used on your car in normal conditions as well as survival conditions.

Hot Weather

Let's say, for example, that you break down in the same situation in the middle of summer, in the middle of the day.

Never leave a sleeping or injured person or your animals in a closed car in the heat – it can kill them. Always leave a window open to ensure ventilation. Heat exhaustion can be lethal. Even if parked in the shade, keep your windows open and don't forget that the sun moves. Not many people will risk breaking into a car with a dog inside, but make sure that the dog will be safe and remember that it is now an offence to leave an animal in a car in the heat.

If the engine is starting to overheat, always stop and allow it to cool. If stopping is out of the question, switch on the heater. It may be absolutely boiling in the car but the engine will be a lot cooler. When convenient, stop and open the bonnet and don't forget and just remove the radiator cap when the engine is running hot because you will get badly scalded.

If the engine overheats, always check the hoses leading to the radiator for leaks. If that is the problem, waterproof tape can be used as a temporary measure. If there is a small leak in the radiator use one of the many proprietary liquids on the market to seal the hole. At a pinch, an egg dropped into a hot radiator will seal the leak.

If there's a big hole in the side of the radiator, flatten one or two of the copper fins that run along the radiator over the hole and then use the sealant. Flattening these fins will make the hole smaller and the sealant can then seal the smaller hole. If you drive steadily, that kind of rough repair should hold.

Just as metal gets cold in winter, it gets hot in summer. Be careful what you touch on the car because all the metal parts can become so hot they can cause very bad burns and blistering.

General Problems

There are many general problems that can happen to your car that can be solved there and then if you think logically about the problem.

Fan belts have a habit of going when you least expect them to. Get into the habit of keeping a spare fan belt in the car and don't forget to replace it when you use it. If you don't have one, you can improvise with string or a pair of tights.

If your high tension lead cap bursts, you can repair it and make it last for a few more miles by using a twig to conduct electricity. Willow is the best type of wood to use. Replace it every time it dries out. You must remember that when you switch on you can get 1200 to 1300 volts pouring through that twig, so don't touch it.

A lot of people think that because the battery is dead, the car is dead. You don't need a battery – if you can get up enough speed, either by being towed or going down a slope, you will be able to bump start the car. When you are going at some speed, put the car into second or third gear before letting out the clutch and the engine should come to life. If not, repeat the process.

Accidents

We have been looking at general breakdowns with cars. What happens if you have an accident? You are driving along quite happily when a child or a dog runs out in front of you, or you find yourself ploughing, out of control, into the village pond, off the edge of a motorway embankment, on to a railway line or towards a collision.

We all know that when driving a car, anything can and usually does, happen. Your car could set on fire, the brakes could fail, etc. Your first reaction will be panic but you have to overcome this. I know it's hard, but in most cases of car accidents, you have to do a lot of jobs all at the same time and you need to be calm to do that.

If you find yourself heading for a collision, don't just close your eyes and pray, steer the car so as to do as little damage to yourself or anybody else as possible. If you have a choice, don't just crash it into a wall, drive into something that will give, something that will slow you down. You don't want to go crashing through the windscreen. Head for fences or up bankings. Many motorways are lined with saplings and I don't think the local council would do anything too drastic if you ploughed down five or six of them. A mature tree is a different matter however; it could do a lot of damage to you if you hit it.

Don't believe that bracing yourself will stop you going through the windscreen. In rare cases it does but it is better not to try and brace yourself against collisions because when the car stops, you could just keep ploughing on and there is every possibility that if you have braced yourself, something will break – usually bones.

If you can, put your arms around your head and twist sideways, away from the steering wheel. Fling yourself towards the point of collision. If you just let nature take its course you will probably hit the steering wheel and smash your ribs in. People in the back should also take these precautions and protect their heads. Get them to lie against the back of the front seat, keeping as low as possible.

If you plough into a pond or river, try and get out before the car sinks. It will take a while to sink, because it's got to fill up first. The water pressure on the outside of the doors will make it difficult to open them, so wind down the windows and try to escape that way.

It takes a lot of courage, will power and presence of mind to sit in the car and do all these jobs when you have just gone through, or are going through, a traumatic experience. Don't try and save your belongings from the car, the most important things are the people. Young children can be sent out of the windows. If you find that you are sinking rapidly, say the windows were already open, and you haven't managed to get out, close the windows and wait for the car to sink before you open the doors and escape.

Children will not be able to open the doors, especially if child locks are fitted. Try and get the children out before it sinks. If they can't swim, they can hold on to the car until you can get out.

If you haven't been fast enough to get people and children out before it sinks, close the windows firmly, make sure everybody takes off their seat belts. Get children to stand up and hold young babies near the roof. Keep them there and keep them breathing until the car fills up. If you have automatic door locks, release them all but don't open the doors. As water fills the interior, air will be trapped near the roof. The water pressure inside the car must almost equal the pressure of the water outside before you can open the doors.

As the car comes to rest and is nearly full of water, tell everybody to take a deep breath, open all the doors together and swim to the surface, breathing out as they swim. As everybody leaves through the door, link arms and keep a tight grip of each other.

All the time on the films, you see stunt men jumping out of moving cars. This is fine on the movies, it is not all right in a situation where you are heading for an accident. Do not try and jump out of a runaway car unless you know that you are never going to be able to survive the impact. A perfect example is if you are headed for a cliff edge or other long drop and you know you will not survive.

What you do in that situation is to open the door and undo your safety belt, begin to roll yourself into a ball, tucking your head against your chest and bringing your feet and knees together. Tuck yourself up nice and tight with your elbows in close to your sides, put your hands up round your ears and head. Bend at the waist and then drop from the car in a rolling movement – just roll out of the car. When you hit the ground, don't try and resist, just keep rolling until you stop.

A Car Survival Kit

Always keep a survival kit in the boot of your car. This should be transferred inside as soon as you get stuck and should contain such items as:

A large clear polythene sheet and/or bag which will keep everything together. This can be used as a shelter, a solar still, a water container, an emergency windscreen, etc.
A nylon washing line at least 16 ft (487 cms) long. It can be used to tow the car, make lashings, lower yourself down cliffs to rescue someone, etc. Good nylon line is fairly unbreakable.
A blanket and/or sleeping bag. Use it to keep yourself warm and it can also be used to improvise a stretcher or a bed.
Spare clothes or at least a warm jumper and dry socks.
Plastic water containers
Waterproof matches
Potassium permanganate
Tins and packets of food

A shovel
A torch
A first aid kit
Emergency repair kit (see next section)
Small gas camping stove
Container of water (changed regularly)
Kendal mint cake, chocolate, etc.
Small saucepan
Quizbook/novel/travel games

Emergency Repair Kit

Torch
Sacking (to get a grip in mud or snow)
Spare fan belt
Spare contacts
Spare spark plugs
Radweld or similar
Insulating tape
Selection of fuses
WD40 or other water repellent spray
Exhaust bandage
Tyre inflator
Soft galvanised wire
Jump leads
Tow rope
Strong elastic bands
Cord
Strong adhesive tape
Wheel brace
Adjustable spanner
Screwdriver
Jack

Starting a Fire

If the car breaks down and you want to start a fire, put a piece of paper, tissue or a spent match in the car cigarette lighter and leave it until it gets hot and use that to light tinder.

If you have no car lighter, disconnect the battery and move it away from the car. Try to find some wire and attach it to the terminals to get a spark and set the spark on the tinder.

It is dangerous to use petrol because it burns explosively, but if you are wet and all the available wood is wet, soak a rag in a bit of petrol and if possible, get some more rag saturated in oil and use this to get the fire started, but be very careful when applying the spark and make sure no petrol has got on to your hands or clothes.

32 The Last Word

There are now many books on the subject of survival. I've not yet come across a bad one. At the end of the day, any informative book is a good book and the fact that information shown in it can be found in other books, is irrelevant.

An instructional book is only useful if it is read, understood and remembered unlike a novel which is disregarded as soon as the book is finished. I hope that this book will be used as a work of reference for learning, revision, discussion and comparison. I have attempted to cover items not often written about but the views featured in the book are my own personal opinions and theories. If you disagree with my opinions and theories, then it will hopefully form the basis of some form of discussion and discussion about a subject invariably causes you to think carefully about the subject.

We live in a society where survivalism is no longer classed as natural instinct by many people and survivalists are frowned upon, yet we all praise the work of the Scout movement and we all depend on the work that our armed forces carry out. Both the armed forces and the Scouts form part of two world-wide survival movements and if they are not wrong then neither are survivalists.

Finally, I hope that you got as much pleasure out of reading this book as I did out of gathering the material and writing it.

Appendices

Appendix 1:   Survivalist's Code of Conduct

1   Abide by and support the law of the land. Fight unjust legislation (existing or proposed) only by constitutional means
2   Respect the Country Code
3   Acquire skills of benefit to yourself and others (first aid, self defence, civil defence, etc.) and be willing to be of service to the public in conditions of emergency
4   Practise 'minimal impact' survival training (i.e. to leave no trace that you have been in the area by litter or damage to vegetation)
5   Respect all life and take life only in cases of necessity
6   Explain the philosophies and techniques of survival to any member of the public showing interest
7   Give aid and support to fellow survivalists
8   As an individual you carry the responsibility for the good image of the entire movement. Do nothing to give British Survivalism a bad name

This Code of Conduct was put together by a magazine called *Survival Weaponry and Techniques* in order that survivalists should have a common aim.

Item 8 of the Code is very important. If you mention survivalism to the vast majority of people, they will invariably conjure up a picture of a Rambo-like psychopathic killer – helped in a lot of instances by the press seeking to sensationalize a story they have unearthed. This image is one which everybody interested in survivalism must help to dispel by always acting in a responsible manner.

The Survivalist's Code is an excellent one to adhere to in a peace-time situation but in an actual survival situation, there is a real possibility that the code would be totally disregarded for a much simpler and condensed Code of Conduct:

Shortened Code of Conduct

1   Survive
2   At all costs

Fig. 106 Common perception of the survivalist!

However survivalism and conservation go hand in hand. Most survivalists are conservation conscious. This is logical because of the value a survivalist places upon his environment. All survivalists must endeavour to save the environment and in a wider aspect, the planet. After all, though the planet can be our worst enemy, it is also our salvation. With the constant increase in roads, motorways, etc., more and more broadleaf trees and open countryside are being destroyed to make way for 'progress' – a progress that will inevitably poison our world with industrial pollution.

Therefore part of any Code of Conduct must be that all survivalists plant trees, extend natural woodlands and support green issues, in an attempt to better our world.

The Country Code

Guard against all risk of fire
Fasten all gates
Keep dogs under proper control
Keep to paths across farm land
Avoid damaging fences, hedges and walls
Leave no litter
Safeguard water supplies
Protect wild life, wild plants and trees
Go carefully on country roads
Respect the life of the country

There are a couple of additional rules that should be added to that code:

Don't go on land with growing crops
Remove turf with care, so it can be replaced

The countryside in Britain is, for the most part, more like a garden than a wilderness. It is farmed and forested over most of its area and close to the towns, on mountains, moorlands, heaths and marshes, you can see by the walls, dykes and hedges and by the cattle and sheep grazing that the land is used as much as possible.

The countryside is largely what man has made it through centuries of toil and care, but there is still much natural scenery. The work of conservation and improvement creates in the countryside a spirit and a way of life which is of great value to the nation. All who understand this spirit will preserve the beauty and order of the countryside, which is held in trust by us for future generations.

As survivalists you will use the countryside a great deal and therefore must have a special responsibility to:

Keep the Country Code
Encourage others to keep it
Act where you find that others have broken the code

Survivalism, like military training is inundated with keywords to help you remember rules and regulations, orders of preference, etc.

PERSPEX is a word used in the scouting movement.

P Personal Fitness
   Speaks for itself – keep yourself fit.
E Equipment
   Make sure the equipment you use is in good order. Also covered in this category is clothing.
R Risks
   Never take them. Don't imagine nothing will happen in a survival situation because it would be right to say that something already has. The worst risk you can take is to think you know it all.
S Safety Rules
   The saying 'Rules were made to be broken' does not apply in this instance. Safety must be of the utmost importance. This includes not taking unnecessary risks. Learn the safety rules applying to whatever you are doing, canoeing, abseiling, hiking, etc. Accepting the need to apply safety rules will help to keep you and others safe.
P Planning
   Plan what you are going to do, who is going to do it, plan routes. Planning boosts morale. Everyone feels he or she is taking an active part in whatever is happening to the group you are with.
E Emergencies
   However careful and conscientious you are, there will be times when accidents happen, either to yourself or others. Be prepared for emergencies.
X Unexpected
   You can't plan for everything, a mist suddenly comes down on a moor, someone has an accident and so on. Don't push yourself or your equipment to the limits. Keep something in reserve, so that when the unexpected happens you have the means and the strength to deal with it.

Remember the key word:

PERSPEX

Another similar word is PLAN:

P Protection
Shelters, clothing, equipment, fires
L Location
Signals, distress signals, contact with others
A Acquisition
Food, water, materials for shelter
N Navigation
Terrain, maps, compass, orientation by day and night.

All must be learnt, all must be remembered.

Appendix 2:   Setting up a Community

Leadership

A leader must have the confidence of his followers as well as having confidence in himself. If he shows doubt in his judgement or decisions, so will they. He must be loyal to his superiors if he has any; if not, how can he expect loyalty from his fellows.

In the case of 'The Event', leadership would undoubtedly be based closely upon military-type leadership; therefore it is only to be expected that ex-military personnel would come to the forefront in survival leadership.

There are many theories as to what is or what makes a good leader of men. Let's face it, Napoleon and Hitler were fantastic leaders of men and superb soldiers, so were Genghis Khan and Taras Bulba amongst others, but people only want heroes who were on their side, like Winston Churchill and Wellington.

In my opinion, the greatest warrior was a woman – Boadicea. She not only brought together the tribes of Ancient Britain but led them into battle, wielding a sword as she went. Very few leaders do that, they all tend to sit back and send everybody else to die. In a survival situation, the leader must also 'get stuck in'. Leaders do not necessarily make the rules or have the ideas; however they must be able to motivate the group, uphold any rules made and implement good ideas. This is no mean feat.

If you ask what is a leader, you will get many answers based on past leaders:

A leader is bigger/harder/better than anyone else
A leader is cleverer/richer/fitter than anyone else

In a perfect world, the leader is fair, understanding and would not ask his men to do anything that he has not or would not, do himself. Maybe this is why all officers have at one time dug or cleaned toilet areas on exercise. He works by their side and as hard as his fellows. He accepts the blame and responsibility as well as being able to hand it out and praises his men when needed. He must be in touch with his followers' feelings and needs.

Men will follow a leader they admire, they will also follow a leader they detest. He does not have to be a nice guy, he has to be right for the job. Responsibility will always weed out the weak.

Setting up a Community

This section is only a suggestion and should be used as a guideline only, as it is a fictitious situation and the scenario has been set to make it viable. There is no guarantee that the following would work in practice though in theory it should.

Civil unrest and a war in the Middle East has caused outstanding problems with general law and order in England. Traffic wardens have been seconded into the police force and the police have been armed. Any person in uniform is now used as an authority figure to quell the unrest and riots. The armed forces are away fighting in the deserts and young men are being called up into the forces. Students and ethnic minorities are rioting because of the war. Our young people are being slaughtered in a futile war against a fanatical army who claim they are fighting a holy war. Petrol prices are around £5 a gallon, food and consumer goods are rationed. Inflation is through the roof and an unfair individual tax is causing acute poverty.

(Note: This part was written before Desert Storm took place!)

A small group of friends have taken to the hills in an attempt to get away from the emergency.

The Group

Six men and their families have joined together:

Bob	Age 30	Vehicle mechanic
Jean	Age 35	Housewife
Children:		Carl 16
		Alex 14

Bob spent 12 years as a vehicle mechanic with REME.

Jim	Age 28	TV repair man
Pat	Age 27	Housewife/part-time cook
Children:		Rose 3

Jim enjoys field sports, has two lurchers and ferrets and is partially sighted in one eye.

Ken   Age 43 Builder
Susan   Age 39 Nurse
Children   Steve 17   Apprentice builder
                      Andrew 16   Apprentice builder
                      James 14
                      Sandra 14
Ken did 22 years with Royal Engineers. Discharged as a SQMS.

Bill   Age 36 Farm labourer
Wife died recently
Children   Colin 16   Unemployed school leaver
                      Mick 14
No military experience.

Harold Age 50 Factory worker
Mavis   Age 38 Teacher
Children   Jeanette 23   Care Assistant
                      Amanda 18   Shop Assistant
                      Billy 15
Harold had twenty-two years Infantry. Rank Sergeant.

Austin   Age 45 Plumber
Irene   Age 40 Shop manageress
Children   Graham   Army
                      Roger   Army
12 years with Parachute Regiment. Rank of Corporal.

Total Numbers

Over 16	Under 16
17	6

Group Employment

Name	Job	Secondary Employment
Bob	Soldier	Group vehicle mechanic
Jim	Soldier	Electrician/hunter
Ken	Soldier	Builder/quartermaster
Bill	Soldier	Grower/hunter
Harold	Soldier	Armourer/hunter
Austin	Soldier	Grower/plumber
Pat	Soldier	Cook
Jean	Assistant cook	Seamstress

Susan	Nurse	General helper
Mavis	Teacher	General helper
Irene	QM Assistant	Grower
Carl	Soldier	Assistant vehicle mechanic
Alex		General helper
Rose		Infant
Steve	Soldier	Builder/hunter
Andrew	Soldier	Builder/hunter
James		General helper
Sandra		General helper
Colin	Soldier	Grower/hunter
Mick		General helper
Jeannette	Nurse	Assistant cook
Amanda	QM Assistant	Assistant seamstress
Billy		Hunter

Employment Breakdown

Soldier
To defend the group against any attacker or unwelcome intrusion and to guard the group property and possessions.

Vehicle maintenance
To maintain any vehicle or engine used by the group.

Builder
To maintain any building owned or used by the group and to erect any building needed by the group.

Quartermaster
To keep stock of all items of food and equipment used by the group and to issue accordingly.

Grower
To maintain land owned and used by the group to grow food for the group and to tend these crops accordingly.

Electrician
To maintain or set up an electric system and other power used by the group including batteries and electrical equipment.

Armourer
To maintain and keep in good and clean order any weapons used by the group and to be in direct charge of ammunition and to issue and ration accordingly.

Seamstress
To make or fix any items of clothing where necessary and to make any clothes items required by the group.

Nurse
To care for the medical and health needs of the group.

Teacher
To maintain a practical and high standard of education within the group's children and to ensure that the children meet the standards required.

Hunter
To hunt for the group food needs and to acquire anything that the group may need. This would include scrounging and scavenging trips.

General helper
To help in any way possible within the group as and when needed.

Cook
To prepare and preserve any food needed by the group.

All soldiers will maintain any standard of fitness that may be necessitated for the defence of the group. All hunters would be in two or three groups and some of the younger members could go with hunting groups.

Guard Duty Rosters

Eight-hour shifts, four group members per night. Cook does not do guard duty due to early cooking duties at breakfast. Under 16s can keep watch for intruders throughout the day. Hunters and soldiers can also spend some time on guard and can also use guard duty time to recuperate from any work carried out. However this would no doubt change as the group expands.

Location

The location can be anywhere where the group feel secure and the location would be chosen by reconnoitring before the group move in. This can be a job for the hunters. Examples could be old deserted barns, farm complexes, old factories, quarries, mines, etc. Location should be within easy travelling distance from main homes of group members with an all-round panoramic view of surrounding areas.

Food

In the initial formation of the group, food can be acquired by group members from shops and supermarkets and stored in a dry, safe place ready for transportation or stored in the designated location. The group would make a shopping list and buy equal amounts every week; this could be started as two or three extra tins each week on the weekly shopping bill.

The quartermaster would be responsible for taking charge of storage and keeping check of sell-by dates. If food is close to sell by date, QM makes out a requisition order for items to be replaced. Group exchange new items for old ones thereby ensuring that:

1 All food is fit for consumption
2 All cost is evenly shared
3 All food due for exchange is equally shared and not wasted

Quite soon a large stock of food will have been acquired. This, together with food grown and caught should be sufficient to sustain the group if and when they re-locate to safety.

The same rules will be taken into account when buying equipment. Any equipment purchased for the group could be hired out at the discretion of the group members; for example, Ken wishes to use the group's cement mixer on a job for one of his customers, the savings he makes by not having to hire, could be donated in part or full to group funds; and any surplus crops could be sold on the open market.

Bug outs

This is a term commonly used in the army when a regiment is called out to its defensive location within a designated time. The group could practise while incorporating camping weekends together.

It is imperative that whilst the group maintain a normal quality of life, in case of emergency they can all be called together and reach the safe location together in time to escape any problems and that while they are in hiding they have sufficient resources to be self sufficient for the duration.

Group Expansion

Undoubtedly expansion could happen over a number of years through marriages, births etc. In a peace-time situation other friends could become interested in the group activities and a pyramid effect could take place.

In addition each group member could start a separate group, keeping the original group secret. For example, Austin sets up a group with Bill and Betty Bentley and John and Mildred Price and their families.

This group finds a location, but only Austin's family would know the location of the original group, and in addition Austin would be unaware of any groups that anybody else set up.

Each sub-group would be set up in the same way as the original group and in the case of a real emergency could either come together to form a large community or else remain as separate groups and trade between groups.

Law and Order

Law and punishment would have to be fast, fair and effective.

Because the group is made up of friends, laws must be abided by even more strongly. In effect, a crime against a friend is exaggerated ten-fold. The serenity of the group must be put first and the Ten Commandments would be a good start for any group. Adultery within the group would cause more friction and disruption than normal because the group all live closely together. Banishment would be a possible final option. Loss of privileges another.

Scenario 2

Jim is watching the news when it is declared that small nuclear bombs have been dropped on three cities in England and that enemy troops are forming in large numbers in France. Indications suggest an imminent invasion attempt.

Jim calls the group and implements bug out. The group mobilize within three hours and meet at a rendezvous. When all the group are present they then move to their safe location in convoy. There they have food and equipment to last twelve months.

While in hiding, the invasion has failed but the civilian population has moved from the cities to find refuge from the destruction and a mass exodus is headed from places like Manchester to the rural areas surrounding the town, looting and pillaging as they travel. Security forces have the job of stopping such a movement of bodies, looters are shot and food is in short supply.

The group have been sending out hunting and scavenging parties. Their home town is desolate as local folk move to escape the onslaught and a number of people have joined the group and the location is becoming overcrowded. A unanimous decision has been taken and a new location is being sought.

There is a small estate in their home area which backs onto a wood yard and a brick works. The estate is made up of 175 houses in 2 circles. The group decide to relocate on to the estate because it is on a hill and will be easy to defend. On arrival there are still a few people in residence and these are absorbed into the group.

The houses on the outer ring are gutted and the inner ones inhabited. Defences are set out in the outer perimeter, leaving only two entrances to the inner circle, both of which are guarded. Some houses are set aside as hospitals, stores, etc.

Trade links are set up with other groups, young men are seconded into the group's defence forces and all the people work for the good of the community. Yes it sounds organized and simple to all intents and purposes but we have the technology to start what it took our ancestors hundreds of years to establish, i.e. towns growing from villages or even river crossings.

The Reality of Fantasy

In a peaceful environment, a group could still flourish without the need to go to the trouble of setting up a full blown community. A large number of Vietnam veterans have formed a community in America though not for the sake of survivalism but because of their inability to fit in with a society they feel they no longer belong to.

There is even a legend of a lost tribe in England. During the wars against the Roman legions a tribe suddenly disappeared after the death of the queen, Boadicea. Legend has it that they sleep in a hidden place until the country needs them. Similar legends are told of King Arthur and his knights.

Another legend says that the young travelling people are the descendants of these people. These people are in many ways self-sufficient and come together many times during the year. For the main part of the year they live in squats and buses; others live in the Lakes or the Dales.

Within the reality there is much fantasy and within the fantasy there is reality.

Appendix 3: Associations Useful to the Survivalist

Archery

The Grand National Archery Society, 7th Street, National Agricultural Centre, Stoneleigh, Kenilworth, Warwickshire,CV8 2LZ

National Longbow Society, Rose Cottage, Kingsley Green House, Kingsley Green, Haslemere, Surrey, GU27 3LG

Canoeing

British Canoe Union, National Watersports Centre, Adbolton Lane, Holme Pierrepoint, Nottingham

British Waterways Board, Melbury House, Melbury Terrace, London, NW1 6LA

Amateur Rowing Association Ltd, 6 Lower Mall, London, W6 9DJ

Camping and Caravanning

Camping and Caravanning Club of GB and Ireland Ltd, 11 Lower Grosvenor Place, London, SW1W 0EY

Camping and Outdoor Leisure Association, 1 West Ruislip Station, Ickenham Road, Ruislip, Middlesex, HA4 7DW

Caving

British Cave Rescue Council, 8 Yealand Avenue, Giggleswick, Settle, North Yorkshire, BD24 0AY

British Speliological Association, 4 Kingston Avenue, Acklam,

Middlesborough, Cleveland, TS7 6RS

National Caving Association, c/o Whernside Manor, Dent, Sedburgh, Cumbria, LA10 5RE

Conservation

Association for the Protection of Rural Scotland, 14 Napier Road, Edinburgh, EH10 5AY

British Association of Nature Conservationists, Rectory Farm, Stanton St John, Oxford

British Trust for Conservation Volunteers, 3 St Mary's Way, Wallingford, Oxfordshire, OX10 0EO

Coastal Anti-Pollution League, c/o Marine Conservation Society, 4 Gloucester Road, Ross on Wye

Council for the Protection of Rural England, 4 Hobart Place, London, SW7 0HY

County Landowners Association, 16 Belgrave Square, London, SW1X 8PQ

Countryside Commission, Dower House, Crescent Place, Cheltenham, Gloucester, GL50 3RA

Flora and Fauna Preservation Society, c/o Zoological Society of London, Regents Park, London, NW1

Forestry Commission, 231 Corstophine Road, Edinburgh, EH12 7AT

Friends of the Earth, 26-8 Underwood Street, London

Hawk Trust, Zoological Society of London, Regents Park, London, NW1 4RY

Greenpeace, 30-1 Islington Green, London, N1

Game Conservancy Trust, Burgate Manor, Fordingbridge, Hants, SP6 1EF

National Trust, 36 Queen Anne's Gate, London, SW1H 9AS

Nature Conservancy Council, Northminster House, Northminster, Peterborough, PE1 1UA

Royal Society for Nature Conservation, 22 The Green, Nettleham, Lincoln, LN2

Royal Society for the Protection of Birds, The Lodge, Sandy, Beds, SG19 2DL

Woodland Trust, Autumn Park, Dysart Road, Grantham, Lincs, NG31 6LL

Cycling

British Cycling Federation, 16 Upper Woburn Place, London, WC1H 0QE

Miscellaneous

British Falconers Club, Moonraker, Allington, Salisbury, SP4 0BX

British Society of Dowsers, High Street, Eydon, Daventry, Northampton

Mountaineering

British Mountaineering Council, Crawford House, Precinct Centre, Booth Street East, Manchester

Fell and Rock Climbing Club, The Old Rectory, Bootle, Millom, Cumbria, LA19 5TH

Orienteering

British Orienteering Federation, Riversdale, Dale Road North, Darley Dale, Matlock, Derbyshire, DE4 2JB

Shooting

British Association for Shooting and Conservation (BASC), Marford Mill, Rossett, Clwyd, LL12 0HL

Clay Pigeon Shooting Association, 107 Epping New Road, Buckhurst Hill, Essex, IG9 5TQ

National Rifle Association, Bisley Camp, Brookwood, Woking, Surrey, GU24 0PB

British Sporting Rifle Club, 27 Tancred Road, High Wycombe, Bucks, HP13 5EQ

Walking and Rambling

Back Packers Club, 7-10 Friar Street, Reading, Berks

Ramblers Association, 1-5 Wandsworth Road, London, SW8 2XX

Appendix 4:   Books Useful to the Survivalist

Survival and Outdoor Techniques previously issued as *Survival Weaponry and Techniques*; it is no longer published, but back issues are worth their weight in gold to the avid survivalist

Intermediate Technology Publications Ltd., 103–5 Southampton Row, London WC1B 4HH. Carry a variety of books aimed at making the Third World self-sufficient but which show simply how to make things.

John Barratt and C.M. Younger, *Pocket Guide to the Seashore*
James A. Bateman *Animal Traps and Trapping*
Maggie Black, *Smoking Food at Home*
Bourne, *Wild Harvest*
Iain Brede, *Ferrets and Ferreting*
L.Cameron, *Wild Foods of Great Britain*
V.J. Chapman, *Seaweeds and Their Uses*
Cooper and Johnson, *Poisonous Plants in Britain*
Geoffrey Eley, *Wild Fruit and Nuts*
W.P.K. Findlay, *Observer's Book of Mushrooms, Toadstools and other Common Fungi*
Nat Gordon, *Food from the Shore*
HMSO, *Home Preservation of Fruit and Vegetables*
Phyllis Hobson, *Home Drying Vegetables, Fruit and Herbs*
Loewenfield and Black, *Herbs for Health and Cookery*
Richard Mabey, *Food for Free*
Eddie McGee, *No Need to Die*
Raymond Mears, *The Complete Outdoor Handbook*
Raymond Mears, *The Survival Handbook*
Oliver Perry Medsger, *Edible Wild Plants*
Robin Page, *Weather Forecasting the Country Way*

Roger Phillips, *Wild Food*
Ronald Rayner, *Mushrooms and Toadstools*
Sharon Ann Rhodes, *Cooking of Sea Vegetables*
Kay Sanecki, *Discovering Herbs*
Amoret Scott, *Hedgerow Harvest*
Dorothy and Reg Stiffe, *Survival Out of Doors*
Judy Urquhart, *Living off Nature*
John Wiseman, *The SAS Survival Handbook*
John Wiseman, *The Urban Survival Handbook*
Basic Butchering of Livestock and Game

Appendix 5: Wildlife & Countryside Act 1981

The following is a list of prohibitions contained in the wildlife protection act. It is still not the full Act. Full copies can be obtained from Her Majesty's Stationery Office.

Birds

It is unlawful without a licence to:

- Kill, injure or take any wild bird, except pest species
- Use cruel or indiscriminate methods of killing or capturing wild birds, including pests
- Take, damage or destroy the nest of a wild bird (except pests)
- Sell or show any wild bird
- Sell the body of a dead wild bird except some sporting birds
- Sell the eggs of British wild birds
- Disturb any specially protected bird whilst nesting or disturb the young

The list of protected bird species is extensive and is regularly updated. It is always wise to check the latest version of the Wildlife and Countryside Act and to learn how to identify wild birds as ignorance of the law is no defence.

Plants

Without a licence it is unlawful to:

- Uproot any wild plant without permission of the owner
- Intentionally uproot or pick any flower of protected species

See Act for complete list of protected species.

Animals

Without a licence it is unlawful to:

- Kill, injure, take, possess or sell a specially protected wild animal
- Damage, destroy, disturb or obstruct access to the animal's den
- Sell any protected animal
- Deliberately kill or capture any species other than those protected, without licence, i.e. badger, pine marten, dormouse, hedgehog, shrew
- To use cruel and indiscriminate methods to kill or capture any animal

Again, the list of animals is extensive and needs to be checked before going out to kill. It must be noted, however, that in a dire survival situation it is unlikely that any prosecution would follow the killing of a protected species for self-preservation.

Index

Index